Vulnerable South Asia

This innovatively organized volume brings together reflections on crisis and community in South Asia by some of the most important authors and scholars writing about the Indian subcontinent today.

The various pieces, including the foreword, the poetic interludes, the nine different essays on a range of topics, as well as the afterword, all seek to understand the precarious state of our planet and its population, and the ways to resist – through both writing and teaching – the forces that render us vulnerable; to create "care communities" in which we look out for, and after, each other on egalitarian rather than authoritarian terms. Turning to literary and cultural criticism in precarious times reveals the immense value of the humanities, including volumes such as this one. This collection is a significant intervention in the on-going global conversation on precarity, vulnerability, and suffering, not only because these issues have preoccupied the human race through the ages, but also because our present moment – the now – is characterized by pervasive hazards that writers, readers, teachers, and humanists must call out, talk and write about, and thus resist.

The chapters in this book were originally published as a special issue of the journal *South Asian Review*.

Pallavi Rastogi is Professor of English at Louisiana State University, USA. She has written two books: *Postcolonial Disaster* and *Afrindian Fictions* and is also the co-editor of the volume *Before Windrush*. She has authored various articles on South Asian and South African literature.

Vulnerable South Asia
Precarities, Resistance, and Care Communities

Edited by
Pallavi Rastogi

LONDON AND NEW YORK

First published 2021
by Routledge
2 Park Square, Milton Park, Abingdon, Oxon OX14 4RN

and by Routledge
52 Vanderbilt Avenue, New York, NY 10017

Routledge is an imprint of the Taylor & Francis Group, an informa business

© 2021 Taylor & Francis

All rights reserved. No part of this book may be reprinted or reproduced or utilised
in any form or by any electronic, mechanical, or other means, now known or
hereafter invented, including photocopying and recording, or in any information
storage or retrieval system, without permission in writing from the publishers.

Trademark notice: Product or corporate names may be trademarks or registered trademarks,
and are used only for identification and explanation without intent to infringe.

British Library Cataloguing in Publication Data
A catalogue record for this book is available from the British Library

ISBN 13: 978-0-367-50666-7

Typeset in Minion Pro
by Newgen Publishing UK

Publisher's Note
The publisher accepts responsibility for any inconsistencies that may have arisen during
the conversion of this book from journal articles to book chapters, namely the inclusion of
journal terminology.

Disclaimer
Every effort has been made to contact copyright holders for their permission to reprint
material in this book. The publishers would be grateful to hear from any copyright holder
who is not here acknowledged and will undertake to rectify any errors or omissions in
future editions of this book.

Contents

Citation Information	vii
Notes on Contributors	x
Editorial	1
Pradyumna S. Chauhan	
Guest Editor's Column: Precarities, Resistance, and Care Communities in South Asia	3
Pallavi Rastogi	
Poetic Interlude I: After the Deluge	9
K. Satchidanandan	
Foreword	17
Homi K. Bhabha	

SECTION I

Bodies That Do Not Matter: Gender and Sexual Precarity

1	Brooms of Doom: Notes on Domestic Bodies Gendered to Death in *Mughal-e-Azam*, *Fire*, and *Earth* *Rahul K. Gairola*	18
2	Post-Magic: The Female Naxalite at 50 in Arundhati Roy's *The Ministry of Utmost Happiness* and Neel Mukherjee's *A State of Freedom* *Meghan Gorman-DaRif*	33
3	The Ethics of Representation and the Figure of the Woman: The Question of Agency in Gayatri Chakravorty Spivak's "Can the Subaltern Speak?" *Anirban Bhattacharjee*	46

SECTION II
In A Class of Their Own: Belabouring Precarity

4 The Literary Lumpen: The *Naksha* Narratives of Binoy Ghosh   56
   Auritro Majumder

5 "No One in the House Knew Her Name": Servant Problems in
   R. K. Narayan's Short Stories   70
   Ambreen Hai

   Poetic Interlude II: *Spaces*   89
   K. Satchidanandan

SECTION III
Region and Religion: Eco-Migrant and Minority Precarity

6 Precarity and Resistance in Oceanic Literature   91
   Tana Trivedi

7 Representing the "Other": Minority Discourse in the Postcolonial
   Indian English Novel   105
   Saman Ashfaq

SECTION IV
Teaching Troubles: The Pedagogy of Precarity

8 Teaching Precarity, Resistance, and Community: Rohini Mohan's
   The Seasons of Trouble and Genocide Pedagogy   118
   Colleen Lutz Clemens

9 Teaching Beyond Empathy: The Classroom As Care Community   130
   Matthew Dischinger

   Poetic Interlude III: *Birds Come After Me*   142
   K. Satchidanandan

   Afterword: Precarious Futures, Precarious Pasts: Climate, Terror,
   and Planetarity   144
   Gaurav Desai

   Index   155

Citation Information

The chapters in this book were originally published in *South Asian Review*, volume 39, issue 3–4 (September–December 2018). When citing this material, please use the original page numbering for each article, as follows:

Editorial
Pradyumna S. Chauhan
South Asian Review, volume 39, issue 3–4 (September–December 2018), pp. 265–266

Guest Editor's Column
Precarities, Resistance, and Care Communities in South Asia
Pallavi Rastogi
South Asian Review, volume 39, issue 3–4 (September–December 2018), pp. 269–274

Poetic Interlude I
After the Deluge
K. Satchidanandan
South Asian Review, volume 39, issue 3–4 (September–December 2018), pp. 275–282

Foreword
Homi K. Bhabha
South Asian Review, volume 39, issue 3–4 (September–December 2018), pp. 267–268

Chapter 1
Brooms of Doom: Notes on Domestic Bodies Gendered to Death in Mughal-e-Azam, Fire, *and* Earth
Rahul K. Gairola
South Asian Review, volume 39, issue 3–4 (September–December 2018), pp. 283–297

Chapter 2
Post-Magic: The Female Naxalite at 50 in Arundhati Roy's The Ministry of Utmost Happiness *and Neel Mukherjee's* A State of Freedom
Meghan Gorman-DaRif
South Asian Review, volume 39, issue 3–4 (September–December 2018), pp. 298–310

Chapter 3

The Ethics of Representation and the Figure of the Woman: The Question of Agency in Gayatri Chakravorty Spivak's "Can the Subaltern Speak?"
Anirban Bhattacharjee
South Asian Review, volume 39, issue 3–4 (September–December 2018), pp. 311–320

Chapter 4

The Literary Lumpen: The Naksha *Narratives of Binoy Ghosh*
Auritro Majumder
South Asian Review, volume 39, issue 3–4 (September–December 2018), pp. 321–334

Chapter 5

"No One in the House Knew Her Name": Servant Problems in R. K. Narayan's Short Stories
Ambreen Hai
South Asian Review, volume 39, issue 3–4 (September–December 2018), pp. 335–353

Poetic Interlude II

Spaces
K. Satchidanandan
South Asian Review, volume 39, issue 3–4 (September–December 2018), pp. 355–356

Chapter 6

Precarity and Resistance in Oceanic Literature
Tana Trivedi
South Asian Review, volume 39, issue 3–4 (September–December 2018), pp. 356–369

Chapter 7

Representing the "Other": Minority Discourse in the Postcolonial Indian English Novel
Saman Ashfaq
South Asian Review, volume 39, issue 3–4 (September–December 2018), pp. 370–382

Chapter 8

Teaching Precarity, Resistance, and Community: Rohini Mohan's The Seasons of Trouble *and Genocide Pedagogy*
Colleen Lutz Clemens
South Asian Review, volume 39, issue 3–4 (September–December 2018), pp. 383–394

Chapter 9

Teaching Beyond Empathy: The Classroom As Care Community
Matthew Dischinger
South Asian Review, volume 39, issue 3–4 (September–December 2018), pp. 395–406

Poetic Interlude III

Birds Come After Me
K. Satchidanandan
South Asian Review, volume 39, issue 3–4 (September–December 2018), pp. 407–408

Afterword

Precarious Futures, Precarious Pasts: Climate, Terror, and Planetarity
Gaurav Desai
South Asian Review, volume 39, issue 3–4 (September–December 2018), pp. 409–419

For any permission-related enquiries please visit:
www.tandfonline.com/page/help/permissions

Notes on Contributors

Saman Ashfaq, The Bhopal School of Social Sciences, Bhopal, India.

Homi K. Bhabha, Harvard University, Cambridge, MA, USA.

Anirban Bhattacharjee, Santipur College, University of Kalyani, Kalyani, India.

Pradyumna S. Chauhan, Arcadia University, Glenside, PA, USA.

Gaurav Desai, Department of English, University of Michigan, Ann Arbor, MI, USA.

Matthew Dischinger, Georgia State University, Atlanta, GA, USA.

Rahul K. Gairola, School of Arts and Asia Research Centre, Murdoch University, Perth, WA, Australia.

Meghan Gorman-DaRif, Department of English, University of Texas at Austin, Austin, TX, USA.

Ambreen Hai, Department of English Language and Literature, Smith College, Northampton, MA, USA.

Colleen Lutz Clemens, English Department, Kutztown University, Kutztown, PA, USA.

Auritro Majumder, Department of English, University of Houston, Houston, TX, USA.

Pallavi Rastogi, Department of English, Louisiana State University, Baton Rouge, LA, USA.

K. Satchidanandan, poet, playwright, and essayist.

Tana Trivedi, Amrut Mody School of Management, Ahmedabad University, Ahmedabad, India.

Editorial

To turn to consider the precarities confronting human life is a very normal response when the world seems poised on the brink of disaster. That we teeter at some perilous edge shall be vividly clear to anyone who would pause and think. Unending droughts have long afflicted large swaths of land, leaving masses dead or dying; rising oceans swallow coastal strips, or completely drown out small islands, forcing people to seek a safer perch elsewhere; hurricanes, tornados, and wildfires, earthquakes and attendant tsunamis, uncontrollable all in their natural fury, wipe out towns with all their novel human constructions and possessions. These frightening intimations of an ultimate risk to the human race, made darkly ominous by their frequent visitations, stem not from any specific region of the world. For those who can read the signs, these are portents of the ominous fate that awaits the planet unless we check, and revise, our course.

And these relentless devastations descend not from the natural universe alone. They spring from the human/animal group itself: dengue fever, the Ebola virus, the flesh-eating bacteria, the avian flu, unstoppable at mightiest borders, suddenly overtake populations thousands of miles away from the centers of their origins, thanks to the rapid transportation systems that bind the world together. Human destiny now is, unalterably, a single one.

The cruelest peril to humankind comes from its own chosen leaders, politicians who, out of personal greed or fear, egged on by dreams of glory or driven by a historical mirage, bedeviled by their personal distortions, or misreading the state of affairs, turn upon their own people, goading them to hysteria and to massive brutalities. These flawed saviors, sadly, unleash upon themselves – and others – genocide and wars, destroying innocent millions even as they cripple for generations their own systems and gullible followers. We are witnessing them all, masquerading as messiahs in different garbs, in various parts of the world stage. Parodies of great people, someday, they may turn out to be world's worst monsters.

Literature but notes and critiques these straws in the wind. Literary critics, the intermediaries between the writer and the reader, decipher and unveil the patterns of a world run amok to warn, or to comfort, the readers.

The editors of *South Asian Review*, recognizing the significance of the literature of precarity and care communities, invited Pallavi Rastogi to edit a special issue of the journal based on the theme of the SALA conference in 2018 for a representative view of contemporary social jeopardies, the current modes of resistance, and of the communities that intervene on behalf of the afflicted. Thankfully, Rastogi has reached out to eminent literary and cultural critics such as Homi Bhabha and Gaurav Desai, both of whom have done serious global thinking about our precarious world today. Their deliberations serve as bookends to the diverse articles that cover a wide range of topics.

Since this happens to be the last volume of *South Asian Review* to be published under my editorship, I would much like to acknowledge the debt I owe my wonderful colleagues: Kamal D. Verma, John Hawley, Amritjit Singh, Kavita Daiya, Raje Kaur, and Robin E. Field. They have always been ready with their help and generous with their advice.

The latest team of editorial assistants – Courtney Dunn and Richard Porten – have struggled along with me against several odds. I appreciate their industry and their ingenuity.

My university and its presidents have, over the past five years, given *South Asian Review* a resourceful home and unstinted support. I am indebted to all of them for an abundant grace freely given.

Pradyumna S. Chauhan

GUEST EDITOR'S COLUMN

Precarities, Resistance, and Care Communities in South Asia

August is the cruelest month. In both the country of my birth and my adopted homeland. As I wrote this Guest Editor's Column for the special issue of *South Asian Review* on "Precarity, Resistance, and Care Communities" in August 2018, the Indian state of Kerala was undergoing the worst spate of flooding in a century: nearly 200 people were dead and 80% of the state was powerless, perhaps in every sense of the word. Meanwhile, hurricane season had reached its peak in my home state of Louisiana. We still vividly remember Hurricane Katrina making landfall in the region near New Orleans on August 29, 2005, drenching and drowning this beautiful bowl of a city in what was then the worst ecological disaster in the US in the new century. Eleven years later, Louisiana was in troubled waters again. "The Great Flood of August 2016" dropped catastrophic amounts of rain on the areas around Baton Rouge, washing away homes and livelihoods of people I knew well. Yes, August is the cruelest month. But it is certainly not the only cruel month. We live in precarious times: when each month, indeed each day, brings new horrors into our lives.

In 2013, *The New York Times* ran a story by the Indian journalist Pico Iyer on "the value of suffering."[1] After reciting a long litany of all the terrible things that had happened in just the last few months, Iyer queried, "does the torrent of suffering ever abate – and can one possibly find any point in suffering?" The "torrent of suffering" only surged in the years that followed Iyer's essay – with mass murders in France, Japan, and Germany, heightened racial conflict and catastrophic floods in the United States, earthquakes in Italy as well as a refugee crisis of unprecedented proportions in Europe. In October 2016, Hurricane Matthew claimed nearly 900 lives in Haiti. When it finally clocked in twelve full months, 2016 had been described as the year of untrammeled catastrophe, the *annus horribilis* of global crisis. The following year, 2017, also ushered in one terrible event after the other, each with catastrophic consequences: Donald Trump's hastily-conceived Executive Orders banning immigrants from seven – then six – Muslim countries; terror attacks in Istanbul, Kabul, London, Paris, and Tehran; the US administration pulling out of the Paris Accord on climate control; Hurricanes Harvey and Irma that nearly destroyed Houston and Puerto Rico. We were only two days into 2018, when we learned a new word – *bombogenesis* – a low pressure system that causes snow to fall with explosive force and led to Boston and New York shutting down. Meanwhile, the summer of 2018 had also registered record-burning high temperatures all over the world, with the unprecedented heat *literally* melting Sweden's highest glacier on Kebnekaise mountain. September rolled around this year to pummel the Carolinas with Hurricane Florence while Typhoon Mangkhut shredded the city-state of Hong Kong and necessitated the evacuation of millions of people in China. October brought the Indonesian Tsunami, which registered a toll of at least 800 dead, as well as heretofore unseen political outrage, by women and for women, over the nomination of a judge accused of sexual assault to the Supreme Court of the United States.

Itemizing even a few examples on a very long list from a very short period of time demonstrates the presence of the viruses of future catastrophes that will metastasize into full-fledged disasters in our already precarious existence today.

No wonder that precarity has acquired such quotidian universality, despite the terror-inducing and spectacular imagery with which it is often associated, that crises have created new states of normalcy in which our acceptance of – and living with – this new-normal allows calamities to go quiet in the collective imagination. Yet the cultural products from our precarious lives, including literary writing, local films, and art exhibitions, refuse to silence catastrophe. Literature and the visual arts lodge crisis into the heart of culture, politics, and public consciousness while also invoking new ways of resisting our continuous state of vulnerability. That is exactly the project of this special issue of *South Asian Review*: "Precarity, Resistance, and Care Communities in South Asia."[2]

The various pieces in this volume, including the foreword, the poetic interludes, the nine different essays on a range of topics, as well as the afterword, all seek to understand the precarious state of our planet and its population, and the ways to resist – through both writing and teaching – the forces that render us vulnerable, and to create "care communities" in which we look out for, and after, each other on egalitarian rather than authoritarian terms.[3] That we turn to literary and cultural criticism in precarious times reveals the value of the humanities, especially journals such as *The South Asian Review*, in showing how our work as humanists not only echoes but also soothes the thunderous roll of calamity that would otherwise overwhelm us all.

The value and morality of the role of art in mediating distress has a long history of philosophical and literary deliberation. George Eliot on tragedy, Aristotle on catharsis, Theodore Adorno on poetry after the Holocaust, Berthold Brecht on the numbing effects of bourgeois theatre, and Susan Sontag in *Regarding the Pain of Others* are just five intellectuals who have pondered these questions. In a South Asian context, Ramu Nagappan in *Speaking Havoc* and Amitav Ghosh in *The Great Derangement* have also discussed precarity, vulnerability, and suffering. South Asian literary critics such as Homi Bhabha and Gayatri Spivak established entire fields of study by writing at length on not just the suffering of the subaltern but also how to undermine oppressive regimes, especially through Bhabha's iconic concepts of hybridity, mimicry, and sly civility.

The nine essays presented here examine some of the most dangerous ontological and existential conditions in South Asia and its diaspora to see if we can find some warning, some lesson for living life, perhaps even some literary purpose or some aesthetic pleasure in telling stories about precarity. How we comfort ourselves with the knowledge of a constant resistance to this vulnerability and inspire each other to form affective communal solidarities are also meta-themes running through all the essays. We hope this volume will contribute to the on-going global conversation on precarity, vulnerability, and suffering not only because they have preoccupied the human race through the ages but also because our present moment – *the now* – is characterized by pervasive hazard that we as writers, readers, teachers, and humanists must call out, talk and write about, and thus resist. We must constantly care.

The special issue has been divided into sections that not only characterize some of the hallmarks of precarity but also constitute the core of postcolonial and South Asian studies: those of gender, race, class, migrancy, as well as resisting precarity through care-oriented interpretive hermeneutics and pedagogy. Organized unconventionally, and we hope with productive innovation, this issue offers not just scholarly essays but also poems and critical pieces by some of the most important creative writers and scholars in South Asia today. Homi Bhabha, a name that needs no introduction in postcolonial and South Asian studies, opens the journal with a foreword that speaks to the issue of precarity and the vital importance of the humanities in nurturing "care communities." As a crucial acknowledgment of the cataclysmic floods in Kerala in August 2018, Bhabha's foreword is followed by a poetic interlude. The preeminent Malayalam poet, K. Satchidandan, a former secretary of the Sahitya Akademi, watched his state destroyed by floods and wrote a series of anguished, moving poems about the havoc wreaked upon Kerala. In "After the Deluge," the poet speaks in the broken voices of the wind, the rain, the river, and the mountain and mourns the destruction of his ancestral land. The poem eventually turns to the narrative of the survivors who remained standing in defiance of the rising waters:

> We made forts with our legs
> We broke walls with songs
> Defeated death with our dance.
> Survive we will,
> Like the ancient mountains,
> Like alphabets.

Songs, dance, and alphabets steady us like ancient mountains, holding humanity together in the time of horror, reminding us that we are not alone, even in our utmost anguish. "After the Deluge" sets the tone for the entire double-issue by focusing not only on the event of the disaster itself but also on the resistance and care communities necessary to withstand our precarity.

Section I ("Bodies that Do Not Matter: Gender and Precarity") opens with Rahul Gairola's essay, "'Brooms of Doom': Gendered to Death in *Mughal-e-Azam*, *Fire*, and *Earth*." According to Gairola, there is no future in Bollywood cinema for deviant, particularly queer and gendered bodies, for whom even cinematic representation is precarious. Indian film is often unable to imagine a visual life for those it represents, and therefore renders, as deviant. The xenophobic West, particularly the American empire, acts as an instrument of "surveillance" on cultural production both inside and outside its borders, even imposing its prejudicial norms onto representation that takes place elsewhere. In "Post-Magic: The Female Naxalite at 50," Meghan Gorman-DaRif examines Arundhati Roy's *The Ministry of Utmost Happiness* and Neel Mukherjee's *A State of Freedom*, both published in 2017, or the 50th anniversary of Naxalbari. According to these novelists, the conditions of tribal people remains precarious even five decades after the Naxalbari uprising in 1967. Moreover, the wondrous joy of being part of an uncorrupted movement that promises radical change has gone, leading to a feeling of what Gorman-DaRif describes as "post-magic," amongst female revolutionaries. The two novels reveal a deep discomfort with violent revolution as a form of redressing injustice, especially when it becomes the *only* way of redressing injustice. Anirban Bhattacharjee in "The Ethics of Representation and the Figure of the Woman: The Question of Agency" analyzes an array of Bengali language texts to understand the oppression of the female subaltern perpetuated by the binary logic of both Western and non-Western philosophical universalism, and how, even now, this agency is impossible to acquire. All three essays underscore the continued oppression – in some instances as dire as the "mark of death" – imprinted on queer and gendered bodies in South Asia in a wide range of visual and literary contexts.

Section Two ("In a Class of Its Own: Belaboring Precarity") focuses on the great economic divide in South Asia. In "The Literary Lumpen: The *Naksha* Narratives of Binoy, Auritro Majumdar studies the genre of the *naksha* to show how it incorporated tropes from the British novel along with the genre of Persian poetry – a seamless instantiation of Bhabha's concept of hybridity – to represent the unrepresentable, namely the Calcutta poor. Like Gairola, Majumdar also argues that Ghosh depicts the sexualized poor –

prostitutes, sex workers, transsexuals – with no reproductive destiny and, therefore, no potential to rehabilitate the city unlike the industrious working poor. In "Servant Problems in RK Narayan's Short Stories," Ambreen Hai claims that despite its preoccupation with subaltern figures, South Asian literary criticism has failed to study the literary representation of servants. Hai examines RK Narayan's short stories to argue that Narayan's sympathetic depiction of domestic servants ultimately constitutes a failure in narrative depiction. The upper-class *narrator* describes domestic servants in the same derogatory mocking tone as the other upper-class *characters* even when critiquing their behavior towards those who labor on their behalf.

We then proceed to our second poetic interlude. In "Spaces," K. Satchidanandan renders the plight of refugees in painful, lyrical shards of verse that cuts the reader to the core. Yet, the poet reminds us, again, of the role of art in rehabilitating humanity from crisis:

Only words fall on my begging bowl:

Kindness. Love. Sacrifice.
Words.
The Black Hole of words.

When all is lost, the world reduced to a mere begging bowl, words may only be what is left. Even though words themselves may fall into the vortex of a black hole, the powerful last line of the poem signals back to science and the origin of the universe in black holes, empty spaces that do not engulf and erase but instead clear spaces for starting anew amidst immense destitution.

The essays in the next section ("Region and Religion: Eco-Migratory, and Minority Precarity") take up the preceding poem's concern with human displacement through both the physical pain of the immigrant and the more metaphysical crisis of feeling out of place, even in one's own country. In "Examining Precarity and Resistance in Oceanic Literature," Tana Trivedi explains how Indo-Fijian poetry lyrically evokes the fraught encounter between Indians and indigenous Fijians. Both communities occupy precarious positions: Indians because of their former status as indentured laborers and indigenous Fijians because of their lack of political and economic power. Ultimately, these groups are more united than fractured precisely because of their mutual vulnerability as island inhabitants, and unconsciously form care communities against the atmospheric vagaries of The Ocean that surrounds them. "Representing the 'Other': Minority Discourse in the Postcolonial Indian English Novel" also reflects these tensions between different groups co-existing in the same nation but refracts them through a religious lens. Showing how Hindu-Indian writers have represented the alterity of Indian Muslims, Saman Ashfaq claims that their novels simultaneously deconstruct the notion of the Islamic Other in order to author a new national narrative that functions as a crucial form of resistance in post-Godhra India. Narration imagines new and better nations into being in both Trivedi and Asfaq's essays.[4]

Section Four ("Teaching Troubles: The Pedagogy of Precarity") focuses on what literary critics do best: teach to change minds and hearts. In "Teaching Precarity: Engaging Genocide Pedagogy Through Rohini Mohan's *Seasons of Trouble*," Colleen Clemens not only asserts that the ethnic conflict in Sri Lanka should be taught under the rubric of genocide pedagogy but also provides readers with strategies, tips, and questions on how to discuss precarious lives with our students in sympathetic and humane ways rather than through condescending and patronizing stereotypes that only reinforce the radical alterity of South Asians to relatively privileged American students. In "Teaching Beyond

Empathy: The Classroom as Care Community," Matthew Dischinger argues that the undergraduate humanities classroom can become a space for understanding the lives of others as well as a venue where we as humanists sustain ourselves and our students. Dischinger rejects the hierarchical term of "empathy" in and outside the classroom, arguing that it is based on a narcissistic concept of self-correction, and opts for the term "care community" instead. Based on his own experience of teaching Mohsin Hamid's novel, *Exit-West* (2017), to American undergraduates, Dischinger demonstrates that discussing literature, particularly the dangerous lives of migrants, can transform the often cold bland atmospherics of the classroom into a more nurturing forum, for both the teacher and the taught.

This section ends with a third poetic interlude. In "Birds Come After Me," K. Satchidandan vividly imagines a tree mourning its own loss as "a dictionary of leaves" but is even now the only safe harbor for the screaming birds escaping ecological destruction by human actors. Gaurav Desai's Afterword, presented as the keynote at the annual South Asian Literary Association conference in January 2018, "Precarious Futures, Precarious Pasts: Climate, Terror, and Planetarity," begins with a discussion of Amitav Ghosh's novel, *The Sea of Poppies* (2008), opium production in British India in the nineteenth century, and then moves to climate change events. Urging us to see the origin of refugees from Syria as not just generated from a regime of terror but the regime of terror itself as partially generated by water shortage, Desai comes full circle with a reflection on the crisis in opium cultivation in Afghanistan today. Through the long cycle of historical abuse caused by the opium trade, the colorful seemingly innocuous poppy, stands out as a symbol for how ecological violence created a continuous flow of migration, voluntary and forced, as well as reinforced patriarchal hegemony in Afghanistan. Arguing that larger economic actants – colonizing nations and private companies – clash with susceptible groups to cause great environmental and human damage, Desai asserts that ecological precarity and climate change undergirds each and every aspect of vulnerability today. ISIS was provided fertile ground for its ascension by an acute water shortage in Syria, and many of Boko Haram's depredations were caused by the depletion of Lake Chad. To think about precarity is to always to think ecologically.

The *representation* of precarious lives, and the discussion of how writers and critics must be careful of the way we depict vulnerable communities today, lie at the heart of all the contributions to this edition. In their breaking down of destructive depictions and their creative solutions of sympathetic interpretation, our contributors teach us how to resist the oppression of susceptible individuals and groups and create the "care communities" of the title of our special issue. We as readers must learn here the importance of interpretive solidarities that can represent and deconstruct with respect and understanding – a mode of writing and reading that can only emerge from the humanities and literary criticism. Our hope, therefore, in publishing a special volume of *South Asian Review* on the topic of "Precarity, Resistance, and Care Communities" is to reveal the pervasiveness of precarity, and how reading, writing, and teaching can resist that precarity as well as create care communities that show us how simply to treat each other, and the world we inhabit, in more just and humane ways.

Notes

1. Iyer, Pico. "The Value of Suffering." *The New York Times*. September 7. 2013. https://www.nytimes.com/2013/09/08/opinion/sunday/the-value-of-suffering.html (accessed August 1, 2018).

2. The idea for a special issue of *SAR* on this topic sprang from our annual conference in New York in January 2018, although many of the papers included here were not presented at the conference but were invited articles. I thank the conference organizers, Sukanya Gupta and Afrin Zeenat, for centering the theme of the conference around precarity. I also thank P.S. Chauhan for asking me to edit this special issue as well as Homi Bhabha and Gaurav Desai for agreeing to contribute a foreword and afterword to this volume. Thanks, last but not the least, to Rahul Gairola for helping me develop, what we hope is an innovative structure, for this issue and for his assistance in many other ways.

3. The term "care communities" is taken from Isabell Lorey's idea of a ciudad (24). It is understood that the essays in this collection referencing Lorey are referring to this particular text. Therefore, full citation in this introduction is sufficient. Lorey, Isabell. 2015. *State of Insecurity: Government of the Precarious*. New York: Verso.

4. Here, I am obviously echoing the title of the Homi Bhabha's pathbreaking anthology of edited essays, *Nation and Narration*, Routledge, London and New York: 1990.

Disclosure Statement

No potential conflict of interest was reported by the author.

Pallavi Rastogi

POETIC INTERLUDE

After the Deluge

K. Satchidanandan

What the Rain Said

    I fell, ceaseless, in total oblivion
    When I felt the rivers' greed
    I fell, in endless desire,
    When I gauged the ocean's depth.

    I sang a song and fell
    As clouds crowded the sky
    I fell, dancing, as I saw
    The rainbow's seven colours.

    I fell, in intense pain
    When I failed to meet God
    I fell, with boundless joy
    When I finally saw God.

    I forgot the earth and forgot men,
    Forgot beasts and forgot trees
    I forgot myself and turned into
    A demoness clothed in red.

What the River Said

    I was life. Lands gave me names.
    Children swam in my blues with fish
    I laughed and played hide-and-seek
    Watering poems and paddy-crops.

Poets sang in my praise and
On my shores rose languages and ballads,
Cities and dances.

When human greed encroached upon my paths
Seeking refuge, helter-skelter I ran,
Strayed into the homes and
Streets of Men and gods.
Curses rose and bloomed in me
As blood-red bubbles.

Where will I go dear ones,
When God's sky and men's dams
Burst into me and fill me?
Pardon me, ripe fields,
Beasts the currents washed away,
Dead houses, I ask of you
Only for a little space to spread my
Blue arms and legs and freely flow
So that we may not have another war,
I may once again become your friendly river,
I may recall and sing my old lullabies.

What the Mountain Said

I looked after your frontiers like a
Guardian goddess with fangs,
Full of trees and flowers in my hand.
Springs rose from my love
My breeze cooled the perspiring bodies,
I held children on my shoulders and
Treated them to enchanting sights.

Then some came from the cities
Carrying arms; they chopped off my
Nose and breasts and limbs and
Carted them off for a fortune.

When the heavy rain came,

I had no hands to stop them, I crashed

And fell and flowed with the torrent.

Thus the nourisher became the punisher.

Pardon. I too need some love, some patience.

I too am a divinity: the goddess of the wild

Who you mistook for a demoness.(1)

What the Forest Said

I am not a tree, nor a grove

I am a forest, who turns you green with

An echo when you call into me.

I am full of the spirits of the forest-dwellers.

At times I roar, I chirp at times.

I have doubts about your civilization

Every axe falling on me really falls on you;

In every scream of mine it is you who squirm.

I am a forest that nourished with fruit

Tribes and goddesses, hermits and birds,

The green eternity of youth

Fear my tears: it may drown you.

What the Bird Said

At times it is good to have wings,

To have sky too.

To fly above wars and floods

Watching blood turn into water

And water turn into blood

–Far above philosophies.

What the House Said

In my memory I am still a field.

In my memory there is a pond close by,

And a little stram where frogs and fishes chat.

Water lifting its arms and legs and

Laughing with its naked gums, like the

Little Sita in the furrow.

Beautiful little plants among the paddy

That men denounce as weeds.

A hundred flowers. White. Yellow. Red.

Periwinkle. Tape Vine. Morning Glory.

Rice won't grow in drawing rooms

Paddy won't ripen in bedrooms

Water won't seep into concrete.

Now once again I am a field.

Men need houses.

Fields too,

perhaps.

What the Dog Said

You must have seen me in that

Story on the flood (2). My

spotted solitude, my loyalty, my sacrifice.

Earlier I was the fool who had lost the bone

in my mouth barking at my image in the water.(3)

Then I began to get bones; love almost choked me,

And then the flood did. I floated away

Even before the family did.

I struggled like a canoe caught in a whirlpool;

The current carried my whines away like dry leaves.

I saw death face to face: A black wolf

Approaching me howling, its fangs exposed.
It was then that a hand was extended to me:
A hand, a human hand. Those fingers
Appeared above water like sunbeams.
They gently pulled me back into life.

O, man's hands,
Land's affection,
The song of birds,
Green moonlight,
A pipal leaf.(4)

What the Fishermen Said

Long ago a fisherman threw love's net
To catch men and became a sacrifice.(5)

We who survive on land and in water follow him
Water is our home and we are at home
Even when we row our boats in the deluge.
Death wags its tail when it sees us.

We have seen the dove with the olive branch.
Hold on to these stubborn fingers
Smelling of salt and fish, board this
Calloused palm's canoe, like entering
This heart, as true as the Mother Sea.
This will take you to the bright breezy
Land of mercy, away from this darkness
Where hate's tempest blows.

Those who have lost everything
Have nothing to lose.
To be saviours is our mission,
And to be dispossessed, our destiny.

What the People Who Stood Together Said

We held our hands together

The deluge was trapped in our hands

We bent our backs

Became rocks to climb up

We sat on the floor

Became steps to walk on

We stood up straight

Became ladders to reach the roof

We lay down flat

Became bridges to cross the river

We built ships with our eyes

Our heads became helipads

We made forts with our legs

We broke walls with songs

Defeated death with our dance.

Survive we will,

Like the ancient mountains,

Like alphabets.

What the Retreating Water Said

Here, I am going back,

My dance of death done, my drum silenced,

My anklets untied.(6)

Anger does not suit water

And I never meant to scare you.

The clouds that I let loose like matted hair

Refused to listen to me, and rivers

Like the serpents that fell from my neck

Strayed and stole many a life.

Still you stood together to tame me,

Turned me from red to blue again

And sent me back to streams and rivers.

But please don't rebuild the walls I broke!

Don't poison the days of kindness!

Remember as you go back home:

Man, in order to be human, needs

Rivers, mountains, forests, fields

The endless friendship of the earth

The undying compassion of the sea.

What the Sun Said

I have returned from the remains

Of the eastern hills, to the screams of a land

Where the Onam flowers have drowned.

In my lean rays I have

Warmth, energy, youth, beauty.

The bow I placed over your horizon

Is a promise: a white *Tumpa* flower,

A paddy-spike, a kinder heart

At the end of the deluge

Another shore

Of a new awareness

Unstained by blood.

August, 2018

(Translated from Malayalam by the poet)

Notes

The poem was written as a response to the recent deluge that devastated Kerala where the poet belongs. (1) An implicit reference to the episode in many Ramayanas, of Surpanakha, supposedly a demoness, maimed by Lakshmana, Rama's brother for having sought his love. (2) Reference to a classic Malayalam short story, *Vellappokkathil* (In the Floods) by Thakazhi Shivashankara Pillai. (3) A popular legend about a foolish dog that used to be taught in primary classes in Kerala. (4) An image from Bhagavata: little Krishna floating on the waters of final Deluge on a pipal (also 'peepal' or sacred fig) leaf. (5) Fisher-folk who risked their lives to save many thousands of people trapped in the floods were the real heroes and have been recognised as such by the people and even the government of Kerala. The references to the Holy Bible strewn across the sequence– fisherman who catches men, Noah's arc, the dove with the olive leaf, God's vow appearing as a rainbow– reflect this context. (6) The image is of Nataraja, Siva in his *thandava*, the dance of death.

Foreword

Pallavi Rastogi and her contributors must be congratulated for taking on the challenge of addressing the post-colonial predicament *in extremis*. Today the global worlds, North and South encounter each other in a terrifying symmetry of ethnonationalist majoritarianism. In the name of the nation's "people", minorities and migrants become targets of a tyrannical rule of discrimination that violates their rights and representations, while dissidents are silenced and incarcerated in the name of the national "interest".

Majoritarian populism is a political machinery of disavowal and projection. The failed promises of an era of equitable global connectivity are unjustly attributed to the miscreants of *mondialisation* – "failed states", refugees, minorities, and increasingly, an ill-defined generic category of "muslims". Wars executed by empowered European nations in the Middle East and the Near East, in the name of democracy, have unseated targeted dictators while leaving their peoples in dire states of destitution and denigration amidst geographies of urban and rural destruction.

What is precarious today extends beyond the conditions of political, cultural or natural life to which this special issue rightly draws our attention. Climate-change unleashes its furies against the human abuse of the environment; regime-change catches us on the wrong foot as, for instance, when Obama yields to Trump. Precarity is more than an ontological or governmental crisis; it is the problem of having to think counterfactually – on other grounds towards other means and other ends and in the interests of other peoples – while we are immersed in the emergencies of the factual localities of our present times. And this makes us ask whether the "precarious" condition elicits a response of care or a resitant solidarity premised on convergence. Or both.

What are the agencies of convergence in an era of world vulnerability? Where does the "third world" exist today, not as a category of hierarchical global economic dependency, not even as a prescribed political geography of post-colonial opposition, but as a carefully constructed interventionist platform of anti-hegemonic global solidarity that is both *tropic* and territorial. The "developing" world today is fraught with bourgeoning billionaires who create their own first-world islands amidst oceans of the negative-growth lives of millions who are cast adrift. The developed world, with very few exceptions, has retreated into the xenophobia of self-protection and all you hear is the white noise of racial exclusion and evisceration. The global world, North and South, is rapidly making its peace with a human condition defined by violence and injustice, forcing us to ask again and again, *Where is the Third World now? Who represents the Third World Now?*

This special issue works towards building arguments that attempt to address these questions.

Homi K. Bhabha

Brooms of Doom: Notes on Domestic Bodies Gendered to Death in Mughal-e-Azam, Fire, and Earth

Rahul K. Gairola

ABSTRACT

This essay explores how current trends of xenophobic and class-based violence target women of color in a throwback to postcolonial studies. Representational discourses produce these subjects as gendered bodies whose ultimate difference lies in a postcolonial biology of difference that opens them to death. In particular, I unravel the tight braid of domesticity "at home" with the necropolitical prerogative of patriarchal hegemons in three key Hindi films: K. Asif's *Mughal-e-Azam* and Deepa Mehta's *Fire* and *Earth*. I begin by recalling various theories of representation of women of color in relation to the othering of gendered and racialized bodies, and then link them to regimes of gender that are allegorized by the "brooms" of domesticity. I focus on the women protagonists, and demonstrate that these three films, with respect to their varying historical periods, deposit gendered domesticity as the occasion and justification for women protagonists to encounter obliteration – a sweeping act that renders them "brooms of doom." In conclusion, I return to the present context to frame my readings of these "brooms of doom" that sweep through these films into a history of the present that continues to render precarious the lives of women of color.

Prelude: Opening Minutes

When South Asian scholars and our allies scrutinize the general health of our world today, it appears to be much worse than when the unthinkable occurred – the Twin Towers of New York City collapsed into a crashing shame on September 11, 2001. Many of us hoped that we were forever rid of George W. Bush's "with us or without us" xenophobic rhetoric of exclusion. More than 15 years later and with many more lives lost in perpetual wars and the vacuum of the carceral state, it seems that Mother Nature too has turned her back on humans. Floods that devastate Kerala, wild storms in Europe, vicious hurricanes battering the US's East Coast, drought in southeastern Australia, melting polar caps in the Arctic, tsunamis in Japan, goliath plastic patches in the oceans, etc., mercilessly assault us as interested parties deny climate change.

For all who have challenged rape and Section 377 in contemporary India.

In "Postcolonial Studies and the Challenge of Climate Change," Dipesh Chakrabarty writes, "Climate change is not a one-event problem. Nor is it amenable to a single rational solution … With regard to the climate crisis, humans now exist in two different modes. There is one in which they are still concerned with justice even when they know that perfect justice is never to be had." (Chakrabarty 2012, 13–14).

Even without perfect justice for both precarious lives and an increasingly precarious ecology, however, the quest for reparation is arguably more urgent now than it has ever been before. It is from this sense of urgency that I open with an urgent question: how might South Asian diasporic subjects scattered across the globe return to key texts in postcolonial studies in relation to the rise of #BlackLivesMatter and #MeToo hashtag activism movements? Given the fruition of violent patriarchy in governments around the globe, we might begin by invoking, Gayatri Chakravorty Spivak's "Can the Subaltern Speak?" on the 30th anniversary of its publication this year. I conduct this exploration by critically analyzing representations of gendered bodies in popular Hindi films that have become staple of Western discourses of orientalism even as they are nostalgic bulwarks for South Asian diasporas in the West. Bollywood films, too, have diasporic lives that are imbricated in scopic bias. I propose this analysis in relation to the filmic lives rendered precarious by the infrastructures of surveillance that situate them. I argue that they pose resistance to hegemonic spaces that are domestic yet semi-public. I turn my attention to popular Hindi filmic representation as a cultural critic while simultaneously acknowledging the stifling atmosphere in the U.S. as a sentient being peering in from the southern hemisphere.

I propose such a lens since it offers a comparative juxtaposition from which one can evaluate British colonialism as it has played out in the USA, India, Australia, and beyond in democratic societies whose own brands of nationalism have inherited Empire's gilded stole. Homi Bhabha recognizes the nation's historical ambivalence, simultaneously looking forwards and backwards, in relation to what he calls the "Janus-faced discourse of the nation" (Bhabha 1990, 3). In describing this double feature of the nation, writes Bhabha, the nation "turns the familiar, two-faced god into a figure of prodigious doubling that investigates the nation-space in the *process* of the articulation of elements: where meanings may be partial because they are *in media res*; and history may be half-made because it is in the process of being made; and the image of cultural authority may be ambivalent because it is caught, uncertainly, in the cat of 'composing' its powerful image [original emphasis]" in relation to the nation and its other (Bhabha 1990, 3–4). While the contemporary and forward-looking face of the nation is about post-racial multiculturalism and individual rights, the actions of the nation starkly challenge the antiquated views of nationalism borne from the Enlightenment.[1]

We know that although any*body* and every*body* is ostensibly invited to make the nation home, not every*body* is the same within the *body* of the nation. Different bodies are marked in different ways by histories of segregation, colonialism, apartheid, eugenics, capitalism, etc., and are thus justifiably caught in the crosshairs of necropolitical precarity as decades earlier.[2] While such treatment – the reduction of human life to that of an animal, one worse than that of a pet – of any individual in any context is abhorrent, watchdog scrutiny has concentrated on the fact that these are children and not fully developed adults. That is, many critics widely view this type of incarceration as mixing criminality and innocence attending juvenile bodies, which the Trump administration has deemed anathematic to American democracy. Of course, many well-meaning Americans disidentify[3] with these bodies since the rules of difference create border-jumpers and law breakers identifiable by the color of their skins.

The global focus on certain bodies – be they of migrants, children, women, or people of color – and the challenge that they pose to the established order of white supremacy by materially existing returns us to shifting notions of otherness. In India, for example, vocal critics of the Modi regime have been harassed, trolled, hunted and arrested under the guise of an "urban Naxal" plot to assassinate the prime minister (Apoorvanand 2018). At stake, all around, are the social significations of flesh and blood – covered by epidermal shells whose social signification is also rooted in color-coded hierarchies. In a world under assault by neoliberal capitalism that renders sentient life precarious, skin color has become the fetishized signifier of institutionalized otherness.

The Skin of Subalternity

These horrific events fall on the year that marks the 30th anniversary of the publication of Gayatri Chakravorty Spivak's (1988) foundational essay, "Can the Subaltern Speak?" Spivak's essay challenges the authority of intersecting paradigms of power that ensnare Hindu women and the knowledge production of philosophical stalwarts including Marx, Michel Foucault, Deleuze and Guittari.[4] As I have elsewhere testified, "The immortal question continues to compel us to recognize and interrogate social exclusions in their most muted and incognizant disguises: 'Can the subaltern speak? What must the elite do to watch out for the continuing construction of the subaltern?'" (Gairola and Ali 2017, 3). In Prathima Banerjee's estimation, the adjective does not inherently contain particularity, and thus we may as well ask, "Can one say that the subaltern is by definition not a socially or culturally specifiable figure? That if s/he is socially or culturally marked, it is so only contingently? Is the subaltern then one who claims recognition by virtue of her inherent political and/or oppositional stance and not by virtue of any historical difference as such?" (Banerjee 2015, 20).

While I do not have the space to include more responses to Spivak's reformulation of "Subaltern," we must note that the term's very malleability has birthed scores of variant iterations and applications of the essay around the globe, and even an academic volume of essays edited by Rosalind Morris titled *Can the Subaltern Speak? Reflections on the History of an Idea*. In commenting on her essay some years later, Spivak personally writes to me, "Many people around the world have borrowed that title ['Can the Subaltern Speak?'] but not really understood what I was trying to say. Mostly, they are claiming that, 'Yes, the subaltern can speak!' without any actual involvement with subalterns anywhere in the world" (Spivak 2016). What comes into sharp focus here is how Spivak draws upon certain types of women's bodies in "Can the Subaltern Speak?" to expose their different social meanings.

One type is the mythical body of a goddess who self-immolates herself to avenge her father's mistreatment of her husband while the other type is the misidentified freedom fighter whose suicide might be socially read as testament of her carrying child out of wedlock (she was not pregnant). These are bodies marked by different domestic duties and labor practices with little about them being the same except perhaps their perceived genders despite the fact that some misreadings of Spivak's work conflate differences between women in claiming to be attentive to the plight of the subaltern. We encounter such a misreading, for example, in a recent "feminist angle" (Maurya, Kumar and Mishra 2018, 228) analysis of Advait Chandan's *Secret Superstar* (2018).

Here, the authors allege that "The trend of Indian cinema is now changing through the production of such movies, where [the] stereotype image of woman as a submissive and docile creature suffering silently, traverses to the image of a new woman who raises her voice against her suffering and emerges victorious [sic]" (Maurya, Kumar and Mishra 2018, 233). This sweeping generalization is compounded by an earlier contradiction on the same page: "a serious interpretation of the movie *Secret Superstar* reveals that Insia and Najma are representatives of all women in general" (*ibid*). In making these dubious claims, the authors resurrect the epistemic violence of misogyny by flattening out the differences between women whose common denominator is their gendered body parts.[5] Here, the rush to claim recognition of the subaltern for self-aggrandizing purposes betrays the impulse to speak for others, namely Muslim women, at all costs.

Such facile thinking nurtures gender oppression for it perpetuates the misogynistic illusion that all women are reducible to the sum of their body parts, producing women as exploitative objects of domestic labor whose lives may be obliterated with little consequence or care. Ultimately viewed as necessary to the domestic, heteronormative household yet always open to physical abuse, sexual harassment and violence, psychological and emotional torture, etc., these women might as well be what I hereon call "brooms of doom." The broom is an allegorical vehicle of domestic labor that sweeps some women towards obliteration. These women are literally "gendered to/for death," marked for a specific purpose in and through their perceived gender, although Spivak has cautioned against "uninstructed cultural relativism," arguing instead for the distinct nuances of difference that characterize serious intellectual labor (Spivak 1995, 197). We clearly see this in the example of death, where suicide attends the bodily function of menstruation from which flows the "truth" of a second body that is not incubating within Bhaduri's body.

In the following section, I put further pressure on the postcolonial, Hindu woman's body as a site of ongoing societal violence. While it is not my intention to reiterate the myth of Sati or engage in a literature review of "Can the Subaltern Speak?", I want to refocus on the woman's body as the contemporary nexus of fluctuating yet ubiquitous rage and epistemic violence today as when Spivak first wrote of it. Indeed, here I wish to write as a person who is an "outsider" (Bhabha 1990, 175) to bodies that are gendered as Hindu women even as I witness the terrifying explosion of sexual violence against them on the watch of Narendra Modi and his pro-Hindu, Bharatiya Janata Party (BJP).

The unborn body within a body sparks a social crisis whereas the body of Sati is immolated, at which point she becomes Devi Sati. Death permeates and defines chastity. After all, is not the placement of black and brown children in "cages" an outright act of war against women of color? The current state of affairs in countries around the world and the openly xenophobic and racist comments of many of their politicians compel us to return to Spivak with a focus on the black and brown bodies of women, which have historically been the fraught vessels of miscegenation.

Skin as such is a biological signifier of race, class, and gender that codifies bigotry in the social sphere. It delineates and justifies which lives are deemed to be, in a word, precarious. This essay broaches themes that are frighteningly too relevant today across historical and geographical boundaries: religious zeal, chauvinistic nationalism, racialized hegemony, gendered violence, betraying institutions, and even the refusal to listen. It also asks readers to think comparatively, against the logic of some strands of area studies. The recent theorizing of Deepika Bahri in *Postcolonial Biology: Psyche and Flesh after Empire* is instructive here. For Bahri, the oppressive superstructure of colonialism and its aftermath – completely fraught with racism, casteism, sexism, bigotry, xenophobia, etc. – is mired in even the most mundane of the body's biological processes. These biological processes include the fundamentals of how we "eat, speak, sit, shit, or spit" (3).

Matters that Embody

Bahri nudges contemporary postcolonial studies away from their overdetermination on identity politics, instead examining the anatomical world within, beneath the shell of skin and flesh. Under a critical microscope, she exhumes the situated positions of postcolonial bodies that meet at the corporeal intersection of Michel Foucault's notion of biopolitics[6] and Michel de Certeau's conception of the practice of everyday life.[7] Bahri's premise in *Postcolonial Biology* is both refreshing and chilling; like a blast of arctic air, her study urges readers to view biological plasticity as the hybrid body's parallel to colonial mimicry – a parallel that renders its subject vulnerable to a flexible "projection, manipulation, and product placement" (6). In simple terms, the hybridity of mixed race postcolonial subjects, for example, entails negotiations in the biological processes within that are shaped by the residual vestments of colonial mimicry.[8] For black and brown peoples upon whose backs lie the heavy burden of Empire's histories and normalized necropolitics,[9] the biological impacts of colonialism within are toxic.

For women of color whom society views as brooms of doom, the threat of transgressive reproduction socially translates to anxieties of mixed race subjects in white spaces that suture together race and reproduction (Weinbaum 2004, 4–6). Precarity crosses the thresholds of generation by collating legal discourse here. Yet mongrel subjects[10] still yearn to belong today, and this desire to belong is literally so internalized that it impacts the biological world while signifying exclusion in the social world. Ketu Katrak has aptly argued that "the [post-colonial] female body is in a state of exile including self-exile and self-censorship, outsiderness, and un-belonging to itself within indigenous patriarchy (historicized within different cultures and histories) strengthened by British racialized colonial practices" (Katrak 2006). As such, the imprisonment of black and brown children in the so-called border zones of the United States is little less than a xenophobic assault on the reproductive bodies of women of color.

The space in which certain bodies are racialized is also constitutive of their internal and external lives, especially under the violence of law on unruly subjects today – a violence that has persisted from the colonial period. Radhika Mohanram, for example, astutely notes, "Raced bodies, nations, ideas about places, passports and visas all emerged in the nineteenth century and are inextricably linked. Senses of place are linked with ideas of national identity as well as with the hierarchy of nations" (Mohanram 1999, 4). Bodies are thus placed at certain sites, one of which is history. Other sites of precarious bodies are those that we can think of as "risky bodies" where hybridity and queer sexuality mix and render the subjects threats to finance capitalism (Patel 2016, 65). Both capital and state-sponsored movements racialize bodies at risk by claiming that they, in fact, pose a risk to movement and capital.

In the context of precarious lives in the twenty-first century, the body mired in transnational surveillance beneath the capitalistic gaze of paranoid patriarchy is the fraught locus of social exclusion. In *Online Philanthropy in the Global North and South*, for example, Radhika Gajjala extends the ways in which finance and technology coalesce around the postcolonial woman's body. She writes,[11]

> Speech patterns and embodied performativity are learned in relation to the people and contexts we engage with and enter into. Translating to be heard transforms our subject position and engagement with the world. If we think of the 'subaltern' as a subject position that is outside the mainstream – that subject position really never "speaks" recognizably because the enunciation must transform in relation to the expectations of hearing within dominant structures. Brought into social media space, this idea of subaltern speech and access is further complicated when we begin to note that the spread of mobile gadget use in the subaltern sphere and also to note the how connectivity, access, and neoliberal agendas also don't clearly fit the center/periphery model of power that cultural studies and postcolonial scholars have often implicitly worked with or negotiated and contested. (Gajjala 2017, xi)

Gajjala's observations are useful in the context of popular Hindi cinema, as these consolidate the ways in which many Western viewers see and Indians orientalise themselves through the lavish, visual fantasies of Bollywood. As we know, South Asian literatures, and other forms of cultural production (for example, television shows, film industries, and even digital advertisements), articulate insecurities within bourgeois communities, especially where masculinity and family honour are concerned. Such dramas on the silver screen seem to mirror the real-life death of Bollywood's most famous feminist actor – Sridevi. The recent, mysterious death of the feminist film siren has sparked many retrospective evaluations of the role of women in Bollywood cinema and the ways in which many women actors pioneered important roles that shattered the glass ceiling of Hindi cinema (Habib 2018). But … that shattered glass ceiling has come through death again, the tragic yet common bond.

Three Filmic Texts and a Critique of Gendered Bodies

The socio-political stakes that frame black and brown women's bodies appear as a theme in a few important films: K. Asif's *Mughal-e-Azam* (1960) and Deepa Mehta's films *Fire* (1996) and *Earth* (Mehta 1998). In considering the ongoing urgency of "Can the Subaltern Speak?" 30 years later, in today's era of fascist surveillance and violence around the world, I focus on brooms of doom, or women's bodies that are marked for death, in these films. This marking is not the same as suicide, where, crudely, one marks oneself for death. While it may have been much easier to conduct a reading of Mehta's *Elements* trilogy by including her film *Water* (2005), I want to demonstrate some historical depth to Hindi cinematic representation of brooms of doom while giving readers a comparative view. At the same time, I wanted to recognize that Deepa Mehta, perhaps more than any other Indian diasporic woman filmmaker, has offered viewers around the world jarring visions of the gender chauvinism that Hindu women endure on a daily basis. I moreover wanted to avoid over-determining the ubiquity of "brooms of doom" by focusing on a single filmmaker. The net effect is, I hope, a fascinating juxtaposition of brooms of doom across space and time with differing exposure to socially-sanctioned murders.

What, exactly, braids these three films together in such a fshion that the varying death decrees fashion these tragic brooms of doom into figures of class resistance – even if we accept that lovers are simply a "class" of citizens? The narratives of these three films orbit around forbidden, what we could call queer love (inter-class, same-sex, and inter-religious) and end with male agents consigning the female protagonists' bodies to variations of death. Failed gender expectations and forbidden lust marks the figures of Anarkali, Radha, and Shanta to death although in all three films the women seem narrowly to escape actually dying. In *Fire* and *Mughal-E-Azam*, women protagonists are pressured to follow social rules and expectations, while in *Earth,* one person's expectations about relationships and whom one woman should love leads to death and abduction. *Mughal-E-Azam* and *Fire* feature female protagonists who, despite patriarchal society's demands, cannot hide their desires to love whom they want. These women are expected and required to fulfil their duties as wives, and in the case of *Mughal-E-Azam,* a courtesan and indentured servant.

Gender norms are barriers that demarcate class, caste, religion, and servitude. Let us first consider Madhubala's performance in *Mughal-E-Azam*. Anarkali is a young woman purchased and enslaved by the Emperor Akbar for her beauty and talent. This is love at first sight for his son, Prince Saleem, and Anarkali soon develops feelings for him as well. Anarkali knows that her desire for the prince is wrong; it would not only be fatal for her, but also detrimental to the prince's reputation and status. Class and caste constitute their society and as a low-class woman, let alone a slave, Anarkali knows she will be punished for acting on her feelings. Part of the forbidden, heteronormative romance that textures this narrative is based in the humanization of idolatry. Anarkali is meant to serve as a model for the emperor's request to a sculptor to make the most beautiful sculpture in the world. But due to time constrictions, the latter paints Anarkali from head to toe and places her on a pedestal covered by a veil of beads. Prince Saleem is smitten by her ethereal beauty. The feeling is mutual, and this angers the jealous and watchful Bahar, who means to invigilate the hierarchies of rank and class.

Bahar, who aspires to be queen one day, reveals the couple's love to Emperor Akbar who imprisons Anarkali, abuses her, and violently coerces her to renounce her love for Prince Saleem. When Anarkali tells Saleem that she does not love him, he strikes her across the face. Anarkali wins back Saleem's heart against the Emperor's wishes, and the couple abscond in defiance of the Emperor's orders. In his article "Notions of Gender in Hindi Cinema: The Passive Indian Woman in the Global Discourse of Consumption," Prakash Kona writes, "However in the end the woman has to make way for the men to reconcile and feudal bourgeois male supremacy prevails" (Kona, 10). Kona's summation implicates both class and patriarchy in the conflict between father and son, but more tellingly suggests that the erasure of Anarkali and her mother are requisites for the reconciliation of Emperor Akbar with Prince Saleem. Order can only be restored to the Mughal Empire when the human allegories of its disarray – the brooms of doom – exit the narrative. Indeed, their disruption of the social order of marriage parallels the insurrection of the lower castes against feudal structures.

Of course, the same is true of the reconciliation with transgressive femininity and hegemonic patriarchy, but the narrative of *Mughal-e-Azam* also includes the hyper-emotive mother figure (Queen Jodha) and the sly and cat-like, rival courtesan (Bahar). Anarkali is thus but property, something to fight over, rather than a sentient being with thoughts and feelings. She is a beautiful, submissive woman whom the King recognizes as his property. In the end, Akbar gives his kingdom the impression that he has buried Anarkali alive, but secretly exiles her from the Mughal Empire with her mother, to whom he owed a decades-old boon. Thus, Akbar commutes Anarkali's body from biological death to social death as her exile includes a symbolic death wherein she must live in obscurity and his son must never know that she is alive. As "a broom of doom," Anarkali's physical death is not as crushing as her symbolic death in the mind and heart of Prince Saleem and the implicit death of her potential to ascend the caste/class ladder. As such, the death penalty levelled against Anarkali's sexualized servility is intended to recuperate the kingdom and Prince Saleem as its heir and murder any hope of gender and/or class consciousness.

Domesticity and Death in the Films of Deepa Mehta

In both of Deepa Mehta's films, we witness different kinds of violent, patriarchal threats of death. In *Fire*, Mehta focuses on queer sexuality in socially acceptable heterosexual relationships that are deemed culturally acceptable in upper middle class, "respectable" families of urban India. Although these relationships and marriages are the only "appropriate" ones in their society, both women and men are unhappy and dissatisfied emotionally or sexually in their relationships. Hindu women must uphold certain gendered expectations, even ideals, to be considered good wives, not only in their community but throughout urban and rural India. In *Fire*, Radha cares for her elderly, mute mother-in-law as her duty involves administering the Hindu homestead along with the men in her family. The women in the film are tools for men rather than companions, lovers, or even friends with thoughts and feelings. Radha's husband demands complete submission and subjugation in the suppression of his desires, and expects Radha to obey without question.

Societal decorum and civility compel Radha to keep her thoughts and feelings to herself, which leaves her longing for someone with whom she can emotionally connect. Radha's solitude is exacerbated by her husband's vow of celibacy, which he took over 10 years earlier after discovering that she is sterile (in the doctor's words, "no eggs, madam"). There is no robust intimacy to any aspect of their relationship, which Radha regards as bland as "boiled rice." Rather than having sex with her as a pleasurable form of intimacy, her husband uses her body to "test" himself for temptation. Throughout the film, both husbands command their spouses to do their duties "as a wife." As a younger foil to Ashok, his hero-like brother Jatin enters an arranged marriage with a beautiful young woman named Sita. Jatin is in love with Julie, a Chinese woman, with whom he has been in a relationship prior to his marriage to Sita, and he continues to see Julie even after his marriage. While many women's bodies are reserved for the pleasure of men and their husbands, Ashok uses Radha's body as a tool to "test" his celibacy. Radha is devoted to her husband and his ways, and goes along with what he – and society expect – her as a "proper" Hindu wife despite her unhappiness.

Jatin, however, sees Sita as just a body through which he can experience an orgasm and/or with whom he can reproduce. Both husbands ultimately use their wives' bodies to satisfy patriarchal transgressions of heteronormative romance. To put this in simple terms, rejection is a prerogative of the chauvinistic, Hindu men in both *Fire* and *Mughal-e-Azam*. As I have elsewhere explained, when Hindu women are given away in marriage, they are essentially "gifted" to the patriarch – an act that demonstrates a woman's worth to herself and to her husband (Gairola 2002, 312–313). These women were also given to their husbands in arranged marriages, and the husbands can use those "gifts" to their liking, put them aside, or do whatever else they please. Radha has always been unhappy in her marriage, as she seems to have lost herself in a dull marriage, living life as her husband's gendered mendicant. Their relationship lacks intimacy, love, and passion, which Radha does not fully realize she is longing for until she bonds with Sita.

Sita and Radha are brought together by their domestic duties. As the women connect emotionally they realize that they share something deeper than friendship with one another. Their passion and desire for intimacy leads them into a socially unacceptable lesbian relationship. Their bodies come together in an emotional expression of physical desire. After their first night together, Sita asks Radha if they did something wrong, although she knows that society, and their husbands, would see their relationship as a sin Radha responds that they did nothing wrong. This demonstrates the age difference between the two where Sita appears to be a carefree and passionate a character who is willing to take risks. The generational difference between these women also reflects in their apparel, in how they cover their bodies. The women in this film wear traditional Indian clothing; these clothes are very colorful, feminine, and delicate looking, just how gendered society expects to look and behave.

In one early scene, Sita dresses in Jatin's jeans and is very giddy and excited in doing so. This scene signifies that Sita deviates from the gender norms of her patriarchal, Hindu household. She is comfortable wearing men's clothing, but she also knows that her transgression of gender norms must be secretive since wearing such clothes would never be acceptable to her family or to outsiders. In another scene, Sita again dresses in men's clothing when she and Radha are singing and dancing to a popular Hindi song in front of Radha's mother-in-law, Biji. The elderly woman is unable to speak, but uses a bell to express herself and her needs. Sita feels safe to dress this way in front of Biji because the mute matriarch cannot normatively express her opinions about the matter. This particular aspect of Mehta's film invokes the gender theories of Judith Butler. In "Imitation and Gender Insubordination," Butler describes the confusion that she experienced because she knew she was a lesbian, but when going off to college she would claim that she is "going to college to be a lesbian" (Butler 1993, 311).

Of course, Butler's anecdote, like her overall theory of gender performance, is overdetermined by its Westcentrism, something to remember when meditating on postcolonial India in the twenty-first century.

However, the confusion between gendered clothing and the desiring body beneath it can travel across geographical and cultural zones. In the context of Sita's dressing in men's clothes, her desire to do so could hint to her lesbianism (although not all lesbians dress in "men's" clothes – or even in "women's" clothes for that matter), or even her class privilege in postcolonial, urban India. It is not clear whether whether Sita and Radha knew they were lesbians before exploring their relationship, but Ashok's discovery of the women whips him up into a murderous frenzy. He averts his eyes and leaves the kitchen when Radha's sari catches on fire. Viewers here acquire a sense of what "becoming Sati" might look like in the domestic confines of the kitchen versus upon the somber coals of the funeral pyre. This "trial by fire" echoes the dubious "kitchen fires" that have claimed the lives of women across India, and takes us back to the ways in which clothes constitute the public shell of the bodies beneath.

Ashok's religious zeal uncovers his murderous inclinations as he watches his wife aflame, then looks away, and walks off with Biji in his arms. Here, mother and son are caustic society's witnesses to the obliteration of a queer, Hindu woman's life. In writing about the film elsewhere, I have observed, "Mehta slows down the action of this scene and engulfs our point-of-view in the flames that spread up the folds of Radha's sari. The sari literally confines Radha to her traditional role of subordinate Indian housewife that makes her subject to a trial by fire/enactment of sati. Sita, in contrast, defies the gender roles expected of her, which we see when she twice wears her husband's Western clothes" (Gairola 2002, 319). Like Anarkali in Mughal-e-Azam, then, Radha in tattered clothing escapes obliteration at the hands of a patriarch due to prohibited sexual desires. As punishment for escaping the iron fist of male privilege, punitive society attempts to strip them like the figure of Draupadi.[12] Like Anarkali, Radha is also left homeless and without any access to money or resources. These women decide to pursue non-heteronormative love that crosses caste and gender boundaries and the men thus swiftly condemn them to death; these women became brooms of doom whose fiery passions must be excised from the social order that threatens caste, as well as gender, hierarchy. With domestic, rather than erotic, labour exhausted, these necropolitical women consequently have the utility of carcasses.

This dystopic vision pans out differently in Deepa Mehta's *Earth*. Here, characters of different religions are affected by the contentions and pressures that come with the division of India following the long process of British colonization. The diverse Indian community members which once lived together in Lahore, the fashionable capital of Punjab, are now targets of the disappearing colonisers' "divide and rule" tactics, namely towards Muslims, Hindus, and Sikhs. Hasan and Dil Nawaaz, who are both Muslims, are in love with Shanta, a Hindu. They anchor a group of friends that comprises people of different faiths. In the beginning of the film, this coterie of friends gets along and even jokes about the impending storm. All the while, Dil Nawaaz and Hasan wittily flirt with Shanta as a means of winning over her affection. As the contentions begin to percolate and quickly reach a boiling point between the different religious groups in and beyond Lahore, the friends start to argue, blame, and divide along sectarian lines. The tension rises, erupts, and ultimately breaks the group apart, just as India's indigenous communities are dividing as rumors of the impending division of the subcontinent into an "India" and a "Pakistan" spread across the city.

The uncertainty and violence among people has everyone on edge as death unfolds on the streets and railways leading in and out of Lahore. Dil Nawaaz is especially consumed by a murderous animus after de discovers his sisters' corpses and severed breasts on a train filled with dead Muslim. Dil Nawaaz's transformation into an unrecognizable thug in Shanta's eyes is catalyzed by his horrific witness of the ghost train and its macabre contents. The dead bodies – of men, women, and children – are a turning point in Mehta's second chapter of the *Elements Trilogy*. The train is an iron hearse on rails lubed with native blood whose arrival inaugurates the death of Dil Nawaaz's heart as he becomes more involved in anti-Hindu and anti-Sikh political violence. Throughout the film, Dil Nawaaz manipulates Shanta, trying to get her to do what he wants, while she usually gives in to his pestering. Dil Nawaaz is unaware of Shanta and Hasan's love for one another and unsuccessfully asks Shanta to marry him. Soon after the rejection of his proposal, Dil Nawaaz sees Shanta and Hasan having sex.

Although Mehta signifies his building resentment, Dil Nawaaz's fury consumes him from the inside out as an inter-faith marriage with Shanta disintegrates in his skewed imagination. Dil Nawaaz feels betrayed by Hasan, Shanta, and his country. Hasan and Dil Nawaaz are of the same faith, yet Dil Nawaaz is so enveloped by his feelings of anger and betrayal and the compounded trauma of his country falling apart that he murders Hasan. Like the various religious groups trying to control India, Dil Nawaaz wants to control Shanta and appropriate her body for himself. And this is indeed how *Earth* ends. As Shanta is preparing to secretly flee Lahore with Hasan and get married in the household servant, Hari, along with Lenny Baby, discovers the corpse body of Shanta's fiance in a gunnysack by the road side on the way home. Hasan's corpse underscores the bloodshed that has driven Dil Nawaaz crazy and implicates him as the murderer. Meanwhile, an enraged group of Muslim men arrive at the estate where Shanta works as a domestic ayah, or nanny, for the child protagonist Lenny Baby. Because the family that Shanta works for is Parsi, who were viewed as neutral during the Partition, the angry mob does not clamour for their blood. But Shanta is a Hindu, so her body is marked for revenge and sexual violence. The angry mob asks where Shanta is, and it seems that she will be spared as her mistress has hidden her.

It is not until Dil Nawaaz appears on the scene and manipulates a child's trust by asking Lenny Baby, "She's here, isn't she?" When the innocent girl reveals that Shanta is hiding in the mistress's closet, the angry mob seizes her, ties her up, and forcefully carries her off into an unknown future as she screams to Lenny's mother to tell Hasan. While the abduction of the servant most clearly leaves her open to punitive death, we also do not know what will happen to Lenny Baby and her mother. As Mehta's film closes, an elderly Lenny reflects on the horrible price of the British Empire's hasty exit from the Indian subcontinent. Metha's filmic turn to the present reminds viewers that the whole story is a memory; moreover, it suggests the different stages of solitude and ostracization that these brooms of doom face across the decades.

Coda: Bodies of Evidence

Children's bodies and abducted bodies, both gendered as women, here open and close the film. But unlike the endings of *Mughal-e-Azam* and *Fire*, the concluding sequence of *Earth* suggests that Dil Nawaaz and his mob have yet to punitively force patriarchal violence on Shanta's body. Although the female characters in *Fire, Mughal-E-Azam,* and *Earth* experience different situations and relationships in their own societies in different times, they are ultimately expected (or forced) to behave how men and society expect Indian women to behave. They are all living in patriarchal societies in which Hindu patriarchs control women regardless of their class or status and the women must obey and fulfil their duties. Each of the women in these films challenge that which society perceives as sinful or dishonorable in the name of love and follow their hearts even though it may put their lives, families, and futures ultimately at risk.

In rejecting the exclusionary axioms of conjugal heteronormativity as articulated though caste and class in Khan's *Mughal-e-Azam*, same-sex love in *Fire*, and rival religions in *Earth*, these women protagonists put their bodies on the line. If we cannot see today that patriarchal facism is putting women of colour and other minorities in the crosshairs of death, then we must continue to read Spivak – again, again, and again until it all sinks in and re-emerges as social action against the production of brooms of doom and normalized regimes of gendered domesticity and violence. With precarity becoming a normalized state of affairs around the globe, the gendered bodies within and beyond South Asia are at the mercy of Anthropocene. What will our collective answer be?

Acknowledgements

I owe great thanks to Pallavi Rastogi and my two anonymous peer reviewers for incisive guidance that greatly sharpened this essay. I moreover thank my SALA colleagues P.S. Chauhan, Robin Field, Christopher Ian Foster, Nalini Iyer, and Amritjit Singh. At Murdoch University,

I am deeply grateful for the collegiality and counsel offered by Tim Flanagan, Helena Grehan, Lian Jenvey, Simone Lazaroo, Melissa Merchant, Vijay Mishra, David Moody, Michael Prince, Ann Schwenkenbecher, Leonie Stickland, Anne Surma, Kathryn Trees, and our wonderful students. In other supportive ways and around the world, I sincerely thank Paul Arthur, Homi K. Bhabha, Ethan Blue, Shae Garwood, Caleb Holmes, Tyler Ray, Nadia Rhook, Tasneem Shahnaaz, and Gayatri Chakravorty Spivak.

Notes

1. For more on perceptions of the nation in relation to slavery and colonialism, see Anderson (1993) and Balibar and Wallerstein (1991).
2. Achille Mbembe describes necropolitics as "subjugation of life to the power of death" (Mbembe 2003, 39).
3. I am using the term "disidentify" by drawing on the concept introduced by Jose Esteban Munoz. For more in the useful notion of strategic use of misalignments of mainstream cultures, see Munoz (1999).
4. Briefly, Spivak exposed the patriarchal assumptions and biases at the hearts of thinking of these influential theorists. These gendered tendencies, exposed Spivak, are also intertwined with class biases that are impregnated with inflections of racialization.
5. Such fetishizations of women's body parts that erase all other discerning aspects of women in India underscores the scores of cases of gang rape, sexual violence, and even the public humiliation and outrage of modesty of foreigners visitors in India. See for example the case of Pulitzer Prize winning author and Fulbright Scholar Nancy Bartley, who testified while guest lecturing at an IIT that "my kindness and personality didn't matter. My breasts did" in *Youth Ki Awaaz* (November 15, 2016): https://www. youthkiawaaz.com/2016/11/iit-roorkee-campus-sexual-harassment/
6. See the last chapter of Foucault (1980), and the complete volume of lectures in Foucault (1997).
7. See de Certeau (1984).
8. For more on colonial mimicry, see Bhabha (1994).
9. See Mbembe (2003).
10. For more on postcolonial diasporic culture in the UK, see Dawson (2007).
11. Gajjala's oeuvre of research has been pathbreaking for feminist studies of technology and agency, as well as the formation of postcolonial digital humanities (#DHpoco) and South Asian digital humanities (SADH).
12. Draupadi is a female character from the Hindu epic *The Mahabharata* who prays to Lord Krishna when a gang of thugs attempt to disrobe her. Hearing her prayers, Krishna makes the folds of Draupadi's sari infinite, thus foiling the thugs' licentious inclination to outage her modesty.

Disclosure Statement

No potential conflict of interest was reported by the author.

References

Anderson, Benedict. 1993. *Imagined Communities: Reflections on the Origin and Spread of Nationalism*. London: Verso.

Apoorvanand. 2018. "'Urban-Naxal' Witch-Hunt: Spectre of Insecurity Haunts Modi Government." *The Quint*. Accessed August 13, 2018. https://www.thequint.com/voices/opinion/bhima-koregaon-activists-arrests-pune-police-urban-naxals

Asif, K. *Mughal-E-Azam*. 1960. https://www.youtube.com/watch?v=rq8MktR_Ctc

Bailbar, Etienne, and Immanuel Wallerstein 1991. *Race, Nation, Class: Ambiguous Identities*. London: Verso.

Banerjee, Prathama. 2015. "The Subaltern: Political Subject or Protagonist of History?" *South Asia: Journal of South Asian Studies* 38 (1): 39–49.

Bhabha, Homi K. 1990. "Introduction: Narrating the Nation." In *Nation & Narration*, edited by Homi K. Bhabha, 1–7. London: Routledge.

Bhabha, Homi K. 1994. *The Location of Culture*. London: Routledge.

Butler, Judith. 1993. "Imitation and Gender Insubordination." *The Lesbian and Gay Studies Reader*, edited by Henry Abelove, Michele Aina Barale, and David M. Halperin. New York: Routledge, 307–320.

Chandan, A., dir. 2018. *Secret Superstar*. India: Aamir Khan Productions.

Dawson, Ashley. 2007. *Mongrel Nation: Diasporic Culture and the Making of Postcolonial Britain*. Ann Arbor, MI: University of Michigan Press.

de Certeau, M. 1984. *The Practice of Everyday Life*. Translated by Steven Rendell. Berkeley, CA: University of California Press.

Dwyer, Rachel. 2017. "Partition in Hindi Cinema: Violence, Loss and Remembrance." *The Wire*. https://thewire.in/film/partition-hindi-cinema

Foucault, M. 1980. *The History of Sexuality: Volume I*. New York: Vintage.

Foucault, M. 1997. *Society Must be Defended: Lectures at the College de France, 1975–6*. Edited by Mauro Bertani and Alessandro Fontana. New York: Picador.

Gairola, Rahul K. 2002. "Burning with Shame: Desire and South Asian Patriarchy, from Gayatri Spivak's 'Can the Subaltern Speak?' to Deepa Mehta's *Fire*." *Comparative Literature* 54 (4): 307–324.

Gairola, Rahul K., and Ashna Ali. 2017. "Ambivalence and Security in the Anglo-American Empire: A Critical Dialogue with Professor Homi K. Bhabha." *JNT: Journal of Narrative Theory* 47 (1): 143–162.

Gajjala, Radhika. 2017. *Online Philanthropy in the Global North and South: Connecting, Microfinancing, and Gaming for Change*. Lanham: Lexington Books.

Habib, Shahnaz. 2018. "Sridevi Obituary." *The Guardian. International Edition*. Accessed July 2, 2018. https://www.theguardian.com/film/2018/feb/27/sridevi-obituary-star-indian-cinema

Katrak, Ketu. 2006. *Politics of the Female Body: Postcolonial Women Writers of the Third World*. New Brunswick, NJ: Rutgers University Press.

Kona, Prakash. "Notions of Gender in Hindi Cinema: The Passive Indian Woman in the Global Discourse of Consumption." *Bright Lights Film Journal*, 30 Apr. 2011. Web. 15 May 2015. https://brightlightsfilm.com/notions-of-gender-in-hindi-cinema-the-passive-indian-woman-in-the-global&#8230

Maurya, P., Kumar, N., and Mishra, B. 2018. "Unveiling the Secret of Secret Superstar: A Feminist Approach." *Daath Voyage* 3 (1): 227–234.

Mbembe, Achille. 2003. "Necropolitics". Translated by Libby Meintjes. *Public Culture* 15 (1 – Winter): 11–40.

Mehta, Deepa, dir. 1996. *Fire*.

Mehta, Deepa, dir. 1998. *Earth*.

Mehta, Deepa, dir. 2005. *Water*.

Mohanram, Radhika. 1999. *Black Body: Women, Colonialism, and Space*. St. Leonards, Australia: Allen & Unwin Publishers.

Munoz, Jose Esteban. 1999. *Disidentifications: Queers of Color and the Performance of Politics*. Minnesota, MN: University of Minnesota Press.

Patel, Geeta. 2016. *Risky Bodies & Techno-Intimacy: Reflections on Sexuality, Media, Science, Finance*. New Delhi: Women Unlimited.

Spivak, G. S. 1988. "Can the Subaltern Speak?" In *Marxism and the Interpretation of Literature*, edited by Cary Nelson and Lawrence Grossberg, 271–313. Basingstoke: Macmillan Education.

Spivak, Gayatri Chakravorty. 1995. "Afterword." in *Imaginary Maps: Three Stories by Mahasweta Devi*, edited by Gayatri Chakravorty Spivak. London: Routledge.

Spivak, Gayatri Chakravorty. 2016. "Re: Response to SALA Invitation." Received by Rahul K. Gairola, 3 February 2016. Email.

Weinbaum, Alys Eve. 2004. *Wayward Reproductions: Genealogies of Race and Nation in Transatlantic Modern Thought*. Durham, NC: Duke University Press.

Post-Magic: The Female Naxalite at 50 in Arundhati Roy's *The Ministry of Utmost Happiness* and Neel Mukherjee's *A State of Freedom*

Meghan Gorman-DaRif

ABSTRACT

In *Gender and Radical Politics in India: Magic Moments of Naxalbari* (2010. New Jersey: Routledge), Mallarika Sinha Roy takes her title from an interview with a former Naxalite woman in which the interviewee declares, "[t]hose were the best days of my life … in those years I lived as a human being … *seta chillo ekta ashchorjyo somoy* (Those were *magic moments*)" (x). The import of this metaphor, Roy explains, is its ability to "convey [the] duality" of "[p]ersecution, pain and tribulation" along with "wonder, surprise and hope" (xi). The early stage of the Naxalite Movement from roughly 1967 to 1975, is often represented as embodying this powerful duality that encapsulates a response to the brutal violence unleashed by the state against the Movement, but also the tangible hope inhering in the late sixties that a revolution was possible.

This paper considers how such representations of, and metaphors for, the experiences of the female Naxalite have changed over time, noting emerging scholarship focused on the gender politics of the movement as well as an increase in literary representations of contemporary female Maoist guerilla fighters. 2017 saw the 50th anniversary of Naxalbari, along with the publication of Arundhati Roy's much-anticipated *The Ministry of Utmost Happiness* (2017. New York: Knopf) and Neel Mukherjee's *A State of Freedom* (2017. London: Chatto & Windus), both of which include the narratives of female guerilla fighters. I argue that the contemporary iteration of this figure is "post-magic," and suggests that despite the authors' sympathies for the current guerilla movement, particularly its female participants, "wonder, surprise and hope" are evacuated from their depiction in the novels. Through a consideration of both literary form and contemporary history, I engage with the reasons for this shift and their consequences when it comes to the potential and imaginary of violent resistance.

Introduction

Two thousand seventeen marked the fiftieth anniversary of the uprising in Naxalbari that sparked an agrarian revolutionary movement, the legacy of which can be seen today in the militancy of the Maoists, famously described as India's "biggest internal security challenge."[1] The anniversary generated renewed debate about the impact, history, and consequences of the 1967 movement. As Alpa Shah and Dhruv Jain argue in a recent article reviewing the "at least 50 scholarly or political books, several novels, and numerous essays," on the subject since 2007, "[t]here are not many other issues that have attracted as much scholarly attention in the last decade as India's Naxalite or Maoist movement" (2017). In addition, the anniversary prompted periodicals across India to run a wide array of articles, memoirs, reflections, and opinions analyzing what caused the early movement's breakdown in the face of state violence and internal disagreements, and where and in what form the movement stands today in relation to escalating state violence and structural inequality in tribal areas targeted for resource extraction.[2]

2017 was also the year Arundhati Roy returned to the fiction scene, releasing the long-anticipated follow up to her prize winning 1997 novel, *The God of Small Things.* Her new novel, *The Ministry of Utmost Happiness*, along with Neel Mukherjee's *A State of Freedom,* published the same month, make two significant contributions to the emerging canon of the Naxal novel in English.[3] Both Roy and Mukherjee have addressed the Naxalite Movement in earlier works,[4] yet these most recent novels represent a shift in focus, not only from the authors' own writings, but from dominant trends in historical and fictional narratives of the Naxalite and Maoist movements, in their focus on female Maoist guerilla fighters.

The Ministry of Utmost Happiness and *A State of Freedom* each feature the narrative of a contemporary female fighter in the People's Liberation Guerilla Army (PLGA), the militant wing of the Communist Party of India (Maoist), who become the voice of the Maoist struggle from within the novels' polyphonic stories of precarious figures struggling to survive on the margins of Indian society. This essay analyzes the nature of these representations, ultimately arguing that the figure of the female Naxalite in both novels can be read as "post-magic," a term I develop in contradistinction to historical and literary representations of the female Naxalite of the earlier 1967 movement due to the novels' interrogation of ascriptions of agency and empowerment to armed female fighters, and their suggestion that fighting is no longer tied to the real possibility of revolution, but merely to a choice of the manner of one's death.

In order to examine how and why such a shift takes place over time, I begin with an overview of gender and the Naxalite Movement, focusing on recent interventions into dominant historiography and highlighting the ways in which critics have maintained attributions of magic to the agential possibilities of historical Naxalite revolutionary violence for women. Against such liberatory imaginings, I analyze how ascriptions of agency slide into ambivalence in the novels of Roy and Mukherjee, as the authors represent the "agency" of contemporary Maoist revolutionary violence as severely limited, suggesting that the only real "choice" afforded their contemporary Naxalite protagonists is the manner of their dying, as opposed to living with hope for revolutionary change that imbued the earlier Naxalite Movement, which, as Bernard D'Mello argues, was "part and parcel of a (then) contemporary, worldwide impulse among radicals embracing the spirit of revolutionary humanism" (2018, 13). Finally, I suggest that this shift occurs in part as an answer to the impasse in our current world order between violence which does not work, and non-violence which cannot win, that these characters serve to draw attention to the work that must be done to promote global possibilities of solidarity, care, and transformative justice.

Gender and Naxalite History

The question of gender and the Naxalite Movement is both timely and fraught. Overlooked in most scholarship until the 2000s, gender has emerged as an important lens through which to interpret the Movement – a fulcrum around which the complexity of Naxalite ideology and practice can be better deconstructed and analyzed. The emerging focus on gender in relation to the Naxalite Movement also relates to broader reinterpretations of revolutionary violence as critics increasingly move away from romantic conceptions of such violence as liberatory that emerged during the anticolonial era, to a more critical engagement with its complexities and complications.[5] These critiques aim to provide the space, as P.K. Malreddy suggests, "to register the ideological and organizational fractures that undermine the liberationalist tendencies of the non-state violence 'from below'" (2016), and to explore the tension between romantic views (particularly on the Left) of revolutionary or resistant violence and the complex realities on the ground. Malreddy further suggests that rather than an "enchanted solidarity" with the Naxalites from afar, as has been the general position of the academy, a more useful engagement would be "disenchanted" – capable of critiquing and interrogating the Movement. Along with such a "disenchanted" position, centering gender in the critique and interrogation of the Naxalite Movement achieves a similar outcome in affording a clearer view of the Movement's "ideological and organizational fractures."

Pushing back on romantic and ultimately flattening understandings of the figure of the Naxalite and the justifications for the violence of the Movement, new scholarship on gender is attentive to the complexities of history, cultural memory, and the multiplicity of experience. Two main concerns that emerge in this scholarship are, first, how normative conceptions of gender (that cast women as victims and men as either protectors or perpetrators) function to provide a moral imperative to revolutionary violence cast as male/protective/good against the bad/rapist/violence of the state, and second, how the interrogation of the agency and empowerment ascribed to female guerilla fighters in order to break down the widespread victim/agent binary for women in war, especially in the global south, seem convincing.

Naxalite historiography has long focused, as have accounts of other instances of revolutionary violence, on gender-based assumptions that project women as victims and men as perpetrators of violence. In this binary, men who take part in revolutionary violence arise as protectors of victimized women and the state is cast as the violent threat that creates female victims (Srila Roy 2009, 2012; Sinha Roy 2009; Parashar and Shah 2016). Thus, according to Kimberly Hutchings, gender "provide[s] a kind of ethical shorthand, which helps to render certain kinds of violence intelligible" (2007), i.e., the "good violence" of the revolutionaries is contrasted, though the shorthand of gender, with the "bad violence" of the state.

Due to this narrative of gendered positions of victimhood for women, and good or bad violence for men, Naxalite historiography has overlooked the multiplicity of the experiences of women within the Movement, focusing on female involvement in positions of support (Sinha Roy 2009), and thereby maintaining female participants in what Pratibha Singh describes as "paradigms of domesticity" (2015). Not only is the variety of women's experiences as revolutionaries elided in such a narrative, but everyday gendered violence within the Movement is rendered invisible as the necessity for cohesion within the ranks requires the preservation of violence on the part of the revolutionaries to always be "good" in contrast to the "bad" violence of the state such that instances of sexual violence by party or guerilla members were, according to Srila Roy's analysis of the early Naxalite movement, largely overlooked.

Emerging scholarship on gender in relation to the Naxalite Movement and the contemporary guerilla struggle in India pushes back on such romanticizing figurations of the Movement and its participants, and emphasizes the need to interrogate and look beyond what Pratibha Singh calls the "Naxalite icon" (2015). This figure is middle class, and, as Srila Roy explains, is "essentially a male one that is put into the service of a righteous revolutionary 'good' violence as against the 'bad' violence of the state" (2012, 55). Mallarika Sinha Roy also affirms that this figure, with the "essentialised characteristics of 'urban', 'educated', 'middle-class' […] and 'male'" has "usually go[ne] unchallenged" (2010, 67–68) in Naxalite historiography.

Responding to such elisions, many recent interventions engage specifically with questions of gender in relation to the historical Naxalite Movement and its legacy in the contemporary Maoist guerilla struggle being waged in India today. In addition to the texts mentioned above, there is also increased attention in current scholarship about women within the ranks of contemporary Maoist guerilla fighters, including reflections on and interpretations of the rise in female participation in the armed struggle as members of the PLGA.

What emerges in these critical engagements with contemporary Maoist fighters is an impasse in postcolonial feminist ethics and theory that broadly sets interpretations of revolutionary violence for women as empowering and agential, against concerns of feminist thinkers about the ends of such violence and if they can ever truly empower, or if, instead, they reaffirm and reproduce masculinist violence that ultimately supports patriarchal agendas and justifies increased state violence that largely impacts poor women (Hutchings 2007; Srila Roy 2009; Singh 2015; Parashar and Shah 2016).

As Kimberly Hutchings suggests, "feminist ethics is ultimately a contested negotiation of tensions between the ethical goals of feminism and the conditions of possibility of the realization of those goals in the world" (2007). In the following sections, I explore how literature has responded to this tension between the goals of feminism and the shifting "conditions of possibility" in the realization of the goals of the 1967 Naxalite Movement as compared to the contemporary Maoist guerilla struggle. I argue that whereas the 1967 Naxalite Movement was imbued with an aura of hope and a belief in the material victory of the revolution, contemporary literature on the current Maoist struggle reveals an evacuation of such hope for social transformation, and presents instead a "post-magic" representation of female revolutionary violence centered on the individual, specifically in her choice of how to die.

'Those Were Magic Moments': Women and the Early Naxalite Movement of 1967–1975

In her (2010) book *Gender and Radical Politics in India: Magic Moments of Naxalbari (1967–1975)*, Mallarika Sinha Roy excavates the gender politics of Naxalbari, suggesting that postcolonial feminism offers a way to overcome the impasse of "feminism's monolithic construction of third-world women as victims, and the insistence of nationalist patriarchal systems that women represent traditional cultural values" (11). By framing gender, she argues, one can "represent the heterogenous reality of [the] movement" (37), and she presents literature specifically as a viable source of 'imaginary history' which "captures what might have happened, how the events were visualized, thought through, and identifies what emotions fuelled those visualizations" (38).

As the title suggests, Sinha Roy's text emphasizes the magical quality of the early Naxalite Movement for female participants. She opens her book with an interviewee's description of the years of her participation in the Naxalite Movement in the late 1960s, "[t]hose were the best days of my life … " she says, "in those years I lived as a human being … *seta chillo ekta ashchorjyo somoy* (Those were *magic moments*)" (2010, x). This metaphor "convey[s] [the] duality" of "[p]ersecution, pain and tribulation" along with "wonder, surprise and hope" (xi). The Naxalite Movement, as well as the earlier Telengana People's Struggle of 1946–1951, are often represented in this way, with women highlighting what they call "the magic of that time" (Kannabiran and Lalitha 1989). The magic, or "wonder, surprise, and hope" which inhere in the early Naxalite and Telengana movements for female participants are tied to the potential of revolution to address, not only social and political, but also their gendered experiences of oppression. Sinha Roy explains, "[t]hose magic moments of Naxalbari signify women's expectation from that movement in tearing down all structures of oppression, including gender" (93), and can be tied, as D'Mello argues, to the global revolutionary impulse of the 1968 moment (2018).

In addition to the scholarship cited above, Mahasweta Devi similarly constructs the magic of the 1967 Naxalite Movement in one of the few earlier instances of literature focused on a female Naxalite in her short story "Draupadi", which, as Gayatri Spivak proclaims in a recent piece on the 50th anniversary of the Movement, was the text that "set the seal on Naxalbari for me and for generations to come" (2017).

Significantly, *"Draupadi"* centers on a female Naxalite and the story ends with precisely the duality of "persecution, pain and tribulation" and "wonder, surprise, and hope" that Sinha Roy argues characterizes the early Naxalite period for women participants. Anyone familiar with the story will remember the epiphany of the final scene – the radical triumph of the female Naxalite in the face of state police forces which have just tortured and raped her, expecting through such violence, to defeat her, yet upon summoning her, encounter the following provocation from a naked Draupadi:

> You asked them to make me up, don't you want to see how they made me? […] What's the use of clothes? You can strip me, but how can you clothe me again? Are you a man? […] There isn't a man here that I should be ashamed. I will not let you put my cloth on me. What more can you do? Come on, *counter* me – come on, *counter* me -?

> Draupadi pushes Senanayak with her two mangled breasts, and for the first time Senanayak is afraid to stand before an unarmed *target*, terribly afraid (402).

The unexpected reversal of power dynamics along with the allusion to the mythical figure Draupadi creates the dramatic and magical triumph of the female figure in this scene, who is able to transform her mutilated body into a weapon against the state official, making him, as the final words of the story proclaim, "terribly afraid." Spivak has highlighted the significance of gender in this scene, arguing that

> [i]t is when she crosses the sexual differential into the field of what could *only happen to a woman* that she emerges as the most powerful "subject," who, still using the language of sexual "honor," can derisively call herself "the object of your search," whom the author can describe as a terrifying superobject – "an unarmed target." (2017, 388)

In her gendered specificity, Draupadi is able to accomplish the transformation into "terrifying superobject" in this scene, embodying the "magic" of the early Naxalite Movement as described by Sinha Roy. As Spivak goes on to say, "I can be forgiven if I find in this an allegory of the woman's struggle within the revolution in a shifting historical moment" (389). The specificity of the historical moment of the late 1960s Naxalite Movement, in this reading of Spivak, Sinha Roy, and Mahsweta Devi has a certain magic that inheres in it, and one that is incribed in the memories of female Naxalites as a hope for success in a revolution that would address both structural and gendered oppression.

Yet, this hope, and the manner in which it is achieved in the text, in precisely its historic specificity, does not persist beyond the early phase. In the next section I argue that the representation of the contemporary female Naxalite in the fiction published in 2017 – Neel Mukherjee's *A State of Freedom* and Arundhati Roy's *Ministry of Utmost* Happiness – reflects a shift from the hope nostalgically associated with the earlier movements, to what I call a "post-magic" perspective on revolutionary violence. No longer focused on the hope for, or potential of, a total social and political transformation through a successful revolution, the post-magic perspective on Maoist violence in the novels of Roy and Mukherjee demythologizes the Party in its attention to its flaws, particularly in relation to gender and in its violent excesses. In addition, the representations of contemporary female Maoist fighters, while sympathetic to the precarity of the characters in the context of the material and structural violence faced by tribal women, refuse to justify their choice to take up arms by suggesting that such a choice is agential or empowering. Instead, both novels emphasize that to take up a gun as a member of the PLGA is to choose to die because of that choice, and in their representations of their characters' struggle with that knowledge, draw attention to the problem with attributing agency and self-determination to participation in violence, since, as Srila Roy suggests, "agency does not usually involve the use of violence; 'agency' is rather the freedom from violence or force" (Srila Roy 2009).

Post-Magic: Representations of the Contemporary Female Guerilla Fighter

Gender makes the question of the capacity of violence and the implications of taking up arms complex from an ethical standpoint, as Hutchings has suggested in her analysis of feminist ethics and revolutionary violence (2007). One could easily argue that the choice to join the PLGA for women is a natural and legitimate one based on the widespread structural and material violence faced by women within both private and public spheres. In Mukherjee and Roy's novels, the female characters who join the PLGA do so in large part because of the structural violence around them, yet, their choice to join is devoid of the hope of actual change in the body politic and is centered, instead, on change in the individual body – in the choice to fight and die.

In *A State of Freedom*, Mukherjee develops several distinct narratives that feature characters on the margins of Indian society struggling to survive and to find, in their various ways, small spaces of freedom. One of the sections follows the lives of two childhood friends from a small village, tracing their divergent paths as Milly becomes a domestic worker in the city, and Soni stays behind in the village, ultimately joining the PLGA. This choice is contextualized in the novel by both material and structural violence emerging from the state, the Party, and domestic spaces. This section of the text opens with an act of violence by the Maoists against a local tribal youth, "[t]he first image that came to her when she thought of that day was the way the blood had arced and sprayed as they threw her brother's right hand into the surrounding bushes" (2017, 165).

In starting at this moment, Mukherjee's novel seems to invite the reader to critique the Maoists, yet the remaining narrative of the village and the experiences of Soni, Milly, and their families reveals that the critique is not limited to the Party, but extends to encompass patriarchal violence within the domestic space through Milly's drunk and abusive father, the structural violence faced in the everyday lives of tribal people depicted in the school where the teacher is absent more than present, and in the lack of medical care which leads to the suicide of Soni's mother, who cannot find a doctor to operate on a cancerous tumor. Mukherjee builds upon the structural violence of inequality overseen by the state to the culmination that takes place in the forest, where Soni's sister is violently raped by Forest Department officials as she and Soni collect Kendu leaves. The scene is emblematic of the precarity of the tribal villagers as Soni and her sister are made vulnerable by a new rule they were unaware of: needing a license to collect Kendu leaves, a rule, as the text suggests comes from the government making "their lives more and more impossible […] because big companies wanted the land" (2017, 178).

Soni's sister's rape is presented didactically in the text, explaining to readers the helplessness of the tribal communities, especially the precarity of women, but also, in the narrative of Soni, as the moment in which she learns that the freedom she has is to choose how she dies. After witnessing the aftermath of the rape in her sister's slow recovery and changed demeanor, the turning point for Soni comes when the Maoists put on a play in the village that echoes her sister's rape by the forest officials,

> She sensed an ultimatum in the play that she was seeing. Two of the samaj sewi came onstage, a man and a woman, and asked how long the people here were going to put up with such humiliation, such indignities? Were they not humans, too, or were their lives as nothing to the big people. She noticed that her sister's trembling had transmitted itself – it was she, Soni, who was now the core of the tremor. She was approaching the realization of something fateful in herself. Something her sister had said after she came back, something Soni though she had forgotten, now inserted itself in her head – just a few words: "I didn't put up a fight because they would have killed me otherwise." (2017, 194)

Soni decides to join the Party at this moment; arriving at a decision that is further elaborated in distinction from the helplessness faced at the hands of the state. As the text explains, the Party "found sympathetic audience in the villagers whose lives of unchanging poverty and misery and helplessness needed a radically new kind of hope, which the militants provided" (2017, 195). The language here is almost utopic – radical hope. Yet it turns out that what is radical about this hope is not so what is so often associated with radicalism – its revolutionary potential – but rather that the hope provided by the militants, is merely the decision to fight back, to die (rather than live) on one's own terms. Though not revolutionary in that the overthrow of the state is never represented as possible in the novel, the radical nature of the hope provided by the militants is the equality that comes from the capacity to also inflict violence. As Soni reflects, once she is the forest: "'If you kill, we kill too. If you have guns, we have guns,' as one comrade had put it so simply. Here was a kind of equality, at last" (2017, 198).

The final articulation of the movement's impact on Soni is elaborated the last time we see her character before her death, in her walk through the liminal space of the forest's edge with her friend Milly. Narrated through the perspective of Milly, this scene draws out the tensions inherent in the Party, both between the Party and the villagers, and within the militant figure herself, who, once she joins, has no way out. Though Soni has found a space of freedom, this freedom is severely circumscribed by the inevitability of her death.

Soni's explanation of her choice to fight with the Maoists includes assertions of agency, gender equality, and the decision to choose how one dies and to do so honorably, yet the scene, filtered through Milly's eyes, highlights the tension between the party line and personal affect,

> The revolutionary's mask still intact on her face, Soni repeated her earlier words, 'What's to fear? We'll all die anyway. This death is more honorable [...] The lives of people like us are nothing. But you can make something of *your* life, stop being nothing.' [...] Suddenly, Soni's mask slipped and she said, in a completely different tone, 'Yes, this will take my life. If I go outside the jungle, I'll be killed. I can only get out after the revolution.' Something sounded extinguished inside her (2017, 216).

While agency can be ascribed to the fact that Soni makes this choice, which she claims provides an honorable identity, her choice clearly comes, too, with a different type of constriction and limitation in her acknowledgement that "this will take [her] life." In addition to the complexity of Soni's experience, Milly's conversation with her brother reminds the reader of the complicated relationship between the Maoists and the tribal villagers, who, as Milly's brother explains, "are caught between the police and the Party. They play both. It's a risky game but they – we – have to survive too, naa?" (2017, 217).

Ultimately the question is what kind of power comes from arming oneself against the state? And how has this power changed since 1967? In "Problems of War and Strategy," Mao claims "political power grows out of the barrel of a gun" (1938). This formulation of the liberatory and agential capacity of violence – the capacity to overthrow the state, to achieve a revolution, resonates with anticolonial thinkers such as Fanon, who believed that violence was not only practical, but the necessary way of overthrowing existing structures of power. History supports such claims in some ways, given that armed uprisings and insurgencies were pivotal in ushering in Independence in the former colonies. However, in the war on terror era when globalized capital and the military industrial complex can be perceived as working in tandem to create "death-worlds," what Mbembe refers to places such as the tribal areas of India where mining companies are displacing people, taking up a gun could be argued, not to be a realistic way toward political power, but merely a way to a guaranteed status of bare life – a way of marking oneself outside the protection of the state and ensuring you will be categorized as one who "must die" (Mbembé 2003). Soni's choice does precisely that – places her within the framework of bare life, a consequence she is aware of, and which the text affirms. To choose death hardly seems a positive articulation of agency in the novel, which focuses instead on the limitations of the "radical hope" the Maoists offer, and interrogates the reality of what can be accomplished on the ground.

Roy's novel too establishes the "choice" to join the Maoists for Revathy, her female guerilla character, as limited and circumscribed in such a way as to interrogate the level of agency and empowerment that might be assumed to go hand in hand with revolutionary violence. In *The Ministry of Utmost Happiness*, the gendered representation of the Maoists exposes the problems in mythologizing their revolutionary struggle by reframing it as a desperate response to epistemic violence, that for women circulates through both the quotidian and the spectacular, the private, and the public, both within the forest and the party and outside in the villages or at the hands of the police. In the novel's attention to the Party's own flaws and similarities to dominant hegemonic patriarchy, Revathy's decision to join the PLGA is cast as despairing – a choice she makes knowing she will die in the fight, but, unlike earlier female revolutionaries, a choice that is not inflected with the hope that forms of everyday violence against women and excessive state violence against tribal people will end. Rather than fighting based on a hope for change, or with a sense of magic, Revathy, like Soni, joins the PLGA because there is simply nothing else to do in the face of the material and epistemological violence experienced by tribal people.

Revathy's letter, which appears towards the end of *Ministry* narrates her story, explaining how she became part of the PLGA. The letter begins by situating Revathy's first articulation of the desire to resist as stemming from the violence her father visits upon her mother, "I wanted to be a lawyer and put my father behind bars forever" (Arundhati Roy 2017, 425). The specificity of the gendered experience, and women's vulnerability to violence in the public and private spheres, is emphasized throughout the letter, with Revathy noting the "[m]aximum hatred police had for women workers" (2017, 426). Revathy's rape by the police affirms this intensity while simultaneously connecting it with the private patriarchal violence of her father toward her mother. After being captured in a village outside the forest, Revathy awakes to one of the police officers "cutting my skin with a knife blade," a direct repetition of the violence her father inflicted on her mother, creating an awareness that women are vulnerable across social spaces, from multiple sides, and regardless of their politics. After her rape, she acknowledges, "[t]his is the experience of so many women in the forest. From that I took courage" (2017, 429). It is not merely her role in the PLGA that makes her vulnerable to sexual violence, but her gender, the inclusion of her mother's story, as well as the allusion to the experiences of "many women in the forest" that establishes the universal nature of violence against women.

The Party in *Ministry* is also implicated in the patriarchal structures that make women vulnerable to such violence. Revathy writes, "[p]arty says men and women are equal, but still they never understand" (2017, 431). Importantly, her description has a temporal element: "still they never understand" emphasizes the inability of the Party, over a 50 year period, to grapple with and address the tension between a revolutionary ideology which centers on class and a dominant hegemonic discourse which occludes the everyday violence experienced by women. Whatever hope inhered in the earlier movement that structural change – including the dismantling of patriarchy – would occur has dissipated over the long years of struggle as suggested by the weary and despairing tone, indicating the persistence of such a misunderstanding that, unlike the female revolutionaries of earlier periods, she does not believe can or will change.

The lack of hope, or the quality of "post-magic" revolutionary violence, that I am attempting to draw out is further elaborated in the way Revathy frames her decision to join the PLGA as a negative but necessary choice, rather than one invested in a utopian vision of the future. Revathy offers no description of what she hopes to achieve in the struggle, but rather a canonical list of what she cannot do – live outside, leave her party. Live otherwise:

> I *cannot* live outside like them. My Party is my Mother and Father. Many times it does many *wrong* things. Kills *wrong* people. Women join because they are revolutionaries but also because they *cannot bear their sufferings at home.* Party says men and women are equal, but still they *never understand.* I know Comrade Stalin and Chairman Mao have done many good things and many *bad things also.* But still I *cannot* leave my party. I *cannot* live outside […] I *cannot* go on hunger-strike and make requests. In the forest every day police is burning killing raping poor people. Outside there is you people to fight and take up issues. But inside there is us only. So I am returned to Dandakaranya to live and *die* by my gun. (Arundhati Roy 2017, 431, emphasis added)

Revathy's gendered experience and understanding of the Party's flaws, along with the acknowledgement that the Party "does many wrong things" and "kills wrong people," is a clear critique of contemporary Maoist ideology and its failure to adequately address and reform its gender politics, and reveals that Revathy does not necessarily believe in the Party's capacity to do so – a belief and hope that was central to women's participation in the earlier Naxalite Movement. An additional reason for the evacuation of hope in her choice to fight is explained in the letter through a description of the escalation and radicalization of state violence in tribal areas, "[a]ll police, Cobras, Greyhounds, Andhra Police would be everywhere. Hundreds of Party workers were killed like anything" (2017, 426). A few sentences later, "In 2008 the situation much worse inside the forest. Operation Green Hunt is announced by Government. War against People. Thousands of police and paramilitary are in the forest. Killing adivasis, burning villages" (2017, 426). This situation frames her "choice" to join the PLGA, and she ends her letter by explaining her inability to do anything else, since "in the forest every day police is burning killing raping poor people." Though state violence is framed as necessitating Revathy's decision to "live and die by [her] gun" the implication, simultaneously, is that years of police repression, brutality and violence against tribal communities, which Roy has documented in *Walking with the Comrades*, has pushed the depiction of the Maoist struggle in Roy's novel towards one of futility.

Both Revathy and Soni choose to die through their choice to take up arms. Yet, in addition to their knowledge that to fight is to die, both characters also refuse maternal roles. Of the two novels, *Ministry* is the more specific in this refusal, and Revathy's narrative of her rape, pregnancy, and abandonment of her baby, serves to consciously break down any possible remaining romantic view of the female revolutionary: first, by refusing a redemptive narrative after rape by the state, and, finally, by subverting the image of the mother-warrior prized by Western feminists.

The popular image of the female guerilla with a gun in her hand and a baby on her back, as Srila Roy argues "is one that has a longstanding presence in the imaginary of 'liberatory', especially nationalist struggles in the 'third world', and is an acknowledged part of a revolutionary femininity" (2009). Singh, too, highlights the prevalence of the image of the woman with a baby and a gun, that despite its gender bias, continues to mobilize a kind of feminist pride in female participation in political violence (2015). This image, in relation to the Naxalite Movement persists today, in the figure of the original female Naxalite, Shanti Munda, who participated in the initial violent uprising at Naxalbari with her baby strapped to her back (Jyoti and Giri 2017; Mukherjee 2017).

Revathy's narrative in *Ministry* subverts both the iconic scene of confrontation and redemption in Mahasweta Devi's "Draupadi" and the image of the mother-warrior. Revathy's rape, like Draupadi's, is multiple, and prolonged, but it is cast in her narrative as part of her story rather than as its apex: "Then they all raped me many times." Revathy writes, "One is Udaya's father. Which, how can I say? I was unconscious. When I waked again I was bleeding everywhere. The door was open. They were outside smoking. I could see my sari. I slowly took it" (Arundhati Roy 2017, 428). The inclusion of Revathy's act of clothing herself after her rape and running away echoes but inverts the story of Draupadi. Further, the rape results in a child, complicating the view of the mother-warrior, an image Roy decimates in Revathy's response when the child is born, "When I saw her first I felt very much hatred [...] I thought to kill her. I put my gun on her head but could not fire because she was a small and cute baby" (2017, 430). There is no romance in this scene of the rape victim as mother and her infanticidal fantasy, yet, like her choice to join the PLGA, it is depicted with sympathy by the author.

Conclusion

The end of Revathy's letter encapsulates the critical challenge represented by the nature of Maoist struggle, in as much as it emphasizes the limitations of both nonviolence, in the face of state terror and in the context of consolidated global capitalism, and the problems which inhere in revolutionary violence as a viable response due to the Party's own flaws and in light of the overdevelopment of the state.[6] As Priyamvada Gopal suggests in a recent essay on the Maoist struggle:

None of these, however, addresses the larger question of how radical change, even if not quite the tabula rasa Fanon dreamed of, might be achieved in the context of a capitalism that works through the appropriation of democratic structures and by eliciting the consent of those it exploits. This remains the most frustrating challenge of our own troubled present. (2013)

Both *Ministry of Utmost Happiness*, and *A State of Freedom*, in their depiction of the current "post-magic" moment of revolutionary violence, affirm this challenge, and though they offer no way out for Revathy or Soni, they draw attention to those on the very periphery of Indian politics, and perhaps, by doing so, begin to engage them in a larger community of care. Situated as they are within narratives of alternative engagements with the state and society, Revathy and Soni's narratives, despite their stark realities, are drawn into a web of connection and solidarity with other figures in the text – their experiences, lives, and deaths variously "heard" or transmitted to other characters, suggesting that perhaps in telling the story or attending to these precarious figures, they might be worked into a larger narrative of contemporary India or serve to highlight the desperation of those "inside" the struggle, forging an awareness and solidarity from those "outside". At the very least, they draw attention to the imperative for new thinking that might resolve such an impasse and initiate new modalities of transformative resistance.

Notes

1. Prime Minister Manmohan Singh, 2006.
2. See, for example, "Naxalbari 50" series in *Frontier Weekly*, and opinion pieces and editorials in *The Statesman,* and articles in *The Hindu* and *Hindustan Times.*
3. A category Nina Martyris establishes in her article, "The Naxal Novel" (2014).
4. Roy referenced the Naxalites in *God of Small Things,* but more significantly in her non-fiction work *Walking with the Comrades* (2011), and Mukherjee's 2014 novel, *The Lives of Others* includes a Naxalite character.
5. See, for example, Arjun Appadurai's *Fear of Small Numbers* (2006) and Priyamvada Gopal on the Maoist conflict in India (2013).
6. As Bernard D'Mello argues, the contemporary impasse for the Maoist struggle stems from its confrontation "India's overdeveloped state, particularly the state's repressive apparatus, which is backed by a coercive legal structure and endorsed by a colonial value system" (2018, 21).

Disclosure Statement

No potential conflict of interest was reported by the author.

References

Appadurai, Arjun. 2006. *Fear of Small Numbers: An Essay on the Geography of Anger.* Durham, NC: Duke University Press.

D'Mello, Bernard. 2018. *India After Naxalbari: Unfinished History.* New York: Monthly Review Press.

Gopal, Priyamvada. 2013. "Concerning Maoism: Fanon, Revolutionary Violence, and Postcolonial India." *South Atlantic Quarterly* 112 (1): 115–128.

Hutchings, Kimberly. 2007. "Feminist Ethics and Political Violence." *International Politics* 44: 90–106.

Jyoti, Dhrubo and Promod Giri. 2017. "Naxalbari@50: Maoist Uprising Was Sparked by Tribal Woman Leader." *Hindustan Times*, May 29. https://www.hindustantimes.com/india-news/naxalbari-50-meet-the-woman-who-lit-the-first-fire-of-uprising/story-5ey8bOCHpquwFT33vo9H5I.html

Kannabiran, Vasantha and Lalitha, K. 1989 "That Magic Time: Women in the Telangana People's Struggle." In *Recasting Women: Essays in Colonial History*, edited by Kumkum Sangari and Sudesh Vaid. New Delhi: Kali for Women.

Malreddy, P. K. 2016. "Solidarity, Suffering and 'Divine Violence': Fictions of the Naxalite Insurgency." In *South-Asian Fiction in English*, edited by Alex Tickell. London: Palgrave Macmillan.

Martyris, Nina. 2014. "The Naxal Novel," *Dissent Magazine* 61 (4): 38–44.

Tse-Tung, Mao. 1938. "Problems of War and Strategy." *Marxists.org*, November 6. https://www.marxists.org/reference/archive/mao/selected-works/volume-2/mswv2_12.htm

Mbembé, J.-A. 2003. "Necropolitics." Translated by Libby Meintjes. *Public Culture.* 15 (1): 11–40.

Mukherjee, Jayita. 2017. "Brutality and Dreams." *The Statesman*, June 3. https://www.thestatesman.com/opinion/brutality-and-dreams-1496524534.html.

Mukherjee, Neel. 2017. *A State of Freedom.* London: Chatto & Windus.

Mukherjee, Neel. 2014. *The Lives of Others.* New York: W.W. Norton & Company, Inc.

Ministry of Home Affairs. 2006. "Naxalism Biggest Threat: PM." *Hindustan Times,* April 13.

Parashar, Swati and Janet Andrew Shah. 2016. "(En)Gendering the Maoist Insurgency in India: Between Rhetoric and Reality" *Postcolonial Studies* 19 (4): 445–462.

Roy, Arundhati. 2017. *The Ministry of Utmost Happiness.* New York: Knopf.

Roy, Arundhati. 2011. *Walking With the Comrades.* New York: Penguin Books.

Roy, Mallarika Sinha. 2010. *Gender and Radical Politics in India: Magic Moments of Naxalbari (1967–1975).* New Jersey: Routledge.

Roy, Srila. 2012. *Remembering Revolution: Gender, Violence, and Subjectivity in India's Naxalbari Movement.* New Delhi: Oxford University Press.

Roy, Srila. 2009. "The Ethical Ambivalence of Resistant Violence: Notes from Postcolonial South Asia." *Feminist Review* 91: 135–153.

Shah, Alpa and Dhruv Jain. 2017. "Naxalbari at its Golden Jubilee: Fifty recent Books on the Maoist Movement in India." *Modern Asian Studies* 51 (4): 1165–1219.

Singh, Pratibha. 2015. "Women in the Maoist War in India: Two Sides of Spectrum." Institute for Transnational Studies. https://www.transnationalstudies.org/Article/89

Spivak, Gayatri. 1981. "'Draupadi' by Mahasweta Devi." *Critical Inquiry* 8 (2): 381–402.

Spivak, Gayatri. 2017. "A Few Words About Naxalbari." *Frontier Weekly* 50 (12–15). http://www.frontierweekly.com/articles/vol-50/50-12-15/50-12-15-A%20Few%20Words%20About%-20Naxalbari.html

The Ethics of Representation and the Figure of the Woman: The Question of Agency in Gayatri Chakravorty Spivak's "Can the Subaltern Speak?"

Anirban Bhattacharjee

ABSTRACT

The paper attempts to analyze systematically how Spivak through the notion of the double-bind of racial difference problematizes the neat philosophical universalism of both European and Non-European systems of thought that produces their respective stereotype of 'other' in the very act of thinking. In course of the analysis, the paper takes up a Dalit autobiographical narrative, Manohar Mouli Biswas's "Surviving My World" (2013) to argue that the nature of cognition is structurally incomplete without the recognition of the perception of subalternity. This, in turn, necessitates a more intimate analysis on Spivak's notion of "imaginative activism", i.e., her recent engagement with how we 'learn' to conceive of this alterity in order to 'respond', and here the function of literature appears as the strange institution in which "imagination is trained". The paper then moves to the social text of sati-suicide, the violent production of the female subject, the discontinuity of subjectivity and agency and talks of a certain stylization of being when it is afflicted with the perception of death. It reads Bhubaneswari's act of committing suicide with reference to two parallel narratives; one is Amodini Ghosh's "Foska Gero" ("Loose Ties"), a novella published in 1931 and a recent one, Sibaji Bandyopadhyay's "Latar Din" ("Lata's Day") (2007), to put forward the notion of a radical unbecoming, the feel of an unremitting combustion inside the fleshed being, which unravels how the woman can perform her transcendence by remaining within the structures of immanence. The paper also tries to understand and explore if the experience of unbecoming itself acts out as agency.

In "Righting Wrongs," an article first published in *The South Atlantic Quarterly* in 2004, Gayatri Chakravorty Spivak offered a subtle but forceful critique of the idea of human rights, which ironically may carry within itself the agenda of *a kind of* social Darwininsm – "the fittest must shoulder the burden of righting the wrongs of the unfit – and the possibility of an alibi" (Spivak 2004a, 5). At first glance, Spivak seems to be making two points: i) being possessed human rights means owning or claiming and dispensing rights; ii) the stronger must right the wrongs of the weaker. By twisting this logic, the powerful's claim to protect the less powerful can also become an excuse to dominate them. But a closer read underlines a counter logic. It opens the possibility that the "unfit" may claim and dispense rights for themselves; they may right wrongs for and by themselves. Spivak persistently critiques a kind of globalism that gathers and structures information about the world in order to intervene and distribute rights to the underclass through its media and technoscientific networks. This privileged taking upon the righting of wrongs produces subaltern classes as the object of knowledge for the dominant economy. The task is necessarily structured on the complex configurations of differences. The global production of the subjects of rights like the notion of racial difference after Columbus's expedition cannot just be ignored as an artificial construction. In fact, in Spivak's sense, claims for rights are articulated through that artifice of racial struggle. Therefore, Spivak proposes a counter-reading of European enlightenment as a double bind which can be *ab-used* [1] or *read from below* (Spivak 2012a, 3–4) and suggests a model of education where "imagination is trained" as a demand to conceive alterity and responsibility and also as a tactic for "the deliberate ruining of the master's machine from the inside" (Spivak 2012a, 2016). In Spivak's phrase, education in the Humanities attempts to be an *uncoercive* rearrangement of desires (Spivak 2004a, 526). She elaborates: "A training in literary reading is a training to learn from the singular and the unverifiable. Although literature cannot speak, this species of patient reading, miming an effort to make the text respond, as it were, is a training not only in poiesis, accessing the other so well that probable action can be prefigured, but teleo-poiesis, striving for a response from the distant other, without guarantees" (Spivak 2004a, 532–537). It is only when we interest ourselves in this new mode of "imaginative activism" (Spivak 2017) that "the inevitability of unremitting pressure as the *primum mobile* of human rights" (Spivak 2004a, 526) will be questioned. Spivak's text spotlights the "epistemic discontinuity" between the human rights advocates and those whom they protect: "The luxury of an expressive or contaminable mind is implicitly not granted to the subaltern of the global South" (Spivak 2004a, 569).

I would here attempt to read, in a brief scape, how Spivak through the *double-bind* of racial difference problematizes the neat philosophical universalism of both European and Non-European systems of thought that produce their respective stereotype of 'other' in the very *act* of thinking. The paper then moves, by a necessarily circuitous route, to the social text of *sati*-suicide, the violent production of the female subject, the discontinuity of subjectivity and agency and talks of a certain stylization of being when it is afflicted with the perception of death. The paper tries to understand and explore the woman's modes of unbecoming and recognize the ways in which the sense of (bodily) vulnerability and precarity can be an incipient and enduring moment of resistance. Along the way, I will have occasion to suggest that subalterity insinuates the world of an unself-conscious existence, of bare and intimate animality.

In the opening chapter titled "Philosophy" of the book *A Critique of Postcolonial Reason: Toward a History of the Vanishing Present* (1999), Spivak reflects on a kind of short-circuit between philosophy and politics. If philosophy is universal human thinking towards truth, then it transcends the immediacy of politics which is circumstantial and susceptible to change (or "making other") (Spivak 1985). The politics of philosophy has to be thought in terms of how the chaos of politics is transformed into history, as the movement of the spirit towards its perfection. This happens through a negation and management of the *indeterminable*. In Kant's philosophical project, it is the philosopher's duty to help man turn the fearful abyss of Nature into the *sublime*, through reason, thus resolving practically the contradiction between what can be known and what must be thought. Spivak reads that the project of initiation into humanity in Kant is rather the project of culture, with that unacknowledged proviso for the limited access for the non-European (Spivak 1999, 30). A systematic description of practical reason and its project operates in terms of an implicit cultural difference. In Kantian discourse, the axiomatic of imperialism works as a natural argument to indicate the limits of the cognition of 'cultural' man. Kant's analytic of the *teleological judgment*, where an 'intelligent' author is assumed behind the movement of history occupying the site of desire itself, purports that the untutored ab-original 'raw-man' (Spivak 1999, 12–13) cannot be the subject of speech or judgment. The subject as such in Kant is geopolitically differentiated. Spivak further reads that this limited access to being-human itself marks the itinerary of the *native informant* into the postcolonial, which remains unrecognized through various transformations of the discussions of both ethics and ethnicity (Spivak 1999, 30). In Kant's "Analytic of the Sublime," in the first part of the *Critique*, the terror of a certain 'raw man' stands in, metaleptically, as a precursor to rational subjectivity. That man in the raw (*dem rohen Mensche)*is as yet unnamed. The raw-man accommodates, in its signifying reach, "the savage and the primitive" (Spivak 1999, 12–13). The raw-man exists in the shimmering space of an unwilled receptivity, susceptibility, precarity and vulnerability, implying a way of being exposed to language prior to any possibility of forming or enacting a speech-act.

Spivak has argued that to claim that the moral impulse in us is cognitively grounded is then to fail to recognize that its origin is a supplement. And uncritically to name Nature *sublime* is to fail to recognize the philosophical impropriety of the denomination (Spivak 1999, 14). She contends that those who are *cooked*[2] by 'culture' (*Kultur* rather than *Bildung* – education or formation) can denominate nature *sublime*, although necessarily through a metalepsis. To the raw man the abyss comes forth as merely 'terrible' (Spivak 1999, 11–14). The raw man has not yet achieved or does not possess a subject whose programming includes the structure of feeling for the moral. In other words, he is not yet or simply not the subject *as such* – the only example of the concept of a natural yet rational being. This gap between the subject *as such* and the not-yet-subject can be bridged under propitious circumstances by culture. Spivak's determination of racial difference exists in this gap between the ontic and the ontological – between what exists as chaotic and indeterminate and the existence which is rationalized in its singularity. What is left-over in this neat scheme of philosophical determination (*Bestimmung*) is its dangerous supplement – the negated other. Who is the other of philosophy is surely a political question. In "Acting Bits/ Identity Talk" (1992), Spivak captured the raw man's existence in the gap between the ontic and the ontological with the analogy of a fart. She writes: "The ontic as fart or belch, the signature of the subject at ease with itself decentered from the mind to body, which writes its inscription. [This also is the level at which word has no meaning], and indeed the embarrassment often offered by the subaltern victim in the flesh, scratching herself and picking her nose" (Spivak 2012a, 159–181). The fart is an effervescent anal product, one that erases itself; its immediacy verges on vanishing; not only does the fart remain invisible, it does not even remain. The subaltern in each of us engages in such bodily activities without embarrassment only in solitude (Sengupta, forthcoming). Subalternity insinuates a space of interiority. It is "the end of public sphere" (Spivak 2012a). The mention of public sphere is significant as this particular bodily function beyond ontological speculation is, by a circuitous logic, linked to the foundational violence of reason – reason that attempts to appropriate everything by means of a strategic error of negation of the *undecidable* and then is forgetful of that error (Sengupta, forthcoming). This self-made, sovereign public sphere exists through such workings of erasure. The space of the intimate induces the glimpse of a world where nothing is posited beyond the present, a disturbing interstice of an immanent animality and the undivided realm of the sacred.

Animality, Subalternity, Death

To push the thought of interiority to its extreme, I will briefly focus on one Dalit autobiographical narrative, Manohar Mouli Biswas's *Amar Bhubane Ami Benche Thaki* ("Surviving My World") (2013). This self-writing grapples with re-presencing a Dalit's alienated, self-encircled and captivated world but in a mode of exposure without disconcealment. Biswas's text – "Surviving My World" – continuously harps on a sentiment of deprivation – a wound: that *of having been given a name, an epithet* (Derrida 1995). It is the condition of finding oneself deprived of language, to name oneself and indeed to respond to one's name – "You people are pig-eating *namasudras*" (Biswas 2013, 24–25). The persona is an (unnamed) untutored rawman. The autobiographical account disturbingly presents how the life of the Dalit is substantially entangled with the life of filthy animals such as pigs. Biswas writes: "The pig-sellers at times entered our village with a drove of pigs. We felt a deep proximity with these homeless wanderers and played with them. Dirty and mud-ridden, both of us caress and nuzzle and play with the animals possessing lute-like noses. Our animal activities were surpassingly delightful" (my translation). The human *dasein* shares an ontical closeness with the animal. The state of *dalitude*[3] is conditioned by a constant oscillation between *an anthropomorphization of the animal* and a corresponding *animalization of man* (Agamben 1998, 2004, 56–59). Biswas's text lays bare an unstable disruptive space to attest that this peculiar perception is the singular property of the Dalit/the animal – the other way of being, which is both present and perfectly inaccessible at the same time. The cogito is constantly negotiating with its animality/its *subalternity*/the being's other. Subalternity inaugurates a new constellation of the political, who have not achieved consciousness of their collective economic and social oppression as a class. Subalternity is the experiences of precarity, suffering from failing social and economic networks of support and becoming differentially exposed to injury, violence and death. Subalternity implies the condition of unspeakability; but it is underscored not by complete absence of speech, rather the failure of speech. The ungraspable muteness of the Dalit/animal world is experienced as somewhat similar to our strange relation to death. Just as we must experience death not as an actuality but as a possibility that hovers over life (since my death can never be an event *in* my own life), so there an experience of being remains left out in relation to the animal/ Dalit life. The animal/the Dalit way of being is the undisclosable, which keeps itself open to the closedness of its interior. Animality is primary. Humanity is obtained only through the suspension of animality. It, therefore, must keep itself open to the closedness of animality. But as it ever forgets the primacy of *animalitas* it closes itself to its own openness. Thinking subalternity is thinking the animal. It stays outside the torus of human thinking. It is ineluctably enmeshed with the totality of being. And given this short circuit, I would submit: the nature of cognition is structurally incomplete without the recognition of the perception of the subalternity/the *animalitas*.

Spivak has analyzed how the figure of the *native informant* is foreclosed in postcolonial thinking. In the opening chapter of *A Critique of Postcolonial Reason*, she examines the emergence and foreclosure of the native informant in the three great texts of western philosophical tradition – Kant, Hegel and Marx. The flux of the history of the vanishing present is perhaps the adjustment or negotiation of what Spivak calls the "European discursive production and the axiomatic of imperialism," which continues to influence and instruct our knowledge, culture, literature, economy and pedagogical practices (Spivak 1999, 4). The point of using this psycho-analytic concept-metaphor of *foreclosure* is to register an unacknowledged failure of relation, one amounting to a denial of access to humanity. That is her major critique of postcolonial reason, which *sublates* the enlightenment reason. The negation of the primary negation remains present as an absence, as *erasure*. *Subreption*[4] or suppression of truth (Kant 1929, 1996) in order to acquire meaning becomes indispensable in this case. In "Righting Wrongs," Spivak seriously notes that while global culture permeates the world, there has been a lack of communication between and among the immense heterogeneity of the subaltern cultures of the world. The frontiers of subaltern cultures, which developed no generative public role, have no channels of inter-penetration. Spivak advocates for a kind of secular, aesthetic education *from below* – radically different from the suspect benevolence of national and international organizations – acknowledging the fact that subalterns are able and allowed not only to speak but 'to teach': Spivak's intention of "learning how to learn from the subaltern" can only be put into practice when the ethical (western) subject is ready "to learn how to listen to, in order to learn from the subaltern" (Spivak 2004b). In the following section, the paper would attempt to read and understand the texture of gendered subalternity through the scheme of erasure and an excess.

Two Takes on Suicide

In the revised edition of "Can the Subaltern Speak?", Spivak begins by stating that women outside the mode of production narrative marks the points of fade out in the writing of disciplinary history; and they are insufficiently represented or representable in that narration (Spivak 2010, 22–79). In Rassundari Dasi's *Amar Jiban* ("My Life," 1876), the first full-length autobiography written by a Bengali woman or in Rabindranath's short story *Streer Patra* ("A Wife's Letter," 1914) or *Khata* ("The Exercise-Book," 1912), writing for women operates as a dangerous supplement, producing an emotional surplus (in the body) that transcends a single structure of understanding. Self-writing for women becomes a fatal necessity. It is the space where the textual overlaps the sexual. The auto-biographical space is the hoard of *jouissance* (in terms of rights, property and of sexual orgasm) – a *jouissance* that is hers, that belongs to the "she" that does not exist, signifying nothing. The woman enjoys and awaits its ever arrival which is hauntingly punctuated by the *Real* of death. In Tagore's "Exercise-Book" and Rassundari's "My Life," writing allows the woman to enter the critical moment in the constitution and understanding of her self. Rassundari's *text* is not 'thinkable' in an originary form of presence; it is nevertheless to be reckoned with. But the reckoning is of a singular and strange kind: it is to engage with the *incalculable*. Writing is hiding oneself. The *act* of writing allows the woman approach the limit-point external to patriarchy. The woman can effectuate a rupture only by seizing an access into the symbolic. Crucially, within the limiting frame of patriarchy that denies woman a subjectivity, is it possible to enunciate her selfhood by performing the act of denial of the self and the structure itself? The choice of not-to-live is an impossible choice as one cannot experience how not to live. The woman operates as a precarious *symptom* (Zizek 1989) that covers up the true relations of domination and servitude, framing the conditions of production in whose discreet diagram she is ever-absent. Spivak states: "it is only in their death they enter a narrative for us, they become figurable" (Spivak 2010, 22). Rajeswari Sunder Rajan has argued that Spivak's example of Bhubaneswari is constructed as a narrative: so that death can function in it as a closure. Rajan attempted to destabilize this closure by invoking a parallel narrative of prolonged life of not-dying in the characterization of the grandmother in Amitav Ghosh's *Shadow Lines* (Rajan 2010, 130). I read Bhubaneswari's act of committing suicide with reference to two parallel narratives; Amodini Ghosh's "Foska Gero" ("Loose Ties"), a novella published in 1931 and the more recent, Sibaji Bandyopadhyay's "Latar Din" ("Lata's Day") (2005), to put forward my notion of *unbecoming* – the feel of combustion inside the fleshed being.

Bhubaneswari's death, I would argue, implies a life of constant combustion and unbecoming. In both Amodini's and Bondyopadhyay's narratives, we see the female protagonists, Chandralekha and Lata, bored by the ordinariness of today and of repetitious chores, hear unceasingly the call of death, the intimate unknown. Empty of self-willed romance and consensual love, Chandralekha lives, as if, the life of a widow in a regime of harsh and continuous self-flagellation. Lata is overcome by a deep idleness, a "gigantic lassitude" (Bandyopadhyay 2005, 21). At a crisis point of the narrative, they determine that suicide is a possible behavior to effectively alter their experience of desperation and despaired state of being. *Foska Gero* ends this way: "From the ceiling there was hanging the body of the woman. The wife wore a white dress of a widow, bereft of vermilion" (cited in Dashgupta 2008, 172). In "Lata's Day," the husband and his neighbors discover the disfigured body at the end: "So, Lata has been able to celebrate her dying day without letting anyone know a thing – the scandalous orgasms of her senses, her sensations have not been revealed, not blown their cover then … ." (Bandyopadhyay 2005, 31) The scandalous orgasm of her senses that undulates rhythmically over her body, the formless flow that grips her tight eventually remains a **secret**. In the discursive horizon of hetero-patriarchal expectations, we only encounter the silhouette of completeness of meaning whereas the split within – the already committed suicide – the exit of the everyday remains unknown by structures of meaning. We see Lata experiencing her bodily flows as leaking, uncontrollable and seeping – a feel of outsidedness to the lived reality. The metaphorics of uncontrollability is a gift of the flesh – the flesh that marks the (un)decidable limits of the female body. An indigestible residue that befuddles in an unprecedented explosion in which – "all human ruminations about time-and-place simply dampen down and die out without fuss" (Bandyopadhyay 2005, 31). I read this specific state of being as *unbecoming* – the state of *constant combustion*. The life of *combustion* is the life of *flesh*[5] (Merleau-Ponty 1962, 1968; Irigaray 1985; Grosz 1994, 103–104). Suicide may appear as pseudo-exit within the program of patriarchy. It may fall upon the grammar of re-appropriation rather than rejection. Here is the specificity of the notion of phenomenological suicide – the feel of combustion inside the fleshed being, which unravels how the woman can perform her transcendence by remaining within the structures of immanence. By committing suicide the woman acts upon the possibility to choose her *way* of dying and thus creates a rupture in the limiting possibilities of her being-toward-death. In Chandralekha, Lata or Bhubaneswari's narrative, the woman's act of choosing a specific way of dying empowers her experience the body-as-subject. Bhubaneswari's suicide was, for Spivak, an act of *subaltern* re-writing of the social text of *Sati*-suicide. Yet the "message" self-inscribed on her body was not read. "She *spoke*, but women did not, do not, *hear her*" (Spivak 2010).

The woman, or more specifically, the subaltern as woman, is a figure in whom the question of ideology – as the production of subjects in whom desire and interest are never entirely symmetrical or mutually reinforcing – splits wide open (Morris 2010, 4). This, then, is the incitement to Spivak's explosive historical excavation of two impossible suicides: one that which resides in the mutilated accounts of something called "sati," the rite of widow self-immolation or the 'good wife' who thus escapes the regressive *stasis* of the widow in a regime of harsh and continuous self-flagellation and self-deprivation; and the other that which lurks in the half-remembered account of a young woman, Bhubaneswari Bhaduri, who hanged herself in her father's apartment in North Calcutta in 1926, supposedly after losing heart in the task of political assassination to which she had promised herself (Spivak 1988, 2010, 62–63). Bhubaneswari had known that her death would be diagnosed as the outcome of illegitimate passion. She had therefore *waited* for the onset of menstruation. I read this particular moment as the moment of (self-) combustion, the moment of unbecoming – the moment capturing the self's precarity. Her temporal experience of *waiting* for a foregraspable future implies a politically induced condition that underlines the clash between bodies and states, insecurities within bodies and the force of bio-(political)power. Her act of unbecoming at the horizon of waiting indicates particularly of a non-performative state – a state of *stasis* when the subject is fully occupied by the perception of death as alterity. Bhubaneswari's urge for auto-effacement is impelled and animated by the (political) possibilities of denying the structure which denies woman a subjectivity.

Woman becomes visible in her absence, disrupting and instigating the re-reading of the whole discursive history of subjectivity. Spivak has argued that "Bhubaneswari attempted to *speak* by turning her body into a text of woman/writing" (Spivak 2010, 47). I would submit that her mode of unbecoming, a disguised form of performativity or the tactic of self-fashioning vis-à-vis death/exit/signing out marks an interruption *in* communication, not of communication, ensuring its unshareability through its resistance to language. The experience of unbecoming – the feel of an unremitting combustion inside the fleshed being – itself acts out as *agency*. It is a certain stylization of being when it is afflicted with the perception of death as alterity. Unbecoming is primary. It is an excess that enframes infinite excesses. It allows the eruption of the *unanticipatable* not as *l'avenir*[6] (future/to-comeness) (Derrida 1982, 1994) but as palpable, fleshly, quotidian, endless and *within*. Unbecoming implies a kind of unrelenting self-formation through the un-writing of the self, one that inaugurates neither total negation, nor negation of the negation; but opens the way to a perceptual life that interlaces between plenitude and absence, fullness and non-being.

Subalternity often insinuates an enormously heavy sense of precarity, exposure and risk – the sense of material and psychological vulnerability, "which is neither fully passive nor fully active, but operating in a middle region, a constituent feature of a human animal both affected and acting" (White 2010, 255–62). Subalternity involves the perception of an intimate animality, the other way of being, staying at the limit, yet intrinsic to the structure of human reason. Spivakian subalternity is a *secret* – the (im)possible. If subaltern speaks, it demands deconstruction; because it is "an Echo" (Spivak 2012b, 218–240). 'Echo' is an attempt to give gendered *subaltern* a space to deconstruct her out of the representation and non-representation, however imperfectly. As it is exemplified in the case of Bhubaneswari Bhaduri, it is beyond our gaze, cognition, and representation, because it lies in the realm of death. It lies 'in-between' human right slogans and the desire for the infinite justice – the *justice to come*.

Notes

1. As Spivak argues, "I suggested that we learn to use the European Enlightenment from below. I used the ex-pression *ab-use* because the Latin prefix *ab* says much more than *below*. Indicating both *motion away* and *agency, point of origin, supporting*, as well as *the duties of slaves*, it nicely captures the double bind of the postcolonial and the metropolitan migrant regarding the Enlightenment" ("Introduction" in Spivak 2012a, 3–4).

2. As Spivak states "Did this metaphor leap to my eyes because of the Vedic tradition of cooking the world in/as sacrificial fire as the specific task of the *brahmana,* who might loosely translate as *the philosopher?* Charles Malamoud has masterfully laid out this tradition for the Western reader in *Cuir le monde: Rite et pensie en Inde ancienne* (Paris: Decouverte, 1989), although he does not comment on its role in sustaining social hierarchy." (Spivak 1999, 14).

3. "Dalitude" implies a framework of literary, philosophical and cultural critique of the Dalit culture, identity and way of being.

4. "*Subreption* is rather a strong word that, in Ecclesiastical Law, means the "suppression of truth to obtain indulgence" ("Philosophy" in Spivak 1999, 11). As Spivak states, "by analogy with the accepted meaning of the term subreption, Kant is hard on *the*

metaphysical fallacy of subreption .... *Such hybrid* axioms *(hybrid, in that they proffer what is sensitive as being necessarily bound up with the intellectual concept) I call a surreptitious axiom. Those principles of intellectual error that have most harmfully infested metaphysics have, indeed, proceeded from these spurious axioms* (Kant, *Inaugural Dissertation and & Early Writings on Space,* tr. John Handyside (Chicago: Open Court, 1929, p. 74). On the next page Kant goes on to propose *[t]he principle ... of the reduction of any surreptitious axiom.* I consider its elaboration in the text" (Spivak 1999).

5. Arguably, the phenomenology of the *flesh* – understanding (feminine) 'being' in terms of the flesh – creates a rupture in the dynamic of authoritarian discourse, particularly in three ways: a) that the privileged, status of vision/sight in western/ Indian culture, in overpowering and acting as a model for all other perceptual relations, submits to a phallic economy in which the feminine figures as a *lack* or a blind spot; b) that the concept of the flesh is implicitly coded in terms of the attributes of femininity; and c) a related point on the debt that flesh owes to maternity. For a detailed critical reading of the phenomenology of flesh see Merleau-Ponty (1962, 1968). Also see Irigaray (1985) and Grosz (1994).

6. Here my point of intervention is different from Derridean notion of "l'avenir" as the unpredictable future coming from the *outside* (see Derrida 1994).

Disclosure Statement

No potential conflict of interest was reported by the author.

References

Agamben, Giorgio. 1998. *Homo Sacer: Sovereign Power and Bare Life. Translated by Daniel Heller-Roazen.* Stanford, CA: Stanford University Press.

Agamben, Giorgio. 2004. *The Open: Man and Animal,* edited by Werner Hamacher. Translated by Kevin Attell. Stanford, CA: Stanford University Press.

Bandyopadhyay, Sibaji. 2005. *"Latar Din" ("Lata's Day") Translated by Ipsita Chanda. Madhyarekha: Ekti (Bi-Chitra) Somabesh.* Kolkata: Anustup.

Biswas, Manohar Mouli. 2013. *Amar Bhubane Ami Benche Thaki ("Surviving My World").* Kolkata: Chathurtha Duniya.

Dashgupta, Rahul. 2008. "Bangla Upanyaser Nirbachito Abhidhan". In *Disha, Barsha 2, Sankhya 3,* edited by Anindya Ray. Kolkata: Disha.

Derrida, Jacques. 1982. *Margins of Philosophy. Translated by Alan Bass.* Chicago. IL: University of Chicago Press.

Derrida, Jacques. 1994. *Specters of Marx: The State of Debt, the Work of Mourning, and the New International*. Translated by Peggy Kamuf. New York: Routledge.

Derrida, Jacques. 1995. *On the Name*, edited by Thomas Dutoit. Translated by David Woodet al. Stanford, CA: Stanford University Press.

Grosz, Elizabeth. 1994. *Volatile Bodies: Toward a Corporeal Feminism*. Bloomington, IN: Indiana University Press.

Irigaray, Luce. 1985. *The Sex Which is Not One. Translated by Catherine Porter, Carolyn Burke*. Ithaca, NY: Cornell University Press.

Kant, Immanuel. 1929. *Inaugural Dissertation and & Early Writings on Space*. Translated by John Handyside. Chicago, IL: Open Court.

Kant, Immanuel. 1996. "Groundwork of the Metaphysics of Morals." In *Immanuel Kant. Practical Philosophy*, translated and edited by Mary J. Gregor. Cambridge: Cambridge University Press.

Merleau-Ponty, Maurice. 1962. *The Phenomenology of Perception*. Translated and edited by Colin Smith. London: Routledge and Kegan Paul.

Merleau-Ponty, Maurice. 1968. *The Visible and the Invisible*. Translated and edited by Alphonso Lingis. Evanston, IL: Northwestern University Press.

Morris, Rosalind. 2010. "Introduction". In *Can the Subaltern Speak?: Reflections on the History of an Idea*, edited by Rosalind Morris. New York: Columbia University Press.

Rajan, Rajeswari Sunder. 2010. "Death and the Subaltern". In *Can the Subaltern Speak?: Reflections on the History of an Idea*, edited by Rosalind Morris. New York: Columbia University Press.

Sengupta, Samrat. Forthcoming. "The Trajectory of Race in G. C. Spivak's Thought".

Spivak, Gayatri Chakravorty. 1985. "Subaltern Studies: Deconstructing Historiography." In *Subaltern Studies IV: Writings on South Asian History and Society*, edited by Ranajit Guha. Delhi: Oxford University Press.

Spivak, Gayatri Chakravorty. 1988. "Can the Subaltern Speak?" In *Marxism and the Interpretation of Culture*, edited by Lawrence Grossberg and Cary Belson. Urbana, IL: University of Illinois Press; Basingstoke: Macmillan.

Spivak, Gayatri Chakravorty. 1999. *A Critique of Postcolonial Reason: Toward a History of Vanishing Present*. Cambridge, MA: Harvard University Press.

Spivak, Gayatri Chakravorty. 2004a. *"Righting Wrongs". The South Atlantic Quarterly*. 103 (2/3, Spring/Summer). New York: Duke University Press.

Spivak, Gayatri Chakravorty. 2004b. "The Trajectory of the Subaltern in My Work". In *Keynote Speech in the Seminar on "The Subaltern and the Popular"*. Santa Barbara, CA: University of California. https://www.youtube.com/watch?v=2ZHH4ALRFHw

Spivak, Gayatri Chakravorty. 2010. "Can the Subaltern Speak?" In *Can the Subaltern Speak?: Reflections on the History of an Idea*, edited by Rosalind Morris. New York: Columbia University Press.

Spivak, Gayatri Chakravorty. 2012a. *An Aesthetic Education in the Era of Globalization*. Cambridge, MA: Harvard University Press.

Spivak, Gayatri Chakravorty. 2012b. "Echo". In *An Aesthetic Education in the Era of Globalization*. Cambridge, MA: Harvard University Press.

Spivak, Gayatri Chakravorty. 2016. *"When Law is Not Justice": "Dialogues by Brad Evans and Gayatri Chakravorty Spivak"*. New York: *The New York Times*.

Spivak, Gayatri Chakravorty. 2017. "What is It To Be a University?" A Special Lecture in the session on "Global Education Summit: The Future of Languages" at Presidency University, Kolkata.

White, Hayden. 2010. "Writing in the Middle Voice". In *The Fiction of Narrative*. Baltimore, MD: Johns Hopkins University Press.

Zizek, Slavoj. 1989. *The Sublime Object of Ideology*. London, New York: Verso.

The Literary Lumpen: The *Naksha* Narratives of Binoy Ghosh

Auritro Majumder

ABSTRACT

This essay outlines the condition of emergence of a cultural phenomenon in India which may be called "the literary lumpen." Karl Marx had, famously, disparaged the "lumpenproletariat" as social "refuse," which, for him, included such colorful members as "rag pickers, knife grinders, tinkers, beggars" and numerous other persons incapable of revolutionary class-consciousness. In the first two-thirds of the twentieth century, many participants in international Marxist movements followed Marx's lead in writing about the urban political scene, simultaneously inflecting and nuancing the lumpen in local terms. Here I focus on one such mid-twentieth century Bengali writer and cultural critic: Binoy Ghosh. I discuss how the literary lumpen emerges as a contradictory inhabitant of urban space in mid-twentieth-century Calcutta, negotiated in Ghosh's refashioning of the literary *naksha*, a nineteenth-century Bengali hybrid of English satire and Persianate *naqshah*. Blending critique, parody, and hyperbole, the literary genre of the *naksha* formally paralleled the interaction between indigenous and colonial cultures, articulating the tensions between the Left's attempt to conceptualize as well as to mobilize the itinerant poor and deviant classes in the postcolonial city. A consideration of Binoy Ghosh alerts us to the imbrication of literary form, precarious subjectivity, and postcolonial nationalism, even as the lumpen prove resistant to representation.

Representing the City and its Underclass

"The Lumpenproletariat are all those who have no secure relationship or vested interests in the means of production." (Cleaver 1970, 8)

Through his provocative framing of the lumpenproletariat as "a sartorial category," Peter Stallybras brings attention to an aspect of the lumpen (literally, "rags and tatters") that has eluded Marxian discussions rooted exclusively in political economy, namely, ways of seeing or representation. Stallybras contextualizes Marx's infamous description of the lumpen – "pickpockets, tricksters, gamblers …" (Marx 1975, 75) – in relation to contemporary literary representations by "nineteenth century commentators, novelists and painters" (Stallybras 1990, 70), thereby highlighting the dialectical tension between the political – the so-called superstructure – and the economic base. In nineteenth-century Paris and London, the staggering volume of literary representation of the urban poor by the likes of Honoré de Balzac, Victor Hugo, Charles Dickens, Elizabeth Gaskell, and Harriet Martineau, among many others, grew out of and, in turn, informed the economic relations of an emergent capitalist modernity. As Stallybras writes, "the homogeneity of the bourgeois subject is here constituted through the spectacle of heterogeneity [of the poor]" (1990, 73). Further, there were multiple ways by which such representations negotiated the social distance between the bourgeois narrator and the underclasses: at times, by claiming "irreducible class difference," but also at other times through "theatrical" modes of masquerade, "co-extensive with the homogenization of the city's poor as a distinct *race*" (1990, 74, original emphasis). For Stallybras, specific attention to literary forms – masquerade among others – nuances the Marxian notion of the racialized lumpen that, later on, came to be so finely articulated by the likes of Frantz Fanon.

Beyond the metropoles of Western Europe, the centrality of race to the marginalized lumpen subject, as Fanon observed in *The Wretched of the Earth*, followed from the historic situatedness of the colony: "Decolonization unified this [divided] world by a radical decision to remove its [class] heterogeneity, by unifying it on the grounds of nation and sometimes race" (2004, 10). In an interesting and provocative twist on the Fanonian notion of racialized, rather than bourgeois, subject formation, Eldridge Cleaver illustrates the phenomenon of the "Black lumpen" in the "internal colonies" of 1970s America (2004, 6). The Black lumpen is the "left-wing of the proletariat," Cleaver avers, unlike the predominantly white unionized working class of "the right" (2004, 6). Writing in the context of the Black Panther movement, Cleaver extended Fanon's insights to conceptualize urban Black America as the lumpen class of an internally colonized settler society, the revolutionary class par excellence, "without vested interests in the means of production" (2004, 8).

I utilize these insights to focus on the literary work of the Bengali Marxist writer, historian, and sociologist Binoy Ghosh (1917–1980). Ghosh presents the urban underclasses in two mutually contradictory ways: as marginal human subjects who exemplify the postcolonial and socialist possibilities of the future, and as aberrant, "lumpen," social types who threaten the very fabric of urban sociality. This essay outlines the condition of emergence of the lumpen figure, in the city of Calcutta, India, and in the literary genre of the *naksha*. Attention to literary representation, I argue, reveals the contradictory ways in which the lumpen is conceptualized at the moment of its "emergence" (Williams 1977, 121 ff.). I posit, moreover, that such contradictions follow from the unifying impulse "of nation and sometimes race" that Fanon observed in the case of Algerian decolonization. In extending transnational frameworks of the figure of the lumpen, I depart from contemporary interventions such as that by Nicholas Thoburn, who writes that, "the lumpenproletariat is actually … oriented toward the maintenance of *identity*, and that it is the proletariat where difference emerges" (2003, 48, original emphasis). My essay emphasizes the dialectical analysis of difference and identity. The lumpen in Calcutta is constituted as "the Other," by its internal differentiation from a unitary, heteronormative working class;

the former is coded as precarious and contingent, and unlike the latter does not belong to the nation. One needs to pay attention to the specificity of the lumpen in Calcutta, in terms both of culture as well as the literary genre of the *naksha*. As a narrative form originating in the colonial city, as we see in the subsequent section, the *naksha* is well suited to represent the city's diverse populations.

The *Naksha* and Binoy Ghosh

As a member of both the Progressive Writers' Association (PWA) and the Indian Peoples' Theatre Association (IPTA), Binoy Ghosh worked as a short story writer and journalist alongside renowned Marxist literati such as Saroj Dutta and Samar Sen in various Left wing and avant-garde journals. Furthermore, as a sociologist and historian, Ghosh was a preeminent scholar of colonial modernity. His study of nineteenth century Bengal, *Banglar Nabajagriti* (*The Bengal Renaissance*, Ghosh 1993 [1947]), was a significant intellectual milestone, alongside historian Sushobhan Sarkar's (1946) shorter English language *Notes on the Bengal Renaissance*. Such texts were representative of a generation of pioneering Marxist scholarship in the 1940s, one that analyzed colonial Indian and especially Bengali history in terms of capitalism and its restructuring of social relations. Ghosh's interest in colonial modernity led him to another study, *Kolkata Shaharer Itibritta* (*The History of Calcutta*, 1975), which focused specifically on the rise of Calcutta, the second city of the British Empire, in the eighteenth and nineteenth centuries.

Ghosh's scholarly work on the history of Calcutta was complemented by his literary depiction of contemporary urban life. Along with scholarly monographs, he composed a series of witty and experimental literary texts on the city of Calcutta. These include the sketches published in book form as *Nabababu Charita* (Ghosh 1979 [1944], *Biography of the Nouveau Riche*, hereafter *Biography*) and *Kalpenchar Rachanasamagra* (Ghosh 1968, *Musings, or the Collected Writings of the Black Owl*, hereafter *Musings*). Spanning the late colonial period to the first two decades after Independence, these texts provide some of the most detailed accounts and fascinating observations on the city and its people, especially the *itar* or "lower" classes.

In terms of style and literary form, *Biography* and *Musings* draw from a nineteenth century Bengali literary tradition of satire or the *naksha*. This includes texts such as Bhabani Charan Bandyopadhyay's *Nabababu Bilas* (*Amusements of the Modern Rich*, 1825), and Kaliprasanna Singha's *Hutom Penchar Naksha* (*The Musings of the Barn Owl*, 1861). Bengali readers of *Biography* would not have missed Ghosh's appropriation of these earlier texts, especially given the thematic focus on the new *babu*, the elite class created by colonial capital. In particular, Ghosh derives the fantastic textual device of the narrator as an all-observing owl directly from Kaliprasanna Singha, as well as the overall narrative structure of the *naksha*. Singha's 1861 *Hutom* was a landmark in depicting the varied social classes and colorful goings-on of colonial Calcutta. The all-seeing owl is a nocturnal creature; it comes alive when the city goes to sleep.

The literary form of the *naksha* was a hybrid colonial form that drew on both English prose satire, such as Charles Dickens's *Sketches of Boz*, and Persian/Farsi *naqshah*, literally "sketches" or "maps." The *naksha* negotiated the heterogeneous multiplicity of the new urban space that was British Calcutta, and which made it a useful genre to depict the lumpen. The *naksha*'s relationship to standard prose narrative is ambiguous: the frequent intermixing of prose and verse characteristic of the *naksha* troubled Europeanist understandings of modern Bengali prose genres. The noted scholar of Bengali letters, Srikumar Bandyopadhyay, thus described the *naksha* in 1938: "[It] is as if the just born prose child were excessively prone to whimsically returning again to the fluidity and melodiousness of verse" (Qtd. in Herder 366). The *naksha* was partially derived from but not wholly dependent on English prose form, as Bandyopadhyay's somewhat exasperated remark about its "whimsical," "just born" prosaic nature indicates.

The specific aspects of the *naksha* that Binoy Ghosh would embrace in his literary sketches of the city include the eschewal of formal prose in favor of lower-class idiom (*itar bhasha*), as well as the constant use of "crude" humor that poked fun at the pretensions of the city's elite. Here, the politics of language is connected to the historical context of nationalism and the literary movement of Bengal modernism. The historian Ranajit Guha has underscored in a discussion of Singha's 1861 *Hutom* that "[i]t is the [*naksha*'s] emphasis on the now, the vehicle of its circulation, rather than the messages circulated … [involving] the instantaneous exchange of information in myriad bits, with no particular demand to make on reflection … that enable[d] this discourse to weld the mass of its interlocutors together into an urban public" (2008, 341–42). In this respect, Guha adds, the *naksha* serves a function similar to the European "penny dreadful" novels in the twin contexts of print culture and modern-day nationalism (2008, 340–44; see also Anderson 1991). Such generic qualities are crucial for Binoy Ghosh. These enable him to critique the late colonial and postcolonial elite of his own time. Ghosh articulates a civic community through the deployment of distinctly lowbrow form and language. Thus, the *naksha* incorporates non-elite viewpoints on the city, thereby representing precarious lives. In this regard, Ghosh is part of a broad constellation of Bengali writers who combined anti-colonialism, Marxism, and modernism (Majumder 2016, 417–18).

Biography of the Nouveau Riche, as can be imagined from the title itself, consists of satirical pieces on the new *babu* – those who had made their wealth during the Second World War. By 1941–42, Calcutta became a central site of the war efforts as the first significant Allied-controlled city in South Asia facing advancing Japanese troops, who had defeated British forces all over southeastern Asia. The native *babus* serving the Allies profited heavily from various mercantile and intermediary business enterprises. Not surprisingly, the wealth of the *babus* stood in sharp contrast to the majority of the population as a massive famine in rural Bengal, a direct result of wartime rationing, resulted in the death of over three million people (Mukherjee 2015, 13–16). In *Biography*, Ghosh's narrator testifies to this state of affairs in crisp colloquial idiom:

> The unemployed of yesterday is either busy working as a store-clerk calculating stocks and supplies, or is employed in the weapons making factories that have been bolstered by the war … And the Bengali *babu*, second to none in being the comprador middleman, has resumed his historical role. They haunt the lanes and by lanes of the "black-market," when night falls on the city. He who had a penny in his pocket has

bundles of fresh currency in his pocket. They have hidden in their secret storages thousands of tons of rice grain, pulses, and essential medicines! These are the very people who would wax eloquent on patriotism and the nation tomorrow! (*Biography* 21–22)

While it is difficult to convey the full flavor in translation especially the innovative use of language, the passage resonates with the hallmarks of the Bengali *naksha*: the wry sarcasm and the back-alley lingo, the theme of overnight reversals of fortune, the easy narrative conflation of rumors and facts, and fantasies of secret riches. The accelerated, uneven economic growth, driven by the war industry of the 1940s, brings the contradictions of the colonial city to the foreground, as both a site of cosmopolitan modernity as well as heightened inequality. The *naksha* grasps both aspects, which it describes in lurid and sensational terms:

> The distinction between vulture-ridden rural Bengal scavenging for the dead, and the many delights of [downtown] Chowringhee … On the right pavement of the street, we laugh, play, sing, whistle, go to the cinema, blow away money on the many delights of this earthly paradise of Calcutta. From the left pavement the odor of rotting corpses lying on the ground terrorizes our nostrils, the primitive cries of dying men, women and children rends our ears. We do not stop, we do not stumble – we cover our noses and speed up our walking. (38)

The passage underscores the plight of precarious populations, who had been displaced on to the city's pavements in the aftermath of the Great Famine. Ghosh's narrator combines the Marxist intellectual's antipathy to class-society with the literary *flâneur*'s abiding fascination with the city. *Biography* contextualizes wartime Calcutta within colonial history by drawing attention to the Bengali's *babu*'s "resumption of his historical role as the comprador middleman." The narrator criticizes the *babu* class of the city and those he sees as its historical predecessor, the colonial-era compradors. Yet the literary form of the *naksha* that *Biography* deploys to such great effect is a product of this same history.

For Ghosh, as contrasted to the English bourgeoisie, this class of Indian compradors – who merely profit from imperial collaboration without effecting any change in the social relations of production – has no progressive function. He is careful to distinguish the comprador class from those he terms the "progressive bourgeoisie." Ghosh writes, "It has to be mentioned in this regard that the middle-class (*maddhyabitta*) culture of the nineteenth century, that which was beneficial to the national renaissance, has no relation to this comprador *babu* culture" (46). *Biography* underscores the point that progressives, "such as Rammohan and Bidyasagar [nineteenth century social reformers] adopted the positive values of the new arriving civilization of the British, in the midst of a degenerated, superstition-ridden society and its poisonous atmosphere" (19). At one level, the Marxist critic and narrator of the text – a figure embodying intellectual resistance to elite excess – seems to be a linear continuation of and advancement over the bourgeois reformers of the past. At the same time, there is indeed a difference from English history, since it is the useless compradors rather than the progressive bourgeoisie that have dominated in the colony.

Such a historical attitude marks a crucial – and to my mind unresolved – dilemma in Binoy Ghosh's attempt to showcase the perspective of the oppressed. As Rajarshi Dasgupta (2003) has noted, Bengali Marxists in the 1940s, largely under the influence of Stalinist two-stage theory, subscribed to the non-dialectical notion of "succession." The influence of a dogmatic notion of scientific history is palpable in *Biography*, not only in its praise for the progressive bourgeoisie but also its implied position that socialism marks the final culmination of social development after feudalism and capitalism. Ghosh's condemnation of "a degenerated, superstition-ridden society" is significant. He transposes the degenerative attributes of the elite class to society as a whole, and simultaneously makes claims for his own scientific perspective that is compromised almost immediately.

In the span of a few pages, Ghosh deploys "superstitious" vocabulary by invoking the blood-sacrifice and worship rituals of the Bengali *Tantric* tradition. The Marxist's call for revolution against the new *babu* elite is articulated through copybook *Tantric* rhetoric:

> Until liberation, the only revolutionary duty is to sit in yogic posture (*yogasan*) on a seat of human skeletons surrounded by human skulls (*naramunda*). The *Tantric sadhana* or cultivation of hatred is necessary for the devilish object of revenge. Neither poetry, nor the creation of eternal works of art is a substitute for that. (42)

Tantric rituals and magical practices appear to supply the ethical basis for Ghosh's Marxist politics. The presence of this vocabulary in the narrative also destabilizes the very binary that Ghosh attempts to set up separating the method of "scientific" Marxism from the "degenerated, superstition-ridden" native society that is to be changed (for *Tantra* see, Muller-Ortega 1989; in the colonial era, see Urban 2003).

To summarize: Ghosh's refashioning of the *naksha* serves two ends. Firstly, he adapts an old literary genre for the critique of the new elite and fashions a means of non-elite underclass expression to that end. Secondly, the culturally specific qualities of language and vocabulary of the *naksha* articulate the complex negotiation between backwardness and progress, and tradition and modernity, thereby foregrounding the internal tension of these binaries. Unlike the classic, nineteenth century *naksha*, Ghosh's political and pedagogical commitments lead, moreover, to a third function: the *naksha* incorporates the narrator's journey to different parts of the city and provides Marxist analyses of the different typologies of the urban poor – the precarious and the contingent. In other words, the descriptive insight of the *naksha* is combined with the prescriptive ethos of the Marxist *flâneur* in search of the proletariat.

Such proletarians are not to be found in the factories, mills, or even the slums of the city. Rather, they appear within a familiar quotidian phenomenon in wartime Calcutta, namely, the long lines of people awaiting their rations at "control shops." As Ghosh notes in a sketch titled "Queue" in *Biography*, the masses are brought together by a common need in these long lines. He writes:

> Neither a hosepipe, nor a concrete pipe, but an actual, human flesh and blood pipe - if seen from above it resembles a human pipeline, if seen from below it will appear to be a series of human chimneys. Neither cambis, nor concrete nor steel, but made of human beings, and human flesh. One can see similar pipes today all over the great city, in all its broad avenues and its narrow alleys. (69)

The transformation of the city dwellers to "human pipeline(s)" represents at once the alienation of the capitalist commodity regime, as well as the streamlining of the population under the scarcity conditions of imperialist war. The narrator's own perspective is one of revulsion: "Many a times, I would think to myself, let's blow up this molehill of civilization with dynamite" (50). In his fervor, the narrator ceases to "see" the assembled people as constituents of an industrialized urban space ("neither … concrete nor steel"). Instead, he goes on to imagine them as symbolic representations of evolution (*bibartan*). After referencing the anthropologist Lewis H. Morgan, who influenced Marx and Engels on social evolution, Ghosh claims a few pages later:

> If we take this 200-yard long queue as a metaphor for the 1 billion years of biological history, then each yard of the queue equals 5 million years. This queue then becomes the living testament of the history of biological evolution! I recognize[d] the coal-supplier's wife Rukmini, half-starved and half-dead, standing at the end of the line; she then is the amoeba of life, the first sign! … They go by one after the other … leave alone a two-limbed human there are no signs of quadrupeds. (77–78)

In the narrator's imagination, almost the entire queue of starved suffering humanity embodies pre-human forms of life in the evolutionary scale. The contemporary decline of capitalist "civilization" not only transforms people into non-human beings but also forces their regression into the pre-human. The narrator is an observer of their precarity, but his representation is also precarious, as we shall soon see. It is only at the very front of the queue that the people begin to resemble humans. The closer they are to the shop-counter selling food items, the more human they become. This is an inversion of the higher qualities that distinguish the human, capable of producing its own food, from the animal that merely obtains it. Finally, the narrator inscribes his hope for civilizational progress on the literal body of the human, "Hema, the maid."

The following passage is striking, both optimistic and disturbing, in its treatment of female anatomy:

> The first appearance of a sentient human being is to be found in the fire-singed elbow of Hema the maid. The hunting, gathering classless societies to the Greco-Roman empires of antiquity all start and end by the palm of Hema's hand. At the base of Hema's middle finger America is discovered … the tip of this finger, filled with the sound and sight of the Industrial Revolution, is infected; pus and disease have permeated it. There is no ease without a surgical incision on her infected finger. Sitting there, with his ripe old beard is Karl Marx. Marx explained, "Do not be afraid. Society and civilization are always in progress, but that [progress] is never smooth or mechanical. At every turn of the evolutionary path lies revolution; from one turn to another there is progress." Humanity heard the oracle of salvation (*abhay bani*) for the first time. (79–80)

The dialectical analysis of history, itself tinged with precarity and refusing "smooth," "mechanical" movement, promises hope for the proletariat represented in the figure of Hema, the maid. The narrator's emphasis at this point is on optimism, born out of a Marxist analysis of history that transforms "evolution" to "revolution." The presence of Marx on top of Hema's "infected finger" and Marx's assurance to her combines scientific and mystical salvation, the first represented by "surgery" and the second by the trope of "*abhay bani*" (oracle). This peculiar combination of the scientific-mystical mode of liberatory politics, another example of which we saw in the earlier passage on Tantra, points to Ghosh's complex negotiations of indigeneity and modernity in the colony. The *naksha* testifies to insurgent proletarian consciousness and gendered subjectivity. This consciousness, as articulated by the *naksha,* is unevenly or differently modern from the bourgeois paradigm of individuality.

The members of the long queue, with the exception of the "Neanderthal man," are all women, such as "Rukmini, Jagattarini, Haridasi, Haba's Mother, Manke's Aunt … Ganesh's Granma … [and] Hema the maid" (78). The names themselves indicate that most if not all the women are of humble station, and also, that many acquire identity through association with men, a common practice among the poor classes. Hema with "blood shot eyes" at the front of the line is the only "Homo Sapiens," and her body, in turn, is divided into portions representing epochs of human evolution. At one level, Ghosh's invocation of Darwinist evolution reduces the entire assembled mass of indigent women to the status of pre-human organisms. At another and, perhaps more redeeming, level, testifying to the precarious nature of Ghosh's representation, these women's bodies provide the ground for the imaginative scripting of biological evolution and proletarian history.

The deployment of women and their bodies, in Ghosh, as a metaphor for the degraded present deserves little elaboration. In the case of colonial India and Bengal specifically such a sentiment is found in Hindu nationalism. This is vividly exemplified in Bankimchandra Chattopadhyay's novel *Anandamath* (*The Alley of Bliss,* 1882) through the affective invocation of the degraded woman who is both mother and motherland. The Hindu nationalist deployment of woman as mother/motherland stemmed from a historicism that established a causal link between the depredations of European and Islamic colonialism and the consequent degradation of Bengali and Indian (read Hindu) women. Such a view contributed to the nationalist anxiety around the "Hindu wife, Hindu nation" (Sarkar 2010).

In Ghosh's Marxist account, by contrast, the affirmation of the dialectical logic of (r-) evolution exists in tension with the masculine nationalist anxiety over decay and degeneration. In the contradictory reality of Ghosh's text, Hema and the women behind her in the queue, represent at one and the same time the possible transition from pre-and non-human nothingness to human potentiality, and the opposite idea of the further decay of the colonized nation as embodied in the nation's women. In short, both progressive and conservative tendencies co-exist, in tension, with each other. The fraught relation between gender, class, and nation, and the resistance of each category to dominant appropriation, is sought to be resolved if only briefly through the oracle of Karl Marx.

In another sketch, the *naksha* articulates the dialectics of progress and its fraught possibilities through the twin figures of the "old Talui'ma, [who] would not get into the train, preferring the safety of her traditional *palki* (palanquin)," and "the old gardener Bikal-mian, who would request the children in the household to tell him stories about the wonders of Calcutta – lane bound cars, double-decker bus, electric fans" (*Biography* 102–03). While they are as backward as the waiting women in the queue, "Talui'ma" and "Bikal Mian" (both elderly – one a woman, the other a Muslim) are, equally, as progressive:

> Then we thought that old Talui'ma, gardener Bikal-Mian, were all wild brutes, poor things! With age I have realized that they were progressive, unlike many middle class folk! They did not dismiss the miracles of modern life by drawing recourse to the Vedas

or Koran. They listened carefully to the advancing sound of scientific achievements of man; they realized that their time has passed, and they have implicitly trusted in the powers of man, in the miracles performed by modern science. Even though they themselves believed in magic amulets and headless apparitions, they trusted the airplane and electricity, accepted that the latter represented the breakthrough of knowledge, the victory of man over nature. (103–04)

If the narrator is sympathetic to this putative recognition and submission of the non-"middle class folk" to the "miracles of modern science," he is still unsparing in his criticism of the other significant class of people, the underclass lumpen. They do not productively contribute to society, and yet fill every nook and corner of the city of Calcutta. As I discuss in the next section, compared to the working poor, the lumpen is a similar yet different category: the latter is to be differentiated from the former not only on the basis of the economic relations of production, but also a gendered regime of reproduction. The issue of literary form is crucial to the representation and translation of this lumpen underclass.

The Literary Lumpen

The lumpen underclass forms a significant part of Ghosh's sketches in *Kalpenchar Rachanasamagra* or *Musings* (1968). Published more than two decades after *Biography*, this collection highlights the heightened urban crisis of the postcolonial period in 1960s Calcutta. In stark contrast to the nineteenth century text he adapts, *Hutom Penchar Naksha* (The Musings of the Barn Owl, 1861) by Kaliprasanna Singha, which is merely content to relay the varied activities of the lower classes, Ghosh's narrator *Kalpencha* (The Black Owl) is invested in scrutinizing the immoral and the deviant – the beggars, madmen and prostitutes – who form an integral part of the city. While these outlier groups are somewhat cursorily surveyed in the earlier *Biography*, each of these urban typologies is the subject of individual sketches in *Musings*. For instance, similar to the *Biography*'s "Neanderthal Man" is the figure of the primitive beggar, whose personage and appearance the narrator notes with great dismay in *Musings*:

> He is much like the most primitive man, pithecanthropus erectus: small head sitting on a thick-set shoulder, huge jaw, large incisors and canines grinning through the open mouth, deep-set blood shot eyes red as the hibiscus flower, one leprosy-ridden arm about to fade away to nothingness, and another arm supporting the body on a crutch, no fingers. I am not talking about any primitive beast or discussing the Pleistocene period. I simply have in mind a hapless 'homo sapien' of the twentieth century in the modern city of Calcutta. Not a prince of this 'princely city,' he is a terrible-looking (*bhayanak*) beggar of vile and deformed (*ghrinnya, kutsita*) Calcutta. (*Musings* 26)

The same deployment of lurid and macabre tropes to illuminate the disjunctive contradictions of the city is repeated here. The charm of the colonial "princely city" is gone, replaced by a postcolonial disorder that appears to be considerably worse. Yet there are other new elaborations. Crucially, there is no "Karl Marx" for the salvation of the hapless beggar. The ascription of negative attributes, "terrible," "vile," and "deformed" is revealing, as these can be transferred and transposed from the beggar himself to stand in for the vile and deformed city itself.

Musings draws the reader's attention to the multiplicity and heterogeneity of such primitive forms of life as they intersperse in, dislocate, and ultimately reconfigure the idea of the city. In subsequent sketches the reader comes across *yogi*-like old men, discharged soldiers, and street urchins. These last appear, "In the midst of the fashionable, neon-flooded pavements of the downtown Chowringhee area ... Suddenly from between the crowd of well-rounded calves of *memsahibs* (white women), you will see peering out the outstretched hand of a *nulo* (deformed) child" (28). The descriptions of the beggar as well as the children achieve their powerful de-familiarizing impact through the activation of an indigenous aesthetic effect, that of the *rasa*.

In literary theory, specific literary affects or *rasas* that can be deployed to evoke specific emotions or *bhavas* in the minds of the reader/audience. Divided into eight such types for use in drama and performance by the dramaturge Bharata and the philosopher Abhinavagupta in the eighth and ninth centuries, the deployment of *rasa* was by no means an unfamiliar device in Bengali poetry and prose literature in the colonial and postcolonial periods (Chari 1995; Herder 2004). Ghosh's representation of the beggars and the urchins is dependent on the deployment, and successful impact, of the *bibhatsa* and *bhayanaka rasas:* "He [the beggar] is not to be seen anymore, because I saw his dead body being dragged around by the street mongrels hungry for something to eat. When he would beg, people would turn from him in fear and revulsion (*ghrinna o bhoy*)" (27).

Analogous to the Kantian notion of the "sublime" creating a sense of fear and awe, the *bibhatsa* and *bhayanaka rasas* seek to arouse feelings of disgust and aversion as well as horror and terror. The success of such an aesthetic move is predicated on the formation of overlapping *bhavas* or affects – disgust, aversion, horror, and terror – in the reader. In this account, there is a tacit acknowledgement that the urchins themselves are aware of their impact; they seek to capitalize, through their performance in front of passersby, "[on] the sentiments of mercy and piety (*daya o karuna*), [which] are the mainstays of the beggars ... Many of course are not affected by these two sentiments; they shell out their two cents out of fear" (29). The beggars activate and deploy the *rasas* of *daya*, *karuna* and *bhoy* (fear) to earn a living. This is not simply a cultural turn, however, as the text is quick to point out. Such activities flow into a profit- making industry capitalizing on begging activities in the city (30).

Interestingly, the descriptions of these underclass urban folk show almost no effort on their part to represent themselves. They are entirely silent, with one notable exception of a marijuana-addicted "madman," who asks the narrator to "sit down to listen to some stories of *dharma* (pious tales)" (42). This mad man's apocryphal tale regales the narrator, even though the narrative's recording of what the madman says is marked by the impossibility of *translation*:

> What I heard from the old man was actually a history of sorts, instead of dharma-katha [tales of piety], *it is not possible to reiterate them in my account* – Muslims came to this continent and slaughtered Hindus, prohibited the Hindu way of life, ... Hindus in turn, mouthed the rhetoric of social reform, but practiced human sacrifice in their temples, right in the heart of the city ... (43, emphasis added).

Unlike the examples of Hema, the maid, or old Talui'ma, the failure of translation and representation points to an irreducible difference. The mad man's gory and fantastical counter-history of the present necessarily finds no resonance with the narrator except to arouse feelings of mild amusement. The narrative is unable to properly account for its object; equally, progressive historiography is rendered inadequate in the face of the man's views or personal concerns.

Again, it is in "the heart of the city" in Curzon Park in downtown Calcutta – "the Viceroy's house to the left" (51) – that Kalpencha finds a peculiar space that represents all the diverse elements of the errant lumpen underclass, compressed together and thriving in contact with each other. The sketch is titled "Curzon Park," designating one of the city's more affluent precincts: "In this same area (in Curzon Park), stretching for almost a mile-wide radius, the thieves, robbers, murderers and scoundrels rule – it seems that this is a 'liberated area', cut off from the civilized society outside" (51). The phrase "liberated area" is in English in this passage, in the midst of the Bengali-language narrative. The English phrase formally parallels, as it were, the lumpen's unique location within the postcolonial city: central yet marginal.

This is, of course, only an illusory liberated area, peopled as they are by the outcasts of society. For Ghosh, this illusion is comparable to the space of *kailash-dham*, the mythical grounds of liberation in Hindu, Jain and Tantric Buddhist thought. He notes, "It can be said without doubt that Curzon Park represents the criminal's *kailash-dham*" (51). By this point, the separation of this space and its inhabitants from the world of the Marxist narrator is complete:

> One will feel like entering a secret *underworld* in the midst of possibly the most public space of Calcutta – there is no day, no night, no weather changes, no plagues, no famines, but all the time, hidden currents of corruption, depravity, adultery, fraud, arson and debauchery are flowing through … Curzon Park during the evening appears like a giant junction station. There is however no ear-splitting noise, only a low constant hum, that lifts itself slowly from the ground up to the clouds. (52, original English in italics)

This inverted and grotesque world is ruled by "Kallu," the Lord of Misrule, "who looks quite like Lord Curzon [the British Viceroy from 1899–1905]" (52). Kallu (whose name is a derivative of *kalo*, meaning Black) is obeyed by the various criminal and immoral elements in Curzon Park, and sought after by "police chiefs and upper class women" (53). The flexibility of his class maneuvers is complemented by Kallu's hold over sexual deviants. The narrator Kalpencha scrupulously describes the "eunuchs," the "trans-genders," and the "cross-dressers" who form the counterpart(s) of a normative sexual order:

> In Curzon Park, the eunuchs of Calcutta … go around in female dress like some deformed monsters [*kutsita rakhshasas*] … observe carefully, and you will find a bunch of young men – all decked up in garish powder and snow-cream like the *bulbul* bird … soon one of them will go off with some huge-sized giant, who scarcely resembles human form … So the general population of Calcutta are shocked when cross-dressing men are found murdered, or the corpse of a young boy is discovered [in Curzon Park], but Kalpencha is not surprised at all …. (53– 55)

This undoubtedly conservative passage, recalls Peter Stallybras' insight that the poor must be, and always is, rendered into spectacular forms of visualization to sustain the coherence of the seeing subject. There is a key difference between the women of the queue that Ghosh writes about in the 1940s, and the personages of deviant sexual orientation who occupy Curzon Park, the veritable *kailash-dham* of Calcutta of the 1960s. The diverse human beings present in the queue and in Curzon Park, similar yet different, are subjected to a process of literary *re*-presentation and translation, whose gender and class implications need elaboration. In the queue, the urban collective is feminized and domesticated by invoking the nationalist trope of suffering motherhood and motherland. The bodies of the assembled pre-human women are the literal and literary sites where the proletarian future can be imagined through the combination of scientific surgery and mystical oracle. The collective is socialized and humanized under a heteronormative, familial order, so that the domesticated female/feminized body can provide a (re-)productive venue for the socialist nation. To retrace Ghosh's account: "Little did old Talui'ma know that her granddaughter's granddaughter will one day drive trains and steer airplanes. Bikal Mian must never have thought his grandson will be the first person in his village to have electricity, and will be able to listen to the radio at home and drive a tractor outside through his lush, wide fields" (*Biography*, 106). Representation of the "now," in other words, translates to an imagination of the future.

In Curzon Park, however, the very absence of such familial figures and notions of domestication render the underclass as incapable of incorporation into the postcolonial national body. The representation of this "underworld" and its differentiation from the "general population of Calcutta" is constituted precisely on the basis of two tropes: impossibility of sexual reproduction, and of literary translation and depiction. The eunuchs, the cross-dressers and the trans-genders cannot be reduced to, or represented, within the heteronormative framework of the familial feminine, and can, therefore, exist only as its counterpart. The lumpen serves as the non-heteronormative, non-translatable "Other": it is this literary construction that allows a feminized, domesticated working class to come into coherence.

To conclude, then: the literary genre of the *naksha* with its attendant question of representing the urban underclasses as either progressive or incorrigible provides, I think, a telling instance of what Raymond Williams describes, in *Marxism and Literature,* as the contradictory and mutually antagonistic relation between "historically varied and variable elements" of the "residual" and the "emergent" (121). In Williams' subtle materialist conception, "new meanings and values, new practices, new relationships and kinds of relationships are continually being created" (123) within the terrain of culture, and in social relations at large. The residual in his account refers to those "element(s) of the past" that are refashioned as "effective element(s) of the present" (122), while the emergent points to the "formation of a new class, the coming to consciousness of a new class, and … the often uneven emergence of a new cultural formation" (124). I have followed Williams in positing that the indigent underclasses of the city can be analyzed in relation to the "dominant" forms of culture, where "elements of emergence may indeed be incorporated [into the dominant], but just as often the incorporated forms are merely facsimiles of the genuinely emergent cultural practice" (126). For Williams, attention to literary form illuminates the multiple ways in which the emergent is negotiated, through "reinterpretation, dilution, projection, discriminating inclusion and exclusion" (123) by the dominant within a cultural formation.

I have tried to show that the interaction of the emergent lumpen and the residual nation-form is negotiated, formally and pluralistically, in relation to the dominant moment(s) of politics and culture in the city of Calcutta. Ghosh's *naksha* writings serve as the literary site of this negotiation. In Ghosh, the relation of the lumpen – and the urban underclasses as a whole – to the nation is a dialectical alternating between the opposite axes of homogeneity and heterogeneity, assimilation and expulsion. This is represented in the literary *naksha* through a series of antithetical binaries: indigeneity/modernity, translation/non-translatability, and inner/outer (the urban/national body and its "other").

In this respect, it is useful to connect Binoy Ghosh to Fanon, whom I invoked earlier in the essay. The emergence of the lumpen for Fanon is tied, similarly, to the past as well as to the post of colonialism, and is in constant tension with the residual refashioning of the nation-form in anticolonial and postcolonial nationalism. As Fanon puts it, the emergent practice of the lumpen militant appropriates and is, in turn, appropriated by the nation-form: "[t]hese vagrants, these second class citizens find their way back to the nation thanks to their decisive militant action" (Fanon 82). Yet Fanon's famous warning of the "Pitfalls of National Consciousness," extends to the lumpen as well, since "colonialism also finds ample material in the lumpen proletariat for its machinations (87). This is because the lumpenproletariat's non-relation to the mode of production (they are "without vested interests" as Cleaver terms it) imparts to the lumpen a political fluidity that is relatively autonomous of economic and social class interests.

On the one hand, in the *naksha*'s deployment of lower-class language or *itar bhasha*, as well as the aesthetics of *rasa*, we see the lumpen "find their way back" to literary representation. On the other hand, the generic emphasis of the *naksha* on the spectacular mode and its formal function of creating an urban public sphere enable the collapse of the lumpen into a conservative nationalism. In manifesting these contradictory pulls and pressures, the *naksha* alerts us to the ways in which literary narrative testifies and contributes to, and alternatively obscures and illuminates, the dynamics of social change.

Disclosure Statement

No potential conflict of interest was reported by the author.

References

Anderson, Benedict. 1991. *Imagined Communities: Reflections on the Origin and Spread of Nationalism*. New York and London: Verso.

Chari, V. K. 1995. "The Genre Theory in Sanskrit Poetics." In *Literary India: Comparative Studies in Aesthetics, Colonialism and Culture*, edited by Patrick Colm Hogan and Lalita Pandit, 63–79. Albany, NY: SUNY Press.

Cleaver, Eldridge. 1970. *On the Ideology of the Black Panther Party (Part 1)*. San Francisco, CA: Black Panther Party.

Dasgupta, Rajarshi. 2003. "Marxism and the Middle Class Intelligentsia: Culture and Politics in Bengal, 1920-1950." PhD Dissertation, University of Oxford.

Ghosh, Binoy. 1968. *Kalpenchar Rachanasamgra [Musings, or the Collected Writings of Black Owl]*. Calcutta: Prakash Bhavan.

Ghosh, Binoy. 1979 [1944]. *Nababbau Charita [Biography of the Nouveau Riche]*. Calcutta: Samprotik.

Ghosh, Binoy. 1993. *Banglar Nabajagriti [The Bengal Renaissance]*. Calcutta: Orient Longman.

Guha, Ranajit. 2008. "A Colonial City and its Time(s)." *Indian Economic and Social History Review* 45 (3): 329–351.

Fanon, Frantz. 2004. *The Wretched of the Earth. Trans. Richard Philcox*. New York: Grove Press.

Herder, Hans. 2004. "The Modern Babu and the Metropolis: Reassessing the Early Bengali Narrative Prose 1821–1862." In *India's Literary History: Essays on the Nineteenth Century*, edited by Stuart H. Blackburn and Vasudha Dalmia, 358–400. New Delhi: Permanent Black.

Majumder, Auritro. 2016. "Can Bengali Literature be Postcolonial?" *Comparative Literature Studies* 53(2): 417–425.

Marx, Karl. 1975. *The Eighteenth Brumaire of Louis Bonaparte*. Ed. C.P. Dutt. New York: International Publishers.

Mukherjee, Janam. 2015. *Hungry Bengal: War, Famine, and the End of Empire*. New York: Oxford University Press.

Muller-Ortega, Paul Eduardo. 1989. *The Triadic Heart of Shiva: Kaula Tantricism of Avinabagupta in the Non-Dual Shaivism of Kashmir*. Albany, NY: SUNY Press.

Sarkar, Tanika. 2010. *Hindu Wife, Hindu Nation: Community, Religion and Cultural Nationalism*. Bloomington, IN: Indiana University Press.

Stallybras, Peter. (Summer 1990). "Marx and Heterogeneity: Thinking the Lumpenproletariat." *Representations* 31: 69–95.

Thoburn, Nicholas. 2003. *Deleuze, Marx and Politics*. London: Routledge.

Urban, Hugh B. 2003. *Tantra: Sex, Secrecy, Politics and Power in the Study of Religion*. Berkeley, CA: University of California Press.

Williams, Raymond. 1977. *Marxism and Literature*. Oxford: Oxford University Press.

"No One in the House Knew Her Name": Servant Problems in R. K. Narayan's Short Stories

Ambreen Hai

ABSTRACT

The invisibility and precarity of domestic servants in South Asia remains a pervasive societal and political problem, not often addressed in South Asian literary studies. This essay analyses four short stories by R. K. Narayan that center on marginal, subaltern servant figures, male and female, young and old. It makes two related arguments: one, that Narayan uses the short story form (as opposed to the novel) to give unusual compassionate attention to these servant figures, and to critique the arrogance and injustice of the employer class; and two, that Narayan's mode of representation, with its limitation to upper class narrators' perspectives, creates a distance from the very figures it seeks to delineate, sometimes reinforcing the very class biases or suspicions of the servants that it attempts to question. Emphasizing attentiveness to forms of narration as well as to content as a reading strategy, this essay assesses both the interventions and limitations of Narayan's portrayal of servants in his fiction.

I want to start with two recent events relating to India that became international news. Both involved the mistreatment of women by women, the abuse of Indian domestic workers by their Indian employers. First, as reported in *The Guardian* (December 18, 2013), Devyani Khobragade, India's deputy consul general in New York, was arrested and "subjected to strip and cavity searches and treated [she claimed] like a "common criminal" with no "dignity" because she was charged with visa fraud, or, more specifically, falsifying a visa application for her maid.[1] According to CNN, Khobragade obtained a work permit for "her nanny Sangeeta Richards" by promising to pay her $9.75 an hour but in fact paid her $3.31 an hour, far below the minimum wage.[2] After Richards fled Khobragade's home and went to the police, American authorities were led to investigate Khobragade's misstatement about the lower-class Indian woman she had brought to the US to care for her children. In India, the reaction was widespread fury, outrage, and vocal protests over the Americans' scandalous failure to treat with respect a female Indian diplomat. But, interestingly, no parallel concern was expressed about the diplomat's treatment of a female Indian domestic worker.[3] While American newspapers highlighted fraud, exploitation and the abuse of privilege by Khobragade, by contrast, Indian newspapers described Sangeeta Richards as "the absconding maid" who was "overpaid" not underpaid; Richards was even accused (by Khobragade's relatives and the Indian government) of attempted extortion, blackmail, and dereliction of duty.[4] While certainly it should be questioned why any woman (regardless of her position, class, race, or nationality) should be subjected to a strip-search, I want to call attention here to the servant, not the diplomat on whose behalf Indian outrage eclipsed empathy or compassion for her servant, and to the normalization of the subjection of servants that created such a blindspot among Indians to a powerful employer's exploitation of her powerless maid, to the extent that the maid was attacked for enacting resistance to the conditions she lived under.

In India, External Affairs Minister Salman Khurshid addressed the Indian Parliament which was united in support of Khobragade: "It is no longer about an individual. It is about our sense of self as a nation and our place in the world."[5] Here, then, are questions to ponder: if the mistreatment of a woman diplomat is a matter of concern for the *nation*, then why is the mistreatment of a servant woman not equally so, a national issue? Why is the "dignity" of a prominent elite professional so vociferously defended while the subjection to routine indignity of a poor voiceless woman not only ignored but the servant also blamed and denigrated in the Indian press while the diplomat claims immunity?[6] What cultural norms enable such attitudes and inhibit others? What produces such extraordinary invisibility? Sumit Ganguly, Professor of Political Science and Indian Cultures and Civilizations at Indiana University, commented: "Something we [Indians] don't want to talk about or think about is how we treat domestic workers. For God's sake, we treat them like chattel ... This is a national shame we have not confronted."[7]

Second, in July 2017, a *New York Times* article titled "Maid's Dispute in India Erupts into Class War" described how a violent riot broke out between maids and their "madams," or the maids' families and their employers in Noida, a gated community outside New Delhi, as a culmination of longstanding disputes. In strikingly discrepant reports, the employer accused her maid of stealing money, whereas the maid and her family accused the employer of withholding two months' wages, and then assaulting her and locking her up overnight in their apartment, not allowing her to return home to the shantytown where she lived. What was rare about this event was the united and public resistance of the poor, the angry protests of her community on behalf of the maid. The *Times* noted that while "conflicts between domestic workers and their employers are a regular feature of Indian crime logs," such a full-scale expression of resentment of the rich by the poor, or confrontation between socially marginalized, precarious domestic workers and affluent, socially powerful employers, is new, given servants' and employers' mutual dependence in a "symbiotic" social system built on inequality, disempowerment, stigmatization, and the threat of police violence.[8] Again, in India, this resistance was met with outrage and seen as uppitiness. *The Washington Post* commented, "For centuries, India's elite have employed servants, but economic liberalization and the rise of the middle class has meant that the number of cooks, maids and drivers has grown exponentially in recent decades... Hundreds of thousands have migrated from villages to India's five major urban centers to tend to the needs of the elite."[9] The *Post* quoted from Tripti

Lahiri's book, *Maid in India* (2017), which describes the routine abuse of servants by employers, lack of legal or social protections, culture of habituated inequality, and performance of deference and subordination: "We eat first, they eat later ... we live in front, they live in the back, we sit on chairs and they sit on the floor, we drink from glasses and ceramic plates and they from ones made of steel and set aside for them, we call them by their names, they address us by titles."[10]

I begin with these two examples to highlight the problem of a pervasive cultural tendency, evinced in South Asian public discourse, not to see the problem of abuse and exploitation of domestic servants by employers, and to ask why contempt for and mistreatment of domestic workers is so normalized that it becomes invisible, and why those who enact resistance are actually further blamed and attacked for doing so. This issue of *South Asian Review* focuses on precarity, conditions of insecurity, and how "othering those at the margins further perpetuates precarity." The call for papers cites Judith Butler's influential definition of "precarity" as "that politically induced condition in which certain populations suffer from failing social and economic networks of support and become differentially exposed to injury, violence, and death. Such populations are at a heightened risk of disease, poverty, starvation, displacement, and of exposure to violence without protection" (2009, ii). It asks how South Asian literatures "depict," "articulate and reflect on," these insecurities, and how they "reimagine" solutions or "propose strategies of resistance," and (quoting Lorey 2015) how "a *ciudadanía*, a care community in which our relationality with others ... is regarded as fundamental," can be formed.

I would say in response that in South Asian literary studies, we have not paid attention to domestic servants as such a vulnerable population. Perhaps this is so because issues of even greater inequality and flagrant abuse have occupied the attention of writers and scholars, such as caste and untouchability, from Mulk Raj Anand's *Untouchable* (1935) to Arundhati Roy's *The God of Small Things* (1997), or, the plight of landless peasants exploited by feudal landowners, as in Kamala Markandaya's *Nectar in a Sieve* (1954).[11] But domestic servitude, I would argue, is also a form of precarity which, like other systemic forms of social injustice and inequality (sexism, racism, etc.), creates groups of the advantaged and disadvantaged, the latter of whom are subjected to prejudice, mistreatment, and dehumanization. In their pioneering study, *Cultures of Servitude* (2009), sociologist Raka Ray and anthropologist Seemin Qayum, describe the "insecurity of in-country migrants" who become domestic servants as follows: "rural migrants who move to urban areas in search of better livelihoods ... are some of the most vulnerable populations, and their lives are precariously close to the edge. ... They are long-term victims of economic decline and failure of land reform who have been hurt, not helped, by present policies of liberalization" (10).

Twenty-first century Anglophone South Asian transnational writers, such as Aravind Adiga, Thrity Umrigar, Daniyal Mueenuddin, among others, have begun to call attention to the habituated invisibility and precarity of domestic servants in South Asia, focusing in their fiction on servants as central protagonists and attempting to render servants' subjectivities and classed and gendered experiences.[12] In this essay, however, I want to explore how an earlier iteration, from twentieth-century

South Asian literature, addresses these questions, how it also attempts to counter that invisibility, calling attention to that blindspot, soliciting concern for individuals on the economic and social margins of the nation, seeking to evoke (and build) a sense of relationality, to defamiliarize abuse within the (employer's) home that may be so familiar that it is unseen, and asking its readers to question and rethink what they may take for granted. Specifically, I examine how R. K. Narayan, a pioneering Indian writer, began in his short stories to explore conditions of servitude in mid-century India; how he highlighted classist and elitist suspicion and mistreatment of servants, as well as the complex of mutually dependent relations between servants (nursemaids, cooks, gardeners, watchmen) and upper-class employers; how he attempted to counteract by calling attention to what is still a culturally rendered invisibility; and how he imagined, in an autobiographical story, both an upper class employer's effort to provide a form of care and its ultimate failure.

For theorizations of domestic servitude in South Asia, I draw centrally on Ray and Qayum's book, where they define a culture of servitude as "one in which social relations of domination/subordination, dependency, and inequality are normalized and permeate both the domestic and public spheres" (2009, 3).[13] As Ray and Qayum argue, domestic servitude in India has "long unbroken histories" that have morphed from feudal to modern systems and imaginaries (2); it is an unregulated "institution" that encompasses a "nexus of relations" (4), hegemonies, and "structures of feeling" (5) that "lies at the bedrock of Indian domestic middle- and upper-class existence" and constitutes class identities, subjectivities, self-identities and perceptions "on both sides of the employer servant relationship" (2). While servitude has clearly evolved and adapted to social changes, some key structural features remain constant and unique to South Asian norms of servitude, such as the dehumanization, expected obsequiousness and self-abasement of servants, the routine abusiveness of employers, and the practices that enforce distance and distinction.

R. K. Narayan's fiction, set mostly in the fictional South Indian town of Malgudi, is well known for its myriad characters from all walks of life. Yet though many of his fifteen novels center on precariously situated subaltern figures (the eponymous tourist guide, the painter of signs, the financial expert, the vendor of sweets), not a single one has a servant as a protagonist. In a few of his short stories, however, Narayan does focus on domestic servants as central figures.[14] Perhaps this is because, as he notes himself in his introduction to *Under the Banyan Tree*, the short story form allows for a brief, intensive exploration of marginal figures, whereas the longer form of the novel calls for protagonists that may better sustain the interest of middle- and upper-class readers:

> I realized that the short story is the best medium for utilizing the wealth of subjects available. A novel is a different proposition altogether, centralized as it is on a major theme, leaving out, necessarily, a great deal of the available material on the periphery. Short stories, on the other hand, can cover a wider field by presenting concentrated miniatures of human experience in all its opulence. (Narayan 1992, viii)[15]

Although Narayan's comment here still casts servitude (by implication) as a minor and not "major theme," and relegates servants to the form of "miniatures," on the "periphery," at least Narayan does focus on servants in the stories I discuss below, and calls for a deeper, more complex understanding of them as human beings. Even so, unlike later writers like Adiga in *White Tiger* (2008) or Mueenuddin in *In Other Rooms* (2009) who, respectively, use a first-person servant narrator's voice or third-person free indirect discourse to convey the servant's interiority, Narayan chooses to tell each story not from a servant's perspective, but from the distanced, humorous, higher-level viewpoint of an upper-class narrator, where the servant is more the *object* of interest, rather than the *subject* as a center of consciousness.

I argue in this essay that in his servant stories Narayan *both* calls upon his readers (assumed to be upper or middle-class, who by definition are themselves employers of servants) for greater understanding of pervasive, habituated and systemic oppression of servants as he satirizes the prejudiced employers he depicts, *and* that nonetheless, Narayan's mode of representation (his tone, style, choice of perspective and narrative situation) undercuts that compassionate portrayal, reinforcing a certain distance from the servant figure, rendering it variously comical, quaint, or remote and inaccessible, sometimes even confirming the very suspicion of the servant figures that he seems to question. The servants in these stories range across age and gender: from an elderly woman who works as an ayah, to a young man hired as versatile household help and childcare provider; to older men who serve single-handedly as all-purpose household servants and odd-job-men.

"A Willing Slave" opens with the emblematic sentence, "No one in the house knew her name; no one for a moment thought that she had any other than Ayah" (Narayan 1982, 136).[16] The story thus begins with an implied critique of the employers and a somewhat compassionate account of this old woman who is defined only by her servant function in the household where, over seventeen years, she has helped raise five children. Yet Narayan himself renders her, from an upper-class employer's condescending and humorous perspective, less as an individual and more as a comical caricature. She is mentally fit only to play with younger children, as if she can never mature, despite her status as grandmother: "The Ayah repeatedly renewed her infancy with each one of them, kept pace with them till they left her behind and marched forward. And then she slipped back to the youngest … It might be said that the limit to which she could go in years was six" (136). She is so officiously devoted to her employers that she takes on "self-imposed duties," zealously monitoring the other servants with whom she appears to feel no sense of solidarity:

> [It was] hard for her to conduct herself in the servant world, which consisted of the cook, two men servants, a maid servant, a gardener and his unpaid assistant. Their jokes fell flat on her, their discussions did not interest her and she reported to her mistress everything she heard. The gardener very nearly lost his job once for his opinion of his master, which was duly conveyed by Ayah. She was fairly unpopular in the servants' quarters. She constituted herself a time-keeper, and those who came late for work did not escape her notice. (136)

Narayan thus presents both the affluence and status of this household, signified by its army of servants with differentiated tasks, and the covert resentment and resistance of servants, who gripe about employers among themselves, except for the Ayah who breaks ranks. She is so protective of the children (or arguably hegemonized by her role as servant) that she guards them from the home-tutor in case he canes them, surveils all the visitors and delivery boys, and plays endless games twelve hours a day with the four-year-old, for all of which she receives minimal remuneration – "two meals a day, fifteen rupees a month and three saris a year" – and a day off once every three months (137). It may seem contradictory that Narayan casts her as both infantile and able to exert power as a (self-appointed) guardian, but in fact both fit with Narayan's ultimately condescending portrayal of a servant woman who cannot think for herself, who is both at the mental level of young children and so loyal to her employers that she cannot differentiate between their interests and her own.

With evocative details, however, Narayan depicts the Ayah's inexhaustible patience with her young charge, how she bends "nearly double" to push the tricycle (138), creatively adapts her aging body to avoid "extreme torture" to engage in pretend play (139), and tells stories of great imaginative power that serve both to entertain and control the child by inculcating fear of "bad men" or "the Old Fellow" from whom she personally promises protection (137, 139). As Narayan remarks in his preface, in each of these modest tales, "almost invariably the central character faces some kind of crisis and either resolves it or lives with it," though "some stories may prove to be nothing more than a special or significant moment in someone's life or pattern of existence brought to view" (Narayan 1982, 8). The Ayah's moment occurs when her long-lost husband unexpectedly returns, sent back from the "Ceylon tea gardens" by the "*circar*" (government), perhaps because he is Tamil, and demands that she give up her job to serve him. "I want Thayi" he says, "She is to cook for me. She must go with me" (141). That Ayah is named for the first time now suggests both her individuality, her identity as extending beyond that of nanny, and that the identity of wife will supersede her role as domestic servant. As "Thayi," Ayah now decides to abandon the family to which she has been so devoted and to follow her husband home.

The title is thus multiply ironic. Ayah, who at first seems the eponymous "willing slave" to the family, turns out to be not that willing, after all, when she exercises agency to return to her husband, to whom she considers she owes a higher loyalty. But there is another turn to Narayan's irony, in that the story concludes with the final impression of the Ayah as a tradition- and convention-bound, somewhat coy and silly old woman who is clearly still a "willing slave" to her husband, and to the patriarchal, gender norms of submission that she has internalized: "she walked out of the house, led by a husband proud of his slave" (141). Narayan's portrayal clearly puts her down: she "giggled," refusing to say her husband's name, other than "shyly" calling him "the Old Fellow" (140). At the same time, there is pathos in the last image of the Ayah waiting for half an hour to say goodbye to a beloved toddler who will not emerge from hiding, and irony in that the fear of the lower-class male that she has fostered in the upper-class child induces the child to flee and refuse to take leave of her at the end.

Narayan's portrayal of this servant woman is, then, both sympathetic and patronizing, as it undercuts what it builds up. On the one hand, he points out how quick employers, particularly women, are to condemn servants unjustly, to suspect the worst, even after years of the servants' impeccable devotion. When the Ayah is late returning from her regular visit home to her sons, her mistress is "furious" and contemptuous even though the family wonders if Ayah has been "run over and killed":

"Such a blundering fool. ... She must have taken it into her head to give herself a holiday suddenly. I will dismiss her for this. No one is indispensable. These old servants take too much for granted, they must be taught a lesson" (140). Here Narayan critiques the upper-class woman's callousness, her instant assumption that a missing servant must be absconding and irresponsible, her resentment at her own dependency, her failure to recognize the relationality between servants and employers. He highlights the servant woman's precarity, her vulnerability to threats, and to arbitrary dismissal and punishment. On the other hand, he also confirms an upper-class sense of superiority to the subaltern figure he depicts, by making Ayah ridiculous, a "willing slave" only willing (or able) to exchange one form of servitude for another, unable (or unwilling) to offer resistance to either form of subjection. Even if we understand why an uneducated old woman like the Ayah might make the choice she does, to sacrifice her economic independence and the child she loves to her sense of self-worth as a good wife, we do not thereby need to be asked to see her as absurd.

In "Leela's Friend," Narayan presents a less ambivalent and more biting critique of employers' injustice and callousness and a more understanding portrayal of a servant's disappearance, possibly because the servant is male.[17] The story opens with the name of the servant who will be its subject: "Sidda was hanging about the gate at the moment when Mr. Sivasanker was standing in the front veranda of his house, brooding over the servant problem" (Narayan 1982, 142). Perhaps, this implies ironically, as the story will show, unfair employers *are* the servant's problem. More obviously, the commonplace phrase, "the servant problem," instantly recognizable to the employer classes, used by employers to reference the apparently ubiquitous difficulties of finding dependable servants, indicates an employer's (biased) perspective: to employers, servants are the problem. This opening presents Sidda as possibly both looking for a job and loafing about lazily, both assertive and possibly mendacious, while the employer is unusually trusting. Their subtly nuanced initial interaction makes manifest their inequality of power: the lower-class man in need must carefully observe and seize the opportunity, using shared, understood codes of deference, while the upper-class man in need retains the upper hand. "Sir, do you want a servant?" inquires Sidda respectfully (142). Mr. Sivasanker "subjects" Siddha to "scrutiny," asks about previous employment, to which Sidda gives the "stock reply" that they have left town, and yet hires him without references because Leela, his five-year-old daughter takes an instant liking to him. Despite its sympathetic bent towards Sidda, the story sows a seed of doubt about Sidda from the start: did his previous employers really leave without giving him references; or is he lying, like presumably others of his ilk, just saying what he needs to in order to get the job?

Narayan clearly represents the precarity and exploitation of this lower-class man, who must singlehandedly do all the housework and childcare for a pittance: Sidda "was given two meals a day and four rupees a month, in return for which he washed clothes, tended the garden, ran errands, chopped wood and looked after Leela" (142). He also presents Sidda as remarkably kind, patient, charming and creative, as Sidda becomes Leela's titular friend, playmate and resource for an extraordinary wealth of oral folklore and inventiveness, telling her "incomparable stories" (like the Ayah in the previous story) "of animals in the jungle, of gods in heaven, of magicians who could conjure up golden castles…," submitting to every demand (144). Teaching her to throw her ball into the sky, he fosters her imagination: "Now this has touched the moon and come. You see here a little bit of moon sticking," he tells her to her delight, and that he has instructed the moon to follow them from the front garden to the backyard (143). Yet none of this is appreciated by Leela's parents, who immediately suspect him of theft when Leela's gold chain goes missing. If Sidda provides care for the employers' child, he receives no care in return, nor does he have recourse to a care community or safety net when trouble arrives.

Via his mode of narration, Narayan leaves no doubt of his implied critique of the upper-class employers and their injustice, highlighting their prejudiced perceptions, making clear how suspicion itself impacts Sidda from the start. When Leela's mother "shouts" to summon Sidda, she thinks "the fellow already looked queer" (144). Narayan gives us, in a single sentence, a hint of Siddha's interiority when asked about the chain: "His throat went dry" (144). The rest of the narration is matter-of-fact, from an external perspective, but the brevity of the sentences conveys the absurdity of the upper-class quick leaps from perceived loss, to suspicion, to threat:

> He blinked and answered that he did not know. She mentioned the police and shouted at him. She had to go back into the kitchen for a moment … When [she and Leela] came out again and called, 'Sidda, Sidda!' there was no answer. Sidda had vanished into the night. (144)

The narrator is as patently sardonic about Mr. Sivasanker, who upon learning of this, "grew very excited," and headed straight to the police (144). Sidda's disappearance is promptly read by his employers as a confirmation of his guilt, but the story suggests the alternative, more likely possibility that he is terrified, despite his innocence, into running away. He knows what happens to accused servants once the machinery of law and state kicks into action. And, indeed, Mr. Sivasanker reports, the police inform him that Sidda "is an old criminal. He has been in jail half a dozen times for stealing jewellery from children. From the description I gave, the inspector was able to identify him in a moment" (145). This is deeply ironic humor – and a dig at upper class readers who may initially believe this report – for Sidda is supposedly "identified" based only on a generic description, not even a photograph. Narayan thus evokes the systemic oppression and vilification of lower class men, and the prejudice and collusion of upper-class men (the employer and the police inspector) who wrongly suspect and slap members of the underclasses with fake criminal records. It also suggests the likely falsity of many such criminal records.

The story affirms that Sidda is innocent, not only because, in a rare moment, once he is apprehended, he speaks and asserts his innocence ("I have not taken it" he says "feebly, looking at the ground," as if he knows that he will not be believed), but also because, days after Sidda has been taken to jail to be interrogated, likely by means of police violence, Leela's mother finds the necklace in the kitchen, where it had been hidden by the child (145). Narayan does not explore the child's motivations, other than to indicate that this is a young child's caprice – his focus is on the adults' unjust and harmful reactions. What is most horrific is Leela's parents' failure to rectify what they have done. Instead of seeking to undo the injustice, to clear Sidda's name or make recompense, they still regard him as a criminal, who cannot possibly be trusted in their house. The story ends with Sivankar's words to his wife: "I will tell the inspector tomorrow ... in any case, we couldn't have kept a criminal like him in the house" (147). The servant not only cannot get his job back (or possibly another one), he is now saddled with a false criminal record.

Narayan uses the child's words to intensify the contrast between Leela's intuitive egalitarianism and trust in Sidda, and the grown-ups' distrust, perhaps to show what is lost as adults are transformed by social convention, and to highlight, from her undegraded perspective, the injustices of those social conventions designed to demean and humiliate servants. "Why should not Sidda sit in our chair, Mother?" she asks, or, "Sidda is gone because he wouldn't be allowed to sleep in the house just as we do. Why should he always be made to sleep outside the house, Mother?" (145). At best, it is Leela who exhibits care for the servant, or a sense of relationality. Narayan also intensifies the pathos of Sidda's defeated posture when Sidda is being taken away by the police: "[Leela] clung to Sidda's hand. He looked at her mutely, like an animal" (146). For all this rendition of the servant's dehumanization, however, Narayan does not give us Sidda's own perspective, or interiority. The perspective favored by the story is that of an upper-class male narrator, who, like Narayan himself, is caustically critical of fellow-upper class arrogance, unfairness, lack of conscience, and is benign to (male) employees, but who nonetheless cannot, or does not, extend his imaginative reach to the empathetic portrayal of a servant's consciousness or inner life from within.[18] It is also worth noting that, unlike Ayah in the previous story, Siddha is not made to seem as foolish, again, perhaps because he is male. Experiences of servitude differ greatly by gender and age, but rather than explore those differences, Narayan seems to focus more sympathetically, and more, on male servants than female. His one story about a woman servant, "A Willing Slave," positions the servant more condescendingly than the ones about male servants.[19]

"A Willing Slave" and "Leela's Friend" are early stories, originally published in 1956. In two later, more open-ended stories, "A Snake in the Grass" and "Annamalai," published in 1985, Narayan is less clear about the servant's innocence or the employer's injustice, and more self-ironic.[20] "A Snake in the Grass" is ambiguous about a servant's possible duplicity even as it shows how a servant is exploited and mistreated. A family living in a bungalow is informed that a cobra has been seen entering their compound. Their instant reaction is to rudely awaken their "old servant, Dasa" (it is unclear if he is elderly or has served them for ages, or both), to blame him for the snake's arrival, and threaten dismissal if he does not get rid of it:[21]

> They shook him out of his sleep... "There is no cobra," he replied. ... They swore at him and forced him to take an interest in the cobra. "The thing is somewhere here. If it is not found before evening, we will dismiss you. Your neglect of the garden and the lawns is responsible for all these dreadful things coming in." (Narayan 1992, 93)

Narayan highlights both the relentlessness of the employers' demands and the systemic pervasiveness of upper-class prejudice, as even the neighbors join in maligning Dasa, calling him the "laziest servant on earth" (93).

At the same time, Narayan's own portrayal of Dasa suggests the servant's recalcitrance and subtle insubordination, as if he deserves this treatment. First, Dasa refuses to believe in the cobra's existence, indicating his desire to shirk the work he is asked to do and, perhaps, a servant's (reciprocated) lack of trust in employers. When handed a stick to scare the creature out, "He kept desultorily poking it into the foliage with a cynical air," comments the narrator (94). "'The fellow is beating about the bush,' someone cried aptly" (94). This humorous literalization of the English idiom indicates both the upper-class employers' education and wit at the expense of the lower-class man, and with the corroboration of Narayan's adverb, "aptly," that it also befits Dasa's actions, as if the servant deserves the mockery. Eventually, after the employers give up and leave the scene, Dasa claims to have caught the snake in a water-pot, and then disposed of the snake. He is hence celebrated and rewarded. "Dasa had the glow of a champion on his face. 'Don't call me an idler hereafter,' he said. … He became the hero of the day" (95). By giving him this speech, Narayan grants Dasa agency, and makes clear the importance to Dasa of clearing his name, of pushing back against the employers' aspersions on his character.

But the story does not end by simply proving the employers wrong. After Dasa has left, they see a cobra slide out of the grass:

> When they recovered from the shock they asked, "Does it mean that there were two snakes here?" The college boy murmured: "I wish I had taken the risk and knocked the water-pot from Dasa's hand; we might have known what it contained. (95)

With this last line, the story's title, which also literalizes a metaphor, reveals itself as a pun. The "snake in the grass," the story suggests, is both literally the cobra hiding in the tall vegetation, but perhaps idiomatically, it is also Dasa who lies and leaves the family vulnerable to being bitten by a snake they believe has been removed. Narayan thus opens up two mutually exclusive possibilities: either Dasa lies and deceives; or he tells the truth and there really was a second snake in the grass. By ending with the perspective of the employer, who wonders if the pot was empty, and denying us access to the perspective of the servant, Narayan allows us no way of knowing for sure. It could thus be read at least two ways: one, that Dasa is in fact a liar, the proverbial snake in the grass who cannot be trusted. Understood thus, the story confirms the deceitfulness and unreliability of servants. Or, two, alternatively, that no matter what a servant does, employers will never trust him and will continue to suspect him of deception and unreliability. I would argue that the latter is too generous a reading, not only because the likelihood of two snakes is low, and because the story offers no evidence that there were two snakes, but because the singular "snake" in the title suggests that there was in fact only one snake.[22] The story thus leans towards suggesting that it more likely that Dasa lied, though that may itself be understood as a powerless servant's sly resistance in response to employers' unreasonable demands. However, even if it carries a hint of sympathy for the reasons for Dasa's deceit, the story still confirms the employers' suspicion that servants are deceitful and not to be trusted. Its humor works at the expense of both the ingenious trickster servant and the employers who are taken in by the duplicitous servant, as it ends with the befuddled employers who are left in perpetual doubt.

"Annamalai" is a more subtle, self-implicating story. It is the only one of Narayan's servant stories told in the first person, by a narrator much like Narayan himself. It is, in fact, autobiographical, as he himself notes, "almost a documentary of a strange personality who served as a watchman in [his] bungalow for fifteen years." (Narayan 1992, viii–ix). In none of the other servant stories is the narrator also a character in the story. This story thus also adds a complicating layer of uncertainty and irony at the expense of the narrator-employer, whose understanding of what he describes is necessarily limited, creating a gap between what the narrator says and what the story itself shows.

"Annamalai" begins with the arrival of a postcard:

> The mail brought me only a postcard, with the message in Tamil crammed on the back of it in minute calligraphy. I was curious about it only for a minute – the handwriting, style of address, the black ink, and above all the ceremonial flourish of the language were well-known to me. I had deciphered and read out to Annamalai on an average one letter every month for a decade and a half when he was gardener, watchman, and general custodian of me and my property at the New Extension. (Narayan 1992, 117)

The narrator's exact details about the card, and precise account of how often he read to the eponymous Annamalai, belie a certain forlornness of tone, and a sense, as he reads this postcard, of Annamalai's remoteness, for while the writing is familiar, it bespeaks the absence of this live-in attendant and man of all work on whom the narrator came to depend, and who cannot even write to him directly himself. On behalf of Annamalai, a paid letter-writer asks for money, outlining, in a recognizable idiom of importunity, Annamalai's precarity and destitution, how he cannot turn to anyone else, least of all the state: "I am in sore need of money. The crops failed this year and I am without food or money. My health is poor. I am weak, decrepit, and in bed, and need money for food and medicine" (118).

Willing to help his former servant, yet knowing that Annamalai cannot read or write, and that "he always affixed his signature in the form of a thumb-impression whenever he had to deal with any legal document," the narrator is unsure if this postcard was in fact sent by the man it purports to represent: "But how could I be sure that he had written the letter? … how could I make sure that the author of the letter was not his brother Amavasai, … who might have hit upon an excellent scheme to draw a pension in the name of a dead brother? How could I make sure that Annamalai was still alive?" (118). The story thus opens with the employer's doubt, his learned mistrust of lower-class men and their claims of need, his fear of being taken advantage of, and his dilemma about what to do. What follows then is a reflective, retrospective account of his memories of Annamalai, and of their relationship, as well as an implicit self-justification, or self-excusal, for his doubts. The story ends without indicating whether the narrator ever responded to the postcard or sent any money.

The narrator – whom I will treat not as the voice of Narayan the author but as a constructed fictional character, even though he is modelled on an employer like Narayan himself — portrays Annamalai with both complexity and humor as a somewhat eccentric, endearing but inept, good-hearted but fiercely independent old man who effectively adopted him when the narrator moved into his new house. As one of the crew of movers who unloaded his belongings, Annamalai takes charge, telling the lorry maker to stop his "donkey noise," and then abandons the lorry driver who had forced him into a kind of bonded labor, and voluntarily, with characteristic independence, decides to look after the hapless narrator instead (123). The narrator thus sets himself up as more benevolent than Annamalai's previous, more exploitative employer. Though "touched by his solicitude," and noting that "there was something fierce as well as soft about him at the same time," the upper-class narrator is wary when Annamalai asks for a small advance to go fetch his baggage: "I had not known him for more than twenty-four hours. I told him, 'I don't have change just at this moment'" (125–26). Annamalai's response is a wry understanding: "He smiled at me, showing his red-tinted teeth. 'You do not trust me, I see. How can you? The world is full of rogues who will do just what you fear. You must be careful with your cash, sir. If you don't protect your cash and wife…'" (126, ellipsis in original). Perhaps this generosity (and man-to-man advice) induces a certain self-consciousness, for the narrator curses his own "suspiciousness" and "lack of grace" (126). As Annamalai takes it upon himself to look after his new employer, oddly protective, as if he was the vulnerable one, the narrator learns to unlearn his distrust, to trust Annamalai.

He describes Annamalai, nonetheless, as somewhat comical and not very knowledgeable, his gardening as effective almost by fluke.

> He followed me about faithfully when I went round to inspect the garden. Whoever had owned the house before me had not bothered about the garden. … Whenever I paused to examine any plant closely, Annamalai also stood by earnestly. … I learnt in course of time that his classifications were extremely simple. If he liked a plant he called it "*poon chedi*" [flowering plant] and allowed it to flourish. If it appeared suspicious, thorny, or awry in any manner he just declared, "This is a *poondu* [weed], and, before I had a chance to observe it, would pull it off and throw it over the wall with a curse. (124)

Yet, despite this "simple" idiosyncratic arbitrariness, with what the narrator describes as excessive watering and manuring, Annamalai manages to produce a lush garden where rose plants "developed into leafy menacing entanglements, clawing passers-by, canna grew to gigantic heights, jasmine into wild undergrowth with the blooms maliciously out of reach" (128). Perhaps this is because the narrator learns to relinquish control, to trust Annamalai to plant "whatever he fancied," to recognize his autonomy and personhood: "I found I could have no say in the matter. I realized that he treated me with tolerant respect rather than trust, and so I let him have his own way" (128). Perhaps, also, this description of Annamalai's gardening suggests an unconsciously parallel ambivalence on the narrator's part, a displaced account of Annamalai himself – as a "menacing entanglement," yet "maliciously out of reach." As if to ward off his own growing dependence on Annamalai, rather than to recognize Annamalai's expertise, he adopts a tone of amused indulgence: "nature was responsible for [the flowers'] periodic appearance, although Annamalai took the credit for it unreservedly" (128–29).

As the narrator details Annamalai's inability to read or write, his consequent dependence on the narrator to read and write for him to communicate with his family, the narrator emphasizes his own kindness in doing this service for his servant for an hour once a month (120). He claims, in other words, to provide the care community that Annamalai has not found elsewhere. He is most condescending, however, about Annamalai's attitude to technology: "One of his urban triumphs was that he could handle the telephone. In distinguishing the mouthpiece from the earpiece, he displayed the pride of an astronaut strolling in space" (132). Irritated by Annamalai's failure to take phone messages, he comments: "The only way to exist in harmony with Annamalai was to take him as he was; to improve or enlighten him would only exhaust the reformer and disrupt nature's design" (133). With such putdowns, the lower-class servant is represented as linked with nature, capable of growing giant plants, himself a creature of nature, but with limited capacity for advancement or progress.

Yet Narayan's portrayal of Annamalai still has a depth and complexity that the servants in the stories discussed above lack. Annamalai becomes deeply indignant about the claims of dishonesty cast upon him by his employer's neighbor, fiercely protective of his name and reputation. The narrator thus showcases (again) the poisonous effects of upper-class suspicion of servants, in contrast with his own more positive, trusting treatment of Annamalai: "Annamalai was believed to earn money by selling my flowers, according to a lady living next door to me, who had constituted herself his implacable enemy" (134). He indicates both the lady's small-mindedness, and his own more generous recognition that even if Annamalai was making small cash on the side, he refused to be territorial or possessive about his flowers, and ruin the good will in his more valuable relationship with his employee, built precisely over time by demonstrating trust. When she accuses Annamalai of stealing her chickens, he reports how Annamali becomes particularly irate, and launches into a speech that address not the lady directly, but the wall between and the connecting sky:

> "You set the police on me, do you, because, you have lost a fowl? So what? What have I to do with it? If it strays into my compound I'll twist its neck, no doubt, but don't imagine that I will thieve like a cheap rascal. ... I am a respectable farmer with an acre of land in the village. I grow rice. Amavasai looks after it and writes to me. I receive letters by post. ... Anyway, what do you think you are? Whom do you dare talk to? ... I am an independent man, madam, I don't stand nonsense from others, even if it is my own father. (134–35)

Narayan gives Annamalai a voice, allowing him to reveal what matters to him, and how he perceives his own identity. This is a form of indirect resistance to upper-class prejudice. Annamalai distinguishes himself with pride from the putative "common rascal" by insisting that he has his own ethic — he does not steal — but will not brook fowl invasion into his turf, and that he is a landowner, who receives mail and is therefore worthy of respect. His tirade becomes unstoppable, and includes an unexpected earlier history of travel and migrant labor, from tea plantations in Ceylon to rubber estates in Penang during World War II. The narrator's tone and attitude towards Anamalai is at once tender and comical: "Although it was beamed in the direction of the lady next door, I gathered a great deal of information in bits and pieces which enabled me to understand his earlier life" (135). However, even here, even as Narayan shows and imagines how a more positive relationship between employers and servants might be built, by the employer's display of trust and care, and the employer's understanding of the servant's heartbreaking vulnerability, Narayan does not clear Annamalai of suspicion. "Once feathers were found scattered around Annamalai's habitat when it was raided by a watchman" (who was pretending to be a policeman, and was actually sent by the lady), reports the narrator, indicating both some culpability on Annamalai's part and the lady's devious action in trying to frighten and intimidate Annamalai (134).

Yet despite this imagined relationship of (limited) care and mutual coexistence, the story shows how the employer ultimately fails the employee. When Annamalai receives a postcard from his brother reproaching him for his absence and reporting the dissolution of a complicated financial arrangement, a loan he had made to the village tailor, his distress is strong enough that he asks for leave to go home to "renew the bond" and sort out the situation (141). For all his understanding and curiosity, however, the narrator refuses to let him go. "I cannot let you go now," he repeats, with a strange obduracy, as if unable (or unwilling) to recognize alternative claims on his servant, to spare him or trust him to return (140, 142). They attempt to negotiate: Annamalai offers to return to guard the house before the narrator has to go on pilgrimage; the narrator reads him the bond and, discovering its fraudulence, even offers to pay Annamali the hundred rupees he wants to recover. But what is more important to Annamalai is that he should be able to save face: "the people in my village will laugh at me," he insists (142). The narrator, however, seems to have difficulty both understanding Annamalai's feelings, and acknowledging his own dependence, psychological and otherwise, on Annamalai. He wants to know that he would be there taking care of his house when he returned from his trip. "Now I felt desolate," he reveals (143). Perhaps the narrator's dependence has grown into possessiveness.

Frustrated, yet exerting his agency, Annamalai finally leaves, not just for ten days, but for good. Shocked to find him packed up, the narrator reproaches him: "Is this how you should leave after fifteen years of service?" (144). Annamalai's response, "I am not well. I don't want to die in this house and bring it a bad name. Let me go home and die," provides a new reason, one different from the original (144). But the story suggests more than the narrator seems to understand. Perhaps Annamalai cannot really tell his employer why he leaves. At the end, he seems hostile, as if that former amity and trust between him and his employer has been broken. Invested in averting suspicion of theft, he insists that the narrator inspect his trunk, and when the narrator refuses, and dashes inside to get him some money, Annamalai does not wait. In the last line of the story, the narrator reports: "When I returned with ten rupees, he was gone" (144). There is pathos in this inconclusive ending, a sense of the inexplicability of a man who remains undecipherable — at least to the narrator. We do not know what happened to Annamalai after this departure, whether the postcard purportedly from him is in fact from him, or whether the narrator responded with money. Told with the benefit of hindsight, from the perspective of the employer, the story conveys his sense of loss, his awareness of having mishandled and messed up a delicate relationship that he cannot rectify, trapped in his ethos of upper-class suspicion.

Compared to the three stories discussed above, "Annamalai" is self-ironic, as the employer-narrator implicates himself in suggesting how upper-class prejudices and stereotypes get in the way to prevent justice and kindness to those vulnerable and dependent, and recognizes his own dependence on his servant. But self-knowing though it is, this story also shows the limitations of Narayan's portrayal of lower-class servants, whom he characterizes with ambivalence and ambiguity. Not only does Annamalai remain ultimately remote, he remains distanced from readers because of Narayan's choice to tell his story through the mediating filter of the upper-class narrator and his inevitably biased, obscuring perspective. As a result, though we can guess at Annamalai's interiority through his reported dialogue, the narration itself does not give us a direct access to the servant figure, who remains at best only partially comprehensible, at times quaint, irascible, annoying, or limited, as seen by his employer. What the story ultimately reveals, then, is not the psyche of the servant *per se* but the limitations of the employer's perspective. The narrator is unable to see, let alone approve of, the tacit resistance offered by Annamalai, who, in the end, rejects the entire position of servitude, and the source of his livelihood, to flee the narrator's unreasonable, controlling grasp. What is tragic, however, is that such resistance becomes self-disabling, for Annamalai likely ends up destitute as a result of the breakdown of communication, and ultimately, of his employer's failure to understand him or allow him to take a short leave of absence.

The contemporary scholarly desire to seek and validate resistance on the part of the oppressed can thus sometimes blunt the nuances of complex realities. In their study of servitude, Kathleen Adams and Sara Dickey point out that the "romanticized" notions of "subaltern resistance" to domination and subordination can be too dichotomous and simplistic, and can fail to address how "hegemonies and their multiple hierarchies" must be "constantly negotiated" (Adams and Dickey 2000, 7). In looking at the nuances of servitude, we need to pay attention to how subordinated persons *negotiate* rather than resist the structures in which they are placed, to how they may assess the costs of resistance. Moreover, if we only validate resistance, how can we recognize or understand the fact of failure to resist? Are some oppressed persons less deserving of concern if they are unable to resist or do not show signs of resistance? Narayan's servant stories reveal such nuances, showing how servitude as a system can itself disable or discourage the possibilities of resistance on the part of (some) servants. Annamalai can leave, but not for any guaranteed future or provision, at the cost of his livelihood and security. Sidda tries to run away, but cannot escape the entanglements of the net of state and upper-class power that catches up with him in the end. Dasa can lie and puncture the certitudes of employers, only to reconfirm their prejudices, but none of these servants can change the structures that disempower and entrap them. Ayah can choose to leave, but only to submit to a husband's demands, substituting one form of extorted care for another, and she is cast – by her employers and by Narayan – as foolish for so doing. Narayan's stories also show, rather bleakly, how there either are no care communities to provide support for these subaltern characters, or that, even the employer who attempts to construct one does so in such a limited way that it is ultimately a failure. The culture of servitude in South Asia, which fosters mutual distrust and the learned contempt of employers for the people they employ for their basic needs, itself seems to disable that care community from forming; indeed, it seems predicated on the lack of care. It is not until the twenty-first century that we see writers who try to imagine alternatives to such systems of servitude — and here I would include, in addition to Umrigar and Adiga, non-South Asian postcolonial writers like Chimamanda Ngozi Adichie, whose main characters in *Half of a Yellow Sun* (2006) include a houseboy who receives the education from his employer that eventually allows him to leave servanthood and become a writer.

Servitude in South Asian literature calls for our attention as an important area that reveals a nexus of concerns around precarity, injustice, exploitation, and the intersections of class, gender, age, among others. Narayan's short fiction is an important pioneer in this area, calling attention to domestic servants' precarity with compassion and unusual attentiveness (though arguably more so for male than for female servants), and to the pernicious effects of employers' lack of trust. However, we also need to pay attention to the narrative strategies that writers use, to their evocation of subjectivity, and to their often inadvertent reinforcement of class and gender biases. Narayan's choice of mode of representation self-contradictorily undercuts that compassion, locking him into narrating from, and thereby limiting himself to, an upper-class perspective that itself casts the servant as either ridiculous (the Ayah), or not entirely trustworthy (Sidda, Dasa), or as remote and inscrutable (Annamalai). At best, in "Annamalai," Narayan offers a self-ironic acknowledgement of that failure. This is by no means an inevitability for writers who themselves hail from privileged backgrounds. Social location does not determine politics.[23] More recent writers, such as Neel Mukherjee in *A State of Freedom* (2017), exemplify the power of fiction to extend imaginatively into the consciousness and experiences of domestic servants, of other selves less privileged than their own, and to imagine alternatives to the habituation of acculturation and tradition. Nonetheless, for its time, Narayan's account of servants is remarkable for what it does achieve, for its ironic, attentive, nuanced portrayals of the dissonances between rich and poor when they cohabit in close proximity and interdependence, and its ultimately heavier placement of responsibility upon those with greater power.

Notes

1. (https://www.theguardian.com/world/2013/dec/18/indian-diplomat-strip-search-us-devyani-khobragade). *The Guardian* continues, Khobragade "pleaded not guilty and plans to challenge the arrest on grounds of diplomatic immunity … If convicted Khobragade faces a maximum sentence of 10 years for visa fraud and five years for making a false declaration." Khobragade was eventually granted diplomatic immunity by the Indian government and enabled to leave the US where she was re-indicted under the same charges. See https://thediplomat.com/2014/01/indian-diplomat-leaves-us-after-being-indicted/.
2. http://www.cnn.com/2013/12/19/world/asia/india-diplomat-politics/index.html.
3. As *The New York Times* reported, "Ms. Richard's lawyer, Dana Sussman of Safe Horizon, a victim services agency, said: "My client is frustrated with how the media has portrayed this story and the response from the Indian government. The victim in this case is not the criminal defendant. The victim is the person who worked incredibly long hours and was severely underpaid." https://www.nytimes.com/2013/12/20/nyregion/fury-in-india-over-diplomats-arrest-in-new-york.html?_r=0.
4. https://www.hindustantimes.com/india/us-embassy-paid-for-sangeeta-richard-s-family-s-air-tickets/story-26pI4LfLlTAT6u8UAB4FOK.html; https://www.indiatoday.in/india/north/story/devyani-arrest-row-devyani-khobragade-sangeeta-richard-india-us-diplomatic-face-off-222241-2013-12-28.
5. https://www.nytimes.com/2013/12/20/nyregion/fury-in-india-over-diplomats-arrest-in-new-york.html?_r = 0.
6. In India, and among Indian Americans, the maid in question, Sangeeta Richards, was blamed for challenging her employer. "Be thankful for what you have," said one Indian

American commentator to *The New York Times*, since she got more than what maids get in India (https://www.nytimes.com/2014/01/10/nyregion/claims-of-diplomats-mistreating-household-staff-are-far-from-the-first.html?_r=0).

7. CNN, ibid.
8. https://www.nytimes.com/2017/07/15/world/asia/at-a-luxury-complex-in-india-the-maids-and-the-madams-go-to-war.html.
9. https://www.washingtonpost.com/world/asia_pacific/maids-riot-at-luxury-high-rise-exposes-class-divide-in-india/2017/07/12/f126b9e0-4f02-49c5-b8c3-f2ebf8d51ab6_story.html?noredirect=on&utm_term=.01353aefcb33
10. Ibid.
11. In my essay, "Postcolonial Servitude" (Hai 2014), I discuss at more length how earlier South Asian writers place domestic servants in the background, and how a new wave of writers has begun to foreground servants as central characters.
12. For a fuller discussion of these, see my essays, Hai (2014) and Hai (2016).
13. "By 'normalized' we mean, first, that these social relations are legitimized ideologically such that domination, dependency, and inequality are not only tolerated but accepted; second, that they are reproduced through everyday social interaction and practice. … In a culture of servitude, servitude is normalized so that it is virtually impossible to imagine life without it, and practices, and thoughts and feelings about practices, are patterned on it" (Ray and Qayum 2009, 4).
14. Scholarly attention has focused on Narayan's novels and relatively neglected his remarkable short stories. For example, in his otherwise perceptive, thoughtful discussion of Narayan's fiction, Pankaj Mishra barely mentions the short stories. A few scholars have addressed irony and humor in Narayan's stories, but not servants, nor how the humor works at whose expense. See for example Gunasekaran (2010), Gupta (2008), Olinder (1989), and Fitz (2006).
15. With more condescension, one critic writes: "India's poor may not bear the burden of a novel but may beautifully fit into the short story" (Gowda 1994, 63).
16. Originally published in *Lawley Road* (1956), republished in *Malgudi Days* (Narayan 1982).
17. Originally published in *Lawley Road* (1956), republished in *Malgudi Days* (Narayan 1982).
18. It may be argued here that Narayan does not presume to represent the subaltern's consciousness. I would respond, however, that that is exactly what imaginative fiction is supposed to do – to extend beyond the self. It would be highly problematic to demand that writers can only write about themselves. It is in fact as an ethical *obligation* for writers with relatively more privilege to speak up for those with less privilege. See my essay "Postcolonial Servitude" (Hai 2014), for a longer discussion of the ethics of representation of socially disadvantaged others.
19. In focusing only on an older female servant, Narayan also does not address the sexual exploitation of younger women servants who are often vulnerable to sexual predation from male employers. Many women writers call attention to this problem of sexual harassment of female servants, notably Hosain (1988 [1961]), and Umrigar (2005).
20. Both republished in *Under the Banyan Tree and Other Stories* (Narayan 1992). Original dates of publication unknown.
21. Dasa also means servant. My thanks to Pallavi Rastogi for this point.
22. Of course, it is possible that the title emphasizes the *belief* that there was only one snake. My point is that the story creates indeterminacy. It is, however, usually read as confirming the servant's duplicity. This is not to say, of course, that servitude inherently creates indeterminacy or the unknowability of servants, but rather, that it is Narayan's mode of presentation that creates the indeterminacy, that Narayan's stories suggest, with overtones of class prejudice, that servants are ultimately unreadable (at least to the upper-class that employs them). Hence the employer's mistrust of the servant, depicted

by Narayan, is ironically mirrored in Narayan's story itself, which echoes that mistrust by leaving the servant's trustworthiness open to doubt.

23. I would clarify that though their social location is not a simple *determinant* of a writer's politics, it is nonetheless a heavy *influence*, as it affects the ideological frameworks that unconsciously structure world view, unless a writer overtly, clearly, consciously struggles against it. In Narayan's case, we see not a case of either-or, but of both-and: we see *both* his attempt to highlight the injustice to lower-class domestic workers by upper-class employers, *and* a tendency to see and cast servants as untrustworthy or inscrutable. It is not inevitable for all upper-class writers to create indeterminacy about a servant character's actions or motivations; Umrigar (2005) and Mueenuddin (2009), for instance, make it very clear in their fiction that the servants accused or suspected of dishonesty by employers are in fact innocent.

Disclosure Statement

No potential conflict of interest was reported by the author.

References

Adams, Kathleen, and Sara Dickey, eds. 2000. "Introduction." In *Home and Hegemony: Domestic Service and Identity Politics in South and South Asia*. Ann Arbor, MI: University of Michigan Press.

Adichie, Chimamanda Ngozi. 2006. *Half of a Yellow Sun*. New York: Anchor Books.

Adiga, Aravind. 2008. *White Tiger*. New York: Free Press.

Anand, Mulk Raj. 1940 [1935]. *Untouchable*. London: Penguin.

Butler, Judith. 2009. "Performativity, Precarity, and Sexual Politics." *AIBR* 4 (3): i–xiii. http://www.aibr.org/antropologia/04v03/criticos/040301b.pdf.

Fitz, Brewster. 2006. "'Gateman's Gift': Self-Reflexive Irony and Allegory in the Narrative of R. K. Narayan." *South Asian Review* 27 (1): 214–218.

Gowda, H. H. Anniah. 1994. "R. K. Narayan and Patrick White as Short-Story Tellers." In *R. K. Narayan: Critical Perspectives*, edited by A. L. McLeod, 53–65. New Delhi: Sterling Publishers.

Gunasekaran, S. 2010. "The Comic Vision in the Stories and Sketches of R. K. Narayan." *Language in India* 10 (1): [no pagination].

Gupta, G. S. Balarama. 2008. "R. K. Narayan, the Ironist (with Focus on His Short Stories)." *Literary Criterion* 43 (3-4): 34–44.

Hai, Ambreen. 2014. "Postcolonial Servitude: Interiority and System in Daniyal Mueenuddin's *In Other Rooms, Other Wonders*." *ARIEL* 45 (3): 33–74.

Hai, Ambreen. 2016. "Motherhood and Domestic Servitude in Transnational Women's Fiction: Thrity Umrigar's *The Space Between Us* and Mona Simpson's *My Hollywood*." *Contemporary Literature* 57 (4): 500–540.

Hosain, Attia. 1988 [1961]. *Sunlight on a Broken Column*. London: Penguin.

Lorey, Isabell. 2015. *State of Insecurity: Government of the Precarious*. New York: Verso.

Markandaya, Kamala. 1956 [1954]. *Nectar in a Sieve*. New York: Signet.

Mishra, Pankaj. 2003. "R. K. Narayan." In *A History of Indian Literature in English*, 193–208. New York: Columbia University Press.

Mueenuddin, Daniyal. 2009. *In Other Rooms, Other Wonders*. New York: Norton.

Mukherjee, Neel. 2017. *A State of Freedom*. New York: Norton.

Narayan, R. K. 1982. *Malgudi Days*. New York: Penguin.

Narayan, R. K. 1992. *Under the Banyan Tree and Other Stories*. Chennai: Indian Thought Publications.

Olinder, Britta. 1989. "Irony in R. K. Narayan's Short Stories." In *Short Fiction in the New Literatures in English*, edited by J. Bardolph, 183–187. Nice: Fac. des Lettres & Sciences Humaines.

Ray, Raka, and Seemin Qayum. 2009. *Cultures of Servitude: Modernity, Domesticity, and Class in India*. Stanford, CA: Stanford University Press.

Roy, Arundhati. 1997. *The God of Small Things*. New York: Random House.

Umrigar, Thrity. 2005. *The Space Between Us*. New York: HarperCollins.

POETIC INTERLUDE

Spaces

K. Satchidanandan

My moon rises in a valley in Damascus,
shedding light on the Arabian Nights.
My sun sets over the Atlantic,
spreading darkness from Lithuania to Liberia
My stars illumine the Pacific,
Turning each of her islands into gold.
My lexicon comes from all over the world
from Iran and China, Portugal and Rome,
from Netherlands and Arabia
The solid gravity of Sanskrit over
the liquid music of Tamil:
a Himalaya in the Mediterranean.
My bread comes from Vidarbha
where peasants commit suicide;
my water, from Ganga
where orphan corpses bob up and down
The song I sing is of the vanishing Nila river,
the death I die, of the pitch-black Yamuna.
I sleep alone, remembering our Syrian driver
Khalid, of Aleppo. Is he alive still?
At times a homeless Kurd appears in a dream;
at times, a Rohingya refugee raises his roofless head.
I do not know Gikuyu,
I haven't even been to Palestine.
I set fire to every proof of my having lived;

only one thought remained in that ash

on earth like a flightless bird.

It still lays eggs;

one day, one of them may hatch

a blazing sun that brightens up my village too,

my memories may reappear as its black spots.

Only words fall on my begging bowl:

Kindness. Love. Sacrifice.

Words.

The Black Hole of words.

Precarity and Resistance in Oceanic Literature

Tana Trivedi

ABSTRACT

This essay examines the writings of Sudesh Mishra and Epeli Hau'ofa to establish how precarity is embedded in Fiji's colonial past and the contemporary internal and well as global geopolitics. Beginning by recounting Fiji's colonial capitalist and territorial history and the segregationist policies of the imperial powers, this essay discusses the impact of nuclear testing on the post-colonial ecology of the Pacific Islands. Cultural and ecological precarity in the island state of Fiji includes colonial capitalism, militarization, and unstable political arrangements of the last two hundred years. An alternative framework that reimagines the oceanic identity, providing sustainable, inclusive solutions for the future, is required urgently. The writings of Mishra and Hau'ofa offer the possibilities of engaging with the history, geography and culture of the islands to create sustainable care communities engaged in preserving the already delicate ecology of the islands.

Introduction

My argument is that it's not just the islands themselves or the land that are important- it's the ocean that is our reality: we touch it, we drink it, we smell it, and the same water that washes our shores also washes the shores of the other islands. (Keown 2007, 75)

Feejee

Exists to give cartographers malignant tumours;

Sometimes they leave it out, sometimes they don't.

Just bits of flyshit on the blue, insignificant,

Yet half-stocked with yahoo taught by rumours

To savour the fashionable turd of nationalism

[…] (S. Mishra 1992, 1)

> In Oceania, problems of globalism are only half-articulated. So far, there are no counter-narratives... A site of resistance, perhaps the site of most effective resistance, of course, is literary production itself. (Subramani 2001, 157)

In an interview with Michelle Keown in 2001, Epeli Hau'ofa, the director of Oceania Centre for Arts and Culture, at the University of Suva, Fiji, clearly outlined the objective of the Center: to recognize the ocean as a visual and physical reality so that it could be protected from nuclear experimentation, and to thwart Western attempts from making it into a global rubbish dump (Keown 2007). Despite being a part of the largest geographical entity, the Pacific Ocean, the Pacific Islands are popu-lated only by a few million people,[1] rendering the islands vulnerable to exploitation on several fronts. Sudesh Mishra, a contemporary Indo-Fijian-Australian poet, reiter-ates this fear of global exploitation in his poem *Feejee*, where he underscores the irony of locating Fiji on the world map giving cartographers "malignant tumours," referring to the islands of Fiji as "flyshit" and "insignificant on the blue of the world map" (S. Mishra 1992, 1). In doing so, he satirically underscores the stereotype of Fiji as an inconsequential group of islands, not worth locating on world map. By referring to the islanders as Yahoos, Mishra ironically comments on the how European impe-rialists transformed a group of humans into unthinking, Yahoo-like figures, meant to be controlled. Mishra and Hau'ofa position their work against these notions, positing Oceanic Studies as a significant intervention in resisting global challenges of eco-logical precarity. In *Precarious Lives*, Judith Butler (2006) describes precarity as a lived condition of vulnerability of people in a hegemonic culture, as those who do not deserve to be remembered as humans, whose loss need not be mourned because they are instruments of war and nation building:

> If there were to be an obituary, there would have had to have been a life, a life worth noting, a life worth valuing and preserving, a life that qualifies for recognition... The matter is not a simple one, for, if a life is not grievable, it is not quite a life; it does not qualify as a life and is not worth a note. It is already the unburied, if not the unburiable" (2006, 34).

Butler's theorization of precarity, although articulated in the context of the "war on terror" in the United States, is applicable to the crises that the Oceanic Islands face against the ongoing threat of global warming and ecological disasters, in that it renders a whole population exposed to insecurities of different kinds, excluded from protection and care. Institutionalized ecological destruction has dispossessed Pacific islanders of their past, and the agency to determine their future, left them precarious, a by-product of unprecedented and non-negotiated globalization.

This essay begins with recounting Fiji's colonial capitalist and territorial history and the segregationist policies of the imperial powers that eventually led to the cul-tural and ecological crises that threaten modern-day Fiji. By highlighting how Mishra and Hau'ofa expose states of precariousness, this essay shows how literary writing can create spaces of resistance and sustainability. Through an analysis of their work, I establish the need for constructing an alternative framework to understand the differ-ent kinds of precarities embedded in Oceania and propose newer ways of reimagining the identity of the islands against existing colonialist and globalist tropes. Amidst ris-ing discourses on the Anthropocene, and its engagement with environmental humanities, an alternative framework, shifting the scholarship from Oceania as a subject of study, to an autonomous site producing its own discourse about itself, is urgently needed.[2] For instance, Mark Goodale's (2006, 634–649) theory of indigenous cosmopolitanism provides a framework to reimagine indigenous civil societies in which marginalized groups across the world are brought together to envision global "belongingness" that surpasses categories of belongingness such as patriotism and national identity. While Goodale examines new forms of indigeneity in Bolivia, Subramani (2001, 149–162), in his seminal essay "Oceanic Imaginary," proposes new epistemologies of examining the space of Oceania, which blur the boundaries between disciplines and involve critiquing oppressive ways of thinking, importantly through literature which he believes, is a critical site of the oceanic imaginary. Subramani posits literary production as an important space of resistance and resilience against unprecedented encroachment of capitalism on the islands. Alternative frameworks such those of Goodale and Subramani present newer ways of examining global citizenship, and provide tools to create sustainable, inclusive expressions of resistance and to counter the growing vulnerability that threatens to engulf world's most precarious populations.

Two significant voices in Oceania that explore the concept of the ocean as a space of origin, sustenance and future, propose ways of resisting not just ecological but also social and cultural precarity that threaten to engulf the already delicate fabric of the islands, are those of Mishra and Hau'ofa. Both the writers use their literary platforms to express their outrage at the precarity that the Oceanic islands have experienced historically, especially post-contact with the European imperial powers. Their works reflect the precarity of the islands at several levels: colonial, post-colonial, cultural, ecological, economical, and political. Mishra employs poetry as an instrument to express ethnic divisiveness within Fijian society and traces it back to the colonial policy of divide and rule; Hau'ofa weaves stories and essays around concerns such as ecological degradation, climate change, and the cultural erosion of indigenous value systems in the present. Both writers trace their ancestry to disparate regions of the world, one to India and the other to Tonga, while engaging with language as means of protest to bring these communities together in the present. Debilitating life conditions caused by indenture and forced labor in Fiji and nuclear testing have made certain islands such Bikini Atoll unlivable, raising significant questions about the civilizational supremacy of the West, and demonstrating its capacity to inflict violence and atrocities on the islands of the Global South. While anxieties, risks, and susceptibilities that impact the island communities affect their responses to global challenges, both Mishra and Hau'ofa's proposal of preserving collective memories offers a means of adaptation and resilience against these challenges. In fact, Mishra's poetry articulates what Hau'ofa believes, that the islanders must see themselves and the spaces between them not as islands in a distant ocean but as a sea of islands in which they themselves participate. To withstand global changes, including economic and ecological exploitation and the unstable political conditions of the present, it is necessary to revisit the past, to investigate memories, and to establish the position of the islands as significant contributors in creating and sustaining world history and culture. Against the backdrop of the ongoing state of political and environmental crises caused by competing imperial powers that have historically posited Fiji as isolated and exotic, as well as well-suited for nuclear testing, Mishra and Hau'ofa establish how precarity is embedded in Fiji's colonial past and contemporary internal and global discriminatory geopolitics. The causes of cultural and ecological precarity in the island state of Fiji include colonial capitalism, militarization, and unstable political arrangements of the last 200 years.

Colonial and Post-colonial Precarity in Fiji

Two events are critical to discerning present-day precarity in Fiji: the first is the practice of indenture established in the late nineteenth century, when laborers from the Indian subcontinent were coerced and transported to the islands to work on sugarcane plantations, with no rights to the land they tilled. The second event is the Cold War, which led to the Pacific's becoming a nuclear testing ground for colonizing nations such as US, Britain, and France, causing large-scale damage to the health of islanders and their ecology, the effects of which are felt even today. Indentured labor to Fiji began after the islands ceded to the British crown in 1874. Shortly after Fiji was colonized, Sir Arthur Hamilton Gordon, its first substantive governor, took it upon himself economically to develop these islands by inviting the Australia-based Colonial Sugar Refining Company (CSR) to start sugarcane farming. Gordon had experienced firsthand the success of the indentured system in Mauritius and Trinidad. With CSR's agreement to lease lands from the Fijian chiefs they began large-scale farming in 1880, which persisted as a large mode of agricultural production for almost a century. Thus began Indian indenture to Fiji from 1879 to 1916, during which 60,965 Indians were transported to work on sugarcane plantations, which now would be described as human trafficking (Srebrnik 2008, 75–95). Conditions of severe drought, and increasing British revenue demands in the state of Uttar Pradesh, in Northern India, from which a majority of the *girmityas* (indentured labourers) were recruited, led to a large-scale migration of labourers to islands such as Fiji and Mauritius in the late nineteenth century. Vijay Mishra, a contemporary Indo-Fijian writer and historian writes that the process of indenture brought together heterogeneous groups without any genealogical basis for membership, alliance or affinity:

> …the Indians themselves were essentially a fragment which had been forcefully wrenched from its centre. For the Girmitiyas (the indentured labourers) their life in Fiji was retrospectively seen as a deception played upon them by recruiting agents (arkatis) who convinced them of future possibilities filled with millenarian expectations. (V. Mishra 1992, 32)

Therefore, the first moment of precarity for the Indo-Fijians can be traced retrospectively to the journey of indenture, when most laborers, essentially landlubbers, were exposed to the ocean, and subsequently to the harsh realities of working on sugarcane plantations for the first time. Deceived into believing that they would lead a better life, the *girmityas* arrived in Fiji as a displaced people, facing five years of servitude and hard labor. Their sense of displacement was so deeply entrenched that even the subsequent generations of Indians born in Fiji continue to recount the pain of indenture.

The Indian migrants experienced extreme precarity, not just physical, on account of hard work in an entirely different topography, but also cultural due to the segregationist policy of the colonizers, who kept the Indians and Fijians apart from each other. The colonial protectionist policy, which leaned towards the islanders, discouraged inter-group contact and promoted ethnic blocks, because of which Fiji evolved into a multi-cultural yet highly fragmented society. Perceived as manipulative and regressive, Indians were treated differently. As James Michener (1951) observed in his collection of short stories *Fiji: Return to Paradise*:

> Nobody can stand the Indians… They are suspicious, vengeful, whining, unassimilated, provocative aliens in a land where they have lived for seventy years. They hate every one: black natives, white Englishmen, brown Polynesians and friendly Americans. They will not marry with Fijians, whom they despise. They avoid the English ways, which they abhor; they cannot be depended upon to support necessary government policies. Above all, they are surly and unpleasant. It is possible for a traveler to spend a week in Fiji without ever seeing an Indian smile. (1951, 123)

Western narratives, such as Michener's, provided ammunition for the continued segregation of the two communities, and reduced the state of Indians to that of *coolies*, or laborers, brought to the islands to build colonial capital,[3] with no access to land ownership. The imperial past of segregationist policies haunts contemporary Fijian politics, which is still marred by recurrent political coups and racial strife.[4] While socio-cultural, political and economic precarity intensified in post-indent Fiji due to the remnants of the colonial racial policies, a new kind of precarity in form of nuclear testing gave rise to ongoing ecological crises.

Nuclear testing in the Pacific started in 1946 and ended in 1996, during which time the former colonial powers United States, Britain, and France had collectively conducted more than 300 detonations. The impact of nuclear testing meant sudden deaths, heart problems, deformities, miscarriages, and mental confusion in the native populations, even as the effects of radiation continue to this day. More recently, colonizing nations have begun compensating Pacific islanders for the havoc wreaked by these tests on their health and environment (AFP 2015). Large-scale nuclear testing in the Pacific continued until 1985, when Fiji and 13 other nations lobbied to sign the Treaty of Rarotonga, also known as the South Pacific Nuclear Free Zone Treaty, calling for a ban on all nuclear testing in the region (2011). The United States refused to ratify any of the protocols of treaty, which remain pending even today. Elizabeth Deloughrey (2001) explains the main reason why these islands were considered suitable for nuclear testing:

> The convergence of imperial, scientific, literary and anthropological discourses have constructed an isolated, atemporal island space which is entirely divorced from its archipelagic neighbors and which suppresses the complex processes of island migrations. (2001, 24)

Creating metaphors of seclusion, leisure, and isolation to describe Islands is a part of a Western ideological project rooted in the imperial and post-colonial policy of claiming land, whether for colonial farming or for nuclear testing, According to Deloughrey, this metaphorical representation traces its roots to the colonial enterprise that sought to expand its shores by building colonies to unburden the overpopulated

English isle.[5] Therefore, the Pacific and Caribbean islands were positioned as isolated, yet susceptible to migration and settlement. The image of the islands as warm, tropical, touristy, and non-industrialized signified the binary of the West as cold, progressive, and industrialized. The construction of the islands as corresponding to ancient European narratives of mythic islands such as Antillia, Atlantis, and Terra Australis Incognita contributed to their being "discovered," "found," and conquered through settlement. The archipelagoes of the Canary and Madeira islands from the East Atlantic, to Mauritius, Galapagos, the Caribbean islands, and the Pacific islands, all have been significant spaces that have contributed not only to the colonial economy, but have also facilitated ecological, anthropological, and biological theories for colonizers, giving rise to ideologies of power and hegemony.

Sudesh Mishra's Poetics of Colonial Precarity

The critique of colonial capitalism and the objectification of the islands finds voice in the works of Sudesh Mishra, whose writing evokes a complex oceanic imaginary, encompassing the history and geography of the islands, in which temporal shifts merge the past and present to reflect the historical and contemporary precarity of Fiji. For instance, in his poem "The Indo-Fijian," from his collection *Rahu* (1987), Mishra captures the anxieties of the fourth-generation Indo-Fijian who recounts and inherits the state of vulnerability that his ancestors experienced:

Born Indo-Fijian I nurse no expectations,

Great or otherwise;

For ten decades I have clung to *Syria's*[6] grisly truth.

[...]

All the same I am gored by the uncertainty

Of a childhood where dungwalls crack

To expose the hysteria of a black ocean,

Where infant hands twisting mother's sari,

Tighten to a fist against the muffled scream

Filtering through partitions.

Only rumours like limericks

Can redeem me from the panic of the cutting season

Or myths, floating as thistledown,

Lighten the post-evening terrors,

When the slightest noise unhinges the mind,

And wrinkles appear at the wrong places. (1987, 11)

In this partly biographical poem, Mishra expresses his angst at being unable to forget the trauma associated with the history of his ancestors as they migrated to Fiji. The images of a hysterical ocean, drowning ship carrying *girmityas*, and the cries of the infants clinging to their mothers, are memories that have been passed on from one generation to the other, while the cane-cutting season still reminds the poet of a dark, ancestral past that continues to haunt him in the present time. By juxtaposing different temporal realities, Mishra captures not just the vulnerability of the displaced *girmityas* by re-imaging their moment of loss and trauma, but also the moment of terror in real time, where evenings are reminders of inherited trauma. The memories of this tragedy continue to profoundly impact the Indo-Fijians, reminding them of the precarity that is embedded in their presence in Fiji. "In Memory of Jarek Woloszyn" (2002, 38), Mishra concludes a poetic account of global historical violence by mourning the partition of cities and nations around the world as they grapple with conflict: "We sit with plugged ears or point the warlock's stick/At another's devilry." Internal strife, metaphorically described as 'inbred golem' in places such as Soweto, Jaffna, Fiji, Bosnia, Angola, Belfast, Punjab, Berlin continue to create ethnic blocks, rendering millions of lives precarious with violence and exclusion. However, the poem's appeal in the end resonates with what can redeem humankind from annihilation:

[…] O citizen

Of the Grave, teach us the common

Dialect of the soil teach us the alphabet of love,

The truth in truisms, tell us there are no separate towers,

Teach us to be simply human. (2002, 42)

Mishra captures in his poetry an inherent indigenous cosmopolitanism that has been a part of the islander identities for centuries. By articulating the dynamic interconnectedness of the islands in their local histories and social practices and by interweaving history, geography, and different temporalities of the islands, he promotes a comprehensive picture of oceanic identity, so that pasts are reconstructed to strengthen selfhood in the present. Positing himself as a multi-located, multi-lingual traveling-native from Oceania, and appealing for peaceful co-existence, he expresses the temporality of his ancestral experience of forced labour on to a larger canvas of violent world politics. In doing so, he proposes a way forward to alleviate the vestiges of historical trauma, and one towards stable and inclusive island communities.

Mishra reimagines the conditions that uprooted his ancestors from the settlements in India, tracing their passage to Fiji, as they slipped into anonymity in a land where they would eventually settle. In "Nightfall" (Mishra 1987), he recreates the trauma of exploitation and displacement-

Evening.

Mynahs are prunes moving against the sky,

The diminishing light holds me together,

Buttressed in retrospect:

A Brahmin Nana[7] rehearsing

His father's dream

Exchanged Lucknow for a vision stretched miles into the ocean.

[...]

Even when the scourge snaked over shoulders

The mind stayed focussed-

Ayodhya[8] was more real than agony or *arkathi,* (1987, 22)

Through the image of an old Brahmin from Lucknow reminiscing about a lost homeland and emphasizing the traumatic reality of his existence on the islands, Mishra describes the pain of the *girmityas* who found themselves betrayed by the false promises of the recruiting agents. The indentured labourers, Mishra explains, were like assembly-line workers, assemblages themselves, misfits on this South Sea island, with no support from their homeland, and also alienated from the ecology that was central to their cultural practices. The homeless Indians, who were inherently terrestrial people, found themselves intertwined in an oceanic ecology and economy over which they had no control. They became participants without agency or belonging, prompting their struggle for political power in post-independence Fiji. By the time Fiji became independent in 1970, indigenous Fijians were already outnumbered by the Indo-Fijians, who constituted 49% of the island population, thus reversing the demographic equation, and creating apprehension about the political and economic domination by the migrant community. Fijians, reduced to a state of representational precarity by their relegation to an almost-minority community in their own nation due to colonial migration policies, created their own means of resistance through political coups. This divide between the Fijians and the Indo-Fijians initiated the first coup in 1987.[9] The precarity of migratory versus ethnic strife was thus embedded in the founding of Fiji as a new nation, and continues to exist even today in the form of multiple coups, which have led to thousands of Indians leaving Fiji, creating a double displacement. While the colonial policy of indenture created a state of precarity in Fiji, the precariousness changed form when the Pacific became a site for Nuclear Testing in the post-colonial period and continues to suffer its consequences even today.

Epeli Hau'ofa and the Politics of Post-colonial Precarity

Postcolonial writers such as Sudesh Mishra and Epeli Hau'ofa have attempted to remap European narratives about the South Pacific, challenging colonial assumptions about the islands as devoid of culture and history. A significant voice in South Pacific Literature and Cultural Studies in the 1980s and '90s, Epeli Hau'ofa's novel *Kisses in the Nederends* (1995) provides a satirical perspective on everyday Fijian life. The central characters in the novel include Oilei Bomboki, a Fijian man who seeks help from Babu Vivekanand, an Indian sage and conman, after he wakes up in severe pain one morning. Describing their interaction, Hau'ofa writes,

> Oilei disrobed and bared his bottom at the holy man, not quite certain that he would do it. But Babu rose into a kneeling position, parted Oilei's buttocks delicately, and in a reverential and sacramental manner, placed his nose inside. He drew back and repeated the action three more times before he resumed his lotus posture, saying, "I have kissed your blessed anus with love and respect. If the presidents of the United States and the Soviet Union do likewise at their next summit meeting, there will be no more threat of nuclear annihilation and there will be set an example for all the leaders of the world to emulate. As in most things we must begin from the top down. When the top meets the bottom, there will be eternal peace."

> Oilei noticed a change in the old man's demeanour as Babu paused before launching himself into something that seemed to have troubled him profoundly.

> "The anus, as you have now seen, is neither revolting nor obscene. The most revolting and obscene thing we live with today is the threat of nuclear annihilation. It is obscene because of the spectre of destruction that it presents to all of us, but more so because it perpetuates, for as long as nuclear weapons exist, the fears, suspicions, and hatreds that blind us to the beauty of creation; that is, the love, trust, and respect that we can have for one another. (Hau'ofa 2008, 130)

In his depiction of Babu as a conman, Epeli mocks the commonly held notion among Fijians that Indians are cheats who will usurp their access to their land and political power and employs him instead as a mouthpiece to ridicule the prejudice of the islands. The comic and distorted image of a holy man sniffing up a naked man's 'nederend' is also a metaphor for the way the powerful nations of the North perceive the Global South, "the Nederend." Epeli satirizes the limited imagination of the powerful North, which renders the Pacific South insignificant and thus dispensable within global geopolitics. Humor and satire are employed as means of deflating and resisting the power wielded by the 'top' countries of the world towards the 'bottom' ones. However, Hau'ofa's writing engagement with nuclear testing in Fiji and its consequent ecological hazards is the most striking aspect of his writing. Nuclear testing created a new form of precarity and remained a crucial part of popular discourse and protest until the end of the 1980s. Referring to British phosphate mining in Banaba and US nuclear testing at Bikini Atoll, Hau'ofa writes in his essay "The Ocean in Us":

> Modern society is generating and accumulating vast quantities of waste matter that must in the near future be disposed of where there will be least resistance. It may well be that for the survival of the human species in the next millennium we in Oceania will be urged, in the way the people of Banaba and Bikini[10] were urged, to give up our lands and seas. (2008, 46)

Cultural and ecological precarity are deeply interconnected in Hau'ofa's work. Hau'ofa argues that the colonizers have expected islanders to cede their land and natural rights to conduct experiments they claim would benefit all of humanity. However, the deep and long-term cultural and ecological damage has only reinforced, and derived legitimacy from, the vulnerability of the islanders and the perceived remoteness of the Pacific. According to Hau'ofa, islanders have been indoctrinated into belittling themselves as savages, and thereafter, to submit themselves to cultural and ecological vulnerability via the force of Western capitalism (2008, 27–40). This sense of historically embedded precarity continues to morph into different forms in various aspects of island culture even today. By exploring diverse colonial and post-colonial temporalities, Mishra and Hau'ofa articulate the state of precarity that haunt the islands, thus establishing the context for creating new ways of resistance and sustenance.

Modes of Resistance: Creating an Epistemology of a New Oceania

Hau'ofa strongly critiques the islanders' rejection of their own traditional approach to ecology, and its replacement with neoliberal globalization instead. He promotes the re-centering of the Oceanic experience and asserts a cultural identity that transcends borders and cartographies to project a much larger and multi-colored picture of Oceania than those derived from Western representations. The metaphor of the ocean captures the essence of the islands as expansive, inclusive, and large, as a space that must be preserved against destruction by imperial capitalist forces that constantly threaten to destroy island ecology by making it a testing ground for nuclear and war-related activities. He also claims that Fiji was an imperial colony taught "nationalism," by colonial culture, which led to replacing an indigenous understanding of the inter-connectivity and heterogeneity of the islands with the concept of a homogenous nation-state. Ironically, imperial governance introduced democracy to Fiji even though it was a dictatorship itself, therefore only imagining an ideal democratic state but never building institutions that would make that possible. By severing the ties of the islands from their own knowledge systems, abruptly introducing an entirely new population that was culturally alien to the islanders, and constructing island identity through a frame of reference from the west, Hau'ofa shows us how Fiji has been rendered precarious, in the past as well as now. Hau'ofa's reconceptualization of the islands as an amalgamation of different races and ethnic backgrounds with a common commitment to building resilient and adaptive island communities acts as a form of resistance to environmental precarity:

> The issue should not arise if we consider Oceania as comprising human beings with a common heritage and commitment, rather than as members of diverse nationalities and races. Oceania refers to a world of people connected to each other. The term Pacific Islands Region refers to an official world of states and nationalities. John and Mary cannot just be Pacific Islanders; they must first be Ni Vanuatu, or Tuvaluan, or Samoan. For my part, anyone who has lived in our region and is committed to Oceania, is an Oceanian ... We have to search for appropriate names for common identities that are more accommodating, inclusive and flexible than what we have today (Hau'ofa 2008, 41–79)

Mishra and Hau'ofa recalibrate acts of belonging to the islands by invoking narratives of migration and indigenous cultures that bring about new ways of understanding kinship and belonging, thereby offering different ways in which the culture and ecology of the islands can be preserved. Hau'ofa writes in his essay "Pasts to Remember":

> With little or no memory, we stand alone as individuals with no points of reference except to our dismally-portrayed present, to our increasingly marketised national institutions, to international development agencies, international lending organizations, transnational corporations, fit only to be globalized and whateverised, and slotted in our proper places on the Human Development Index. (2008, 70–71)

Hau'ofa helps us understand how knowledge has been historically produced by hegemonizing capitalist discourses, which portrayed the islands as spaces for either scientific and cultural experimentation, or as spaces offering leisure and relaxation. Postcolonial Pacific writers, such as Mishra and Hau'ofa, are interested in exploring contemporary experiences that portray the islands as real spaces, instead of the exoticized tourist destinations depicted in colonial discourse. Hau'ofa argues in "Pasts to Remember,"

> Most of our remote and so much of our recent pasts are not documented and therefore lie outside the purview of mainline history. We must in that case devise other methods, based on different perspectives of history, to reconstruct such pasts to suit our purposes, including those of maintaining the depths of our roots and the strengthening of our autonomous identities. We have to bequeath to future generations more memories of our recent past and our present than we ourselves remember of our remote pasts. We must remember and reconstruct as much of our pasts as we can to present to the future. (2008, 69)

Oceanic modern history is the story of an alienated realpolitik, continuously in flux, attempting to engage with its precarity by finding meaning in the lexicon inherited from its colonial past and forgotten traditional way of life. This has fragmented Oceania's understanding of itself and changed its cognitive relationship with time and place. An inclusive framework that encapsulates voices of heterogenous groups with varied histories, and acknowledges them as the "Oceanic citizens," is necessary to create modes of resistance and even care communities, ones that can sustain the island inhabitants against an increasing precarity in the Oceania. (Lorey 2015) One of the greatest challenges posed by human-engineered climate change is the loss of space and familiar surroundings, which can never be recovered through means other than memories and ancestral knowledge. Creating care communities that work not only towards preservation and sustenance of life, but also engage in chronicling memories for future, opens the possibility for healing trauma and displacement and ushering ontological security in times of crises. George Handley (2015, 360–379) in his essay "Climate Change, Cosmology and Poetry: The Case of Derek Walcott's *Omeros*," says:

> What our epoch of the Anthropocene needs is neither a reinforced balkanization of identities and communities nor a facile unity that ignores or obliterates differences. It needs cosmologies whereby we can imagine and then enact a new sense of answerability and belonging in a world that is a much broader and more collective than we can know or imagine. (Handley 2015, 341)

Mishra and Hau'ofa present these possibilities of creating a broad web of inter-dependence and intersubjectivities, thereby shaping futures that can offer resistance against migratory and ecological fragilities. Their accounts of fragmentation and displacement in Fiji provide opportunities for projecting a world that must amalgamate and obliterate differences of the past to create community-based approaches to reduce vulnerability to various forms of precarity. By embedding knowledges of reliance and adaptability from the past and by integrating them with new knowledge and technology, Oceania, or an Ocean-based imaginary, may bring about a sustainable change to world ecology and human habitation.

Notes

1. As per the World Bank census, population of Pacific Islands is about 2.3 million, with Fiji with the highest population of 8,80,000. Spread over a vast area, these islands are scattered roughly over 15% of the globe's surface area.
2. According to the Oxford Centre for the Humanities, Environmental Humanities are a diverse and emergent field of cross-disciplinary research that seeks to analyze and investigate the complex interrelationships between human activity (cultural, economic, and political) and the environment, understood in its broadest sense.
3. The contract of labour stipulated the workers to work on the plantations for five years, and they would be given remuneration, food, clothing, and medical facilities and an optional free passage home after those five years.
4. Four coups have taken place in Fiji since its independence in 1970. The first two took place in 1987, the third in 2002, and the last one in 2006. During these coups Indians suffered economically and psychologically. Once again they were reminded of their dim origins and struggles, instilling in them a deep sense of futility and anger. As Satendra Nandan encapsulates the Fijian experience of Indians in a few words, "As a migrant, stripped much of his history, his human dignity, his roots, once again uprooted by the coups, the twice-banished, thrice-betrayed, had to live by his wits" (Nandan 2000).
5. The Pacific Islands, historically described as "South Sea Islands" by eighteenth century European explorers, were perceived to be isolated spaces that evoked romantic, utopian notions of paradise. This changed after the Second World War, when the region was labeled as "South Pacific" by the Western Alliance military forces, and was popularized as an exotic tourist destination by Michener in his 1946 collection of stories, Tales of the South Pacific (Keown 2007, 11).
6. At 8:30 pm on Sunday, May 11, 1884, an inexperienced crew had allowed the Indian immigrant ship, the Syria, to drift off course, and it was wrecked on the Nasilai reef at Nakelo in Tailevu. Of the 497 men, women, and children on board, many had never seen water. The giant rocky reef was unforgiving and shredded the 200-foot, 1000-ton iron ship. By the time the shipwrecked passengers were brought to safety, 59 had drowned. Drowning of Syria is a recurring theme in contemporary Indo-Fijian literature.
7. Nana refers to maternal grandfather in Hindi language
8. Ayodhya is a city in Uttar Pradesh, India, believed to be the birthplace of Lord Rama
9. On a misty morning on May 14, 1987, at about 10 o'clock, armed rebels barged into the Fijian parliament and claimed power at gunpoint, overthrowing the one-month-old democratically elected government of Prime Minister Timoci Bavadra of the National Federation Party, who had come to power after 17 years of near-continuous rule of the Fijian-dominated Alliance Party headed by Ratu Sir Kamisese Mara. Though an indigenous Fijian, he was elected mostly with the support of the Indo-Fijians, and this became a bone of contention for the Fijians, ultimately leading to the coup. In elegy for Dr Timoci Bavadra, the founder of the Fiji Labour Party, and who served as the Prime

Minster for a month before being deposed in the first coup of 1987. An ardent opponent of the US nuclear testing in the Pacific, Bavadra passed away in 1989, leaving a bereaved Mishra, who recollects his magnanimity and humility to contrast the contemporary state of politicians whom he describes as "hucksters, quibblers and sophists," and the "interim beasts of recent history," who are "leaving an augury of pug-marks/ Which neither man nor Heaven/ May succeed in undreaming." (S. Mishra 1992, 50).

10. The people of Bikini Atoll were moved from their homeland in 1946 to make way for the testing of 23 nuclear weapons by the United States government. Subsequent exodus of the Bikini people included a two year stay on Rongerik Atoll, and six months at Kwajalein Atoll under conditions of starvation, after which, in 1948, they were finally relocated to Kili, a small, isolated, 200-acre island owned by the US. See: https://www.ncbi.nlm.nih.gov/pubmed/9199216 (accessed September 4, 2018).

Acknowledgements

I thank Surabhi Vaya for her all help, without which it would have been impossible to write this essay. I also thank Dr Pallavi Rastogi for patiently providing valuable inputs and feedback for the essay. I am grateful to the South Asian Literary Association for giving me the opportunity to present my research, and I am indebted to my family for their constant love and support.

Disclosure Statement

No potential conflict of interest was reported by the author.

References

Butler, Judith. 2006. *Precarious Life: The Powers of Mourning and Violence.* London: Verso.

DeLoughrey, Elizabeth. 2001."The Litany of Islands, The Rosary of Archipelagoes: Caribbean and Pacific Archipelagraphy." *ARIEL: A Review of International English Literature* 32 (1): 24.

Goodale, Mark. 2006. "Reclaiming Modernity: Indigenous Cosmopolitanism and the Coming of the Second Revolution in Bolivia." *American Ethnologist* 33 (4): 634–649.

Handley, George B. 2015. "Climate Change, Cosmology and Poetry: The Case of Derek Walcott's Omeros." In *Global Ecologies and the Environmental Humanities: Postcolonial Approaches*, edited by Elizabeth DeLoughrey, Jill Didur, and Anthony Carrigan, 360–379. New York: Routledge.

Hau'ofa, Epeli. 2008. *We are the Ocean.* pp. 130. Honolulu: University of Hawai'i Press.

Keown, Michelle. 2007. *Pacific Islands Writing: The Postcolonial Literatures of Aotearoa/New Zealand and Oceania.* Oxford: Oxford University Press.

Lal, Brij. 2004. *Bittersweet.* Canberra: Pandanus Books.

Lal, Brij V. 2015. *Historical Dictionary of Fiji.* Lanham, MD: Rowman & Littlefield.

Lorey, Isabell. 2015. *State of Insecurity: Government of the Precarious.* London: Verso Books.

Michener, James A. 1951. *Return to Paradise: Stories.* New York: Random House.

Mishra, Sudesh. 1987. *Rahu*. Lautoka: Vision International.

Mishra, Sudesh. 1992. *Tandava*. Victoria: Meanjin Press.

Mishra, Sudesh. 2002. *Diaspora and the Difficult Art of Dying*. Dunedin: University of Otago Press.

Mishra, Vijay. 1992. "Satendra Nandan, The Wounded Sea." *SPAN: Journal of the South Pacific Association for Commonwealth Literature and Language Studies* 32.

Srebrnik, Henry. 2008. "Indo-Fijians: Marooned without Land and Power in a South Pacific Archipelago?" In *Tracing an Indian Diaspora: Contexts, Memories, Representations*, edited by Parvati Raghuram, Ajaya Kumar Sahoo, Brij Maharaj, and Dave Sangha, 75–95. Thousand Oaks, CA: SAGE Publishing.

Subramani. 2001. "The Oceanic Imaginary." *The Contemporary Pacific* 13 (1): 149–162. Project MUSE.

Representing the "Other": Minority Discourse in the Postcolonial Indian English Novel

Saman Ashfaq

ABSTRACT

Through an analysis of the postcolonial fiction emanating from acts of violence unleashed in India during the anti-Sikh massacre of 1984, the demolition of the Babri Masjid in Ayodhya in 1992 and the explosion of violence in Gujarat in 2002, this essay examines how literary representation impacts communalism or religious minorities. It underscores the narrative strategies and techniques that fictional constructs use to articulate as well as to challenge the physical, emotional, and psychological dimensions of the marginalization and the exclusion of minorities in India. Emerging as a powerful and radical critique, these fictions can be read as counter-narratives or studies in resistance that interrogate and unravel the politics of suppression that governs nationalist discourses thereby challenging the secular underpinnings of the Indian nation-state.

Underlining the inherently ambiguous nature of the majority-minority configuration in our multi-ethnic, multi-religious and multi-lingual nation, eminent political scientist Rajni Kothari claims that "one way to think about India is as a people and a land made up of a series of minorities" (qtd. in Hasan 2000, 145). Several instances can be cited of communities that defy the overtly numerical basis of this classification[1]. However, with majority-minority configurations generally located in the realm of statistical enumeration, the question of "minority" remains distinctly political in nature. And, in India, the category of "minority" tends to be represented as a religious one. Caste or linguistic identities are not, generally, seen to fall under the rubric of "minority" (Kalin 2005). Thus, Muslims, Sikhs, Christians, and Parsis are commonly identified as minority communities in the nation.

In India, the perpetuation of precarity for the religious minorities has been consolidated through innumerable "cycles of hatred" (Mander 2002, 104) witnessed after 1947. Amongst these, the 1984 Sikh massacre (following Indira Gandhi's assassination by her Sikh bodyguard), the demolition of the Babri Masjid in 1992 and the 2002 Gujarat riots represent the flashpoints of communalism in post-independence India. As macabre reminders of the tenuous relationship between state, religion, and violence which led to the loss of thousands of lives, these incidents continue to jog the nation's memory in unprecedented ways. Signifying moments of rupture that disrupt the "official"/nationalist/dominant histories which assiduously seek to project the nation as a secular and seamless land, these events emerge as markers that articulate the crisis of secularism and point out the aporias in the secular and democratic underpinnings of the nation.

It is against this backdrop of vilification and violence that this essay examines some select texts. Anita Desai's *In Custody* (1984), Rukun Advani's *Beethoven Among the Cows* (1994), Githa Hariharan's *In Times of Siege* (2003) and *Fugitive Histories* (2009), and Raj Kamal Jha's *Fireproof* (2007) can be regarded as deeply-felt imaginative responses to some of the most catastrophic events in post-1947 India. While the novels[2] may or may not directly draw upon any of the three events, nonetheless, their thematic concerns and the timings of their publication inevitably ensure that communalism is the common thread that binds the events and the novels. For example, 1984 saw the publication of Desai's *In Custody*. Though the anti-Sikh riots are neither referred to nor form the background of this novel, it can be said that Desai's novel is a symbolic recreation of the atmosphere of divisiveness and hatred that characterized the early eighties; more to the point, it explores the effects of suspicion and distrust on human relationships. Advani's *Beethoven Among the Cows*, fictionalizes the realities of 1992–93 and its concomitant violence. Hariharan's *In Times of Siege* and *Fugitive Histories*, and Raj Kamal Jha's *Fireproof*, grew out of the Gujarat conflagration.

The present essay analyses these fictional constructs as a discourse of dispossessions and resistances. It documents the impact of communalism on religious minorities and highlights the precarity of their existence by underscoring the strategies of representation and technique that the novels use in order to articulate as well as challenge the physical, emotional, and psychological dimensions of the marginalization and exclusion of minorities in India. In doing so, the essay elucidates how these novelists represent a community of care that maps the growing sense of precariousness of the religious "other," and how it offers an exercise of deep introspection that grapples with issues of identity, history, culture in a nation largely viewed as inclusive, democratic, and heterogeneous.

Desai, Advani, Hariharan, and Jha also symbolize the deeply conflicted majority-minority configuration in the nation. Seen through the prism of religious identity, these writers, raised in the Hindu faith, effectively speak on behalf of the marginalized minority, especially the Muslim. However, to see the issue just in the light of religious affiliations would be erroneous. These writers belong to the tribe of Indians who represent the voice of the Indian liberal/secular tradition pitted against the conservative/religious rhetoric. They foreground the clash between two differing conceptions of the Indian nation and two differing nationalisms. Hence, their novels exist as a fervent appeal to re-imagine India as a pluralist nation, built on ideas of respect for different regional, ethnic, and religious traditions. This undercuts the exclusionary vision of the nation as crystallized by the *Hindutva* forces and reflected in the works of M.S. Gowalkar or V.D. Sarvarkar. Moreover, in pronouncing the nation as a space of diverse and multiple cultural claims, rather than as the sole domain of any one group, they privilege those precepts of Hinduism that are rooted in ideas of acceptance and tolerance. Thus, they attempt to reiterate and reclaim the essence of Hinduism which is insidiously being abandoned by the fervent notion of the nation. Seen from this perspective, these writers constitute a fundamental threat from within as they persistently question and undermine the narrow, chauvinistic and exclusive nature of the Hindu nationalist project. This consequently, marks them as the new "other" in the nation.

Scholars have frequently underlined the fact that like other social groups and communities, Muslims in India are also regionally, socially, culturally and economically diverse (Saberwal 2010). The concept of a unified and monolithic Muslim community is a myth that emanates from colonialist and nationalist discourses which in turn "flowed from a certain understanding of the histories of the Muslim communities in South Asia and their perpetuation by the Muslim elites to legitimize their own claims" (Hasan 2000, 46) Therefore, tracing the responses of the Muslim community to the ever increasing phenomenon of *Hindutva*, and the multi-dimensional and systematic nature of their persecution is not an easy task. Nevertheless, the texts examined here attempt to explore and articulate the community's feelings of powerlessness, dejection, apathy, bewilderment, betrayal, pain, inferiority, resignation, fear, revenge, and its utter loss of faith in the state machinery and the principle of secularism which underpins the Indian nation.

Anita Desai's *In Custody* emerges as a record of a community's frustrations that emanate from desperation to preserve its religious symbols and cultural heritage. The novel, spatially as well as symbolically, mirrors the shrinking world of Urdu in its current socio-political milieu. The fact that the language that once grew up and flourished in courts is now reduced to being appreciated in brothels, "in the back lanes and gutters of the city," in the dark alleys of old Delhi, in the dilapidated *havelis*, and dingy shops surrounding the Jama Masjid, points out to its fast dwindling existence (*IC* 15). People like Murad, who claim to be patrons of Urdu, appear exploitative and not driven by any real love for the language. The protagonist, Deven, a lecturer in Mirpore, though possessed of a keen interest in Urdu, is forced to teach Hindi – a language backed by the state. The novel is replete with images of death to convey, symbolically, that Urdu in post-independence India has become a dying language. Universities are described as "cemeteries" where the language exists only as a "ghost wrapped in a shroud" (*IC* 56).

The novel presents the impact of the marginalization of Urdu on society through the figure of Nur, a renowned Urdu poet. The physical and emotional disintegration of Nur mirrors the disintegration of Urdu in contemporary India. If Nur is seen as a disillusioned, senile poet whose creative days are long since over, so is the fate of Urdu. Both Urdu and Nur are the metaphor of all that has been lost and forgotten. The deterioration of the poet and his language is stark, as Nur, who Deven expected to be like a "serene *tika* on the forehead of a madman," is seen living at the mercy of flatterers, of "clowns and jokers and jugglers" (*IC* 51). They enjoy life at his expense, while in a striking similarity, the language that grew and flourished in the courts is now reduced to find its audience in brothels (*IC* 15). Nur's interview is conducted in a brothel for whatever little remains of Urdu, is to be found there. His final letters in the end reveal the wretched state of affairs where he is helpless in even getting assistance for the treatment and education of his son. Amina Yaqin believes that Desai's characterization of Nur is "conservative as [he] is reluctant to part with the old metaphors and lifestyle of an aristocratic lineage, and his lifestyle appears to be untouched by a progressive outlook" (2006, 115). Nur thus parallels the degeneration that Urdu has come to suffer in the present scenario. Like Nur, Urdu has also become a symbol of a decadent era and lifestyle, having no live relevance in the nation.

Desai's novel also maps the fate of Urdu journalism in post-independence India through the character of Murad – the overbearing, manipulative, shrewd and penny-pinching friend of Deven. The scion of a wealthy family who is the editor of a "leading" Urdu magazine, *Awaaz*, Murad is proud to have dedicated his life to the service of the language. However, as the narrative unfolds, one realizes that Murad is a bundle of contradictions and his lofty ideas are just hollow words. At the very out-set, he acknowledges that Urdu journalism in present-day India is plagued with difficulties:

> Everybody thinks it is an easy thing to bring out a magazine ... Nobody knows of the cost involved. Every month there is a crisis – the printing press refusing to print unless past bills are cleared, the distributor refusing to pay for last month's supplies of copies, the telephone bill, the postage ... Such expenses ... And where are the readers? Where are the subscriptions? Who reads Urdu anymore? (*IC* 14-15)

Therefore, he never pays, or to put it more accurately, is unable to pay Deven for the book reviews or the poems that Deven regularly contributes to his magazine. The office-cum-printing press of his "high class Urdu magazine" is located in the dark alleys of old Delhi; it is actually the rented corner of the balcony of a cluttered shop whose owner has not deigned to give Murad even an electric point for a fan or a lamp (*IC* 34). The only significant order that the printing press has received is the publication of UP government's school text books (*IC* 34). The crowded office space, thus, represents the losing battle the magazine is fighting to maintain its relevance.

In post-independence India, Urdu journalism is often reflective of "Islamist jour-nalism," which exhibits a marked lack of vision, maturity and sensibility to provide viable direction to community thinking and empowerment (Amanullah 2009). This is also reflected in the novel. Murad's dream of reviving "the glorious tradition of Urdu literature" through the poetry of Firaq, Faiz, Rafi, or Nur suggests that he is living in a time warp in which he makes anachronistic attempts to regain the lost glories of the Mughal Empire (*IC* 15–16). His desperate efforts to negotiate with Deven even for the damaged tapes that contain scraps of Nur's poetry emerge as a comic and a pathetic comment on the future of Urdu language.

In Custody reflects the perception that Muslims in post-independence India repre-sent a besieged and a "decapitated" (Raychaudhari 1999) community. The novel presents the predicament of people who chose to live in a nation they considered to be their motherland, but ended up as victims of the politics of men and ideologies in 1947. The experience of Partition foisted sudden change in the lives of the Muslims who chose to stay back in India. Stereotyped as "suspect" and largely considered to be better off on the other side of the Radcliffe Line, the novel delineates the ways in which, socio-politically and psychologically, Indian Muslims found themselves on the fringes of Indian society. Commenting on the predicament of the community, Rakesh Basant and Abusaleh Sharif point out that the situation of India's Muslims is unique in that they "carry a double burden of being labelled as 'anti-nationalists' and being 'appeased' at the same time – a predicament not shared by any of the other ethnic minorities in the nation" (2010, 3). One of Nur's friends considers 1947 as an event that has rendered Muslims vulnerable and powerless. Rebuking a person who talks of "attack" and "vengeance" as far as the propaganda of Urdu is concerned, he says: "he calls for attack thirty years after his claws have been extracted and his teeth filed .... How do you expect to attack? With what weapons? ... Here we live as *hijras*, as eunuchs" (*IC* 53). These interactions present a slice of life of the community's struggles, and underline its heightened sense of powerlessness, insecurity and vulnerability, and the hostility and humiliation that it routinely encounters in everyday life.

While *In Custody* traces the decline of a community through the symbol of language, Githa Hariharan's *In Times of Siege* points to the role that history has played in engendering division and distrust. In contrast to Nur and his friends, who choose to vociferously voice their anger and desperation, the auto driver Suban in Hariharan's narrative, whom the protagonist Shiv encounters in Hampi, is apologetic about his religious identity and has accepted and even internalized the version of religious nationalists who see Muslims as "invaders" and "violators." He is, therefore, "willing to bear an unnecessary burden of guilt" for past sins that his ancestors committed in this country (*ITS* 160). For Suban, Shiv's identity is of nothing but a Hindu, "a custodian of a mythicized Hindu past" (*ITS* 159), and despite repeated assurances by Shiv "that they did not belong to two different sides" (*ITS* 160), the novel shows the distrust and fear deeply embedded within Suban. Like Nur, Suban is also a victim of the contemporary political discourse where the Muslim identity is trapped in a vicious propaganda of hatred and violence. This sense of entrapment and imprisonment of the Muslim figure is further reinforced through the titles of these novels. *In Custody* and *In Times of Siege* point out to the implications of being a Muslim caught in a stranglehold of divisive politics that has led to the alienation of the community.

Hariharan's *Fugitive Histories*, written during a decade that witnessed 9/11 and the Gujarat riots, also belongs to a corpus of literature that dwells on the problematized discourse of Muslim identity in contemporary India. Traversing Delhi, Mumbai, Madras and Gujarat, Hariharan's narrative is a collage that powerfully weaves together several stories of "precarization" of Muslim identity across space and time in India. Of the children of a Hindu mother and a Muslim father, the novel traces Sara and Samar's arduous journey from childhood to adulthood. A school-going Samar is forced to eat his lunch alone as his friends accuse him of carrying meat in his tiffin box. Sara grows up wishing that she were like her other friends, Asha, Lata, Rehana, or Barbara. Her best friend Tripti, is curious to know who she really is – a Hindu or a Muslim. It is a question which immediately sets Sara apart from the others. Sara and Samar are unable to reconcile to the heterogeneity that marks their existence. They feel alienated and confused not knowing what to do with school forms asking them to state their religion. The novel, thus, delineates the dilemma encountered by even a "half-Muslim" in Indian society where labels are based upon one's faith or mother tongue.

In the highly polarised post-2002 Gujarat too, the ways in which Muslims are stigmatized, questioned, maligned, persecuted and subjected to myriad forms of discrimination and violence draw attention to their beleaguered existence. A mother recalls how her son, Nasir, was forced to discontinue his education because the Principal was doing "partition work." His dreams of becoming an engineer are cruelly thwarted as he is relentlessly taunted of being a terrorist and a Pakistani (*FH* 156). Another child is asked by his teacher to use green crayon in his drawing because it is a Muslim colour (*FH* 234). A burqa-clad English speaking woman in Gujarat is considered to be a foreigner because she sounds too educated to be a local Muslim (*FH* 234). On her train journey to Delhi, Sara's travelling companions, a middle-aged couple which insists on sharing their food with her, suddenly look embarrassed, withdraw into silence, and pack the leftover food when they learn of her parentage (*FH* 198). Lastly, Nasreen, a survivor of 2002 riots, recounts how loudspeakers spewed hate with slogans such as "Go to Pakistan!" renting the air (*FH* 167). The incidents described in the novel are neither extraordinary nor can they be termed wholly fictional. Completely common place and credible, what is striking about these incidents is that most of them are not reported from the backwaters of India. Sara and Samar live in Delhi, the national capital, and Gujarat too, despite the scars of 2002, is widely recognized as one of the most developed states in the country.

Fugitive Histories also records the trials and tribulations of a Hindu-Muslim marriage in India against the backdrop of religious prejudices. Hariharan's treatment of the Asad-Mala relationship, and the typically hostile responses that their marriage triggers, is comical, ironic and yet very realistic. After marriage, Mala's family is burdened with the onerous task of justifying and accommodating the "foreigner" Asad within their community. They take great pains to explain to their relatives that Asad and his family are "different" from other Muslims, that they are "modern" and "secular" (*FH* 96). When Asad and Mala visit her ancestral village to meet her dying grandmother Bala, the "outsider" and the "barbarian" Asad is served on a separate plate in order to prevent "polluting accidents." Though Mala's uncle is extremely courteous to Asad, he nevertheless draws a line about eating with him (*FH* 117). When Asad, in keeping with the image of an irreverent, bohemian painter decides to grow a beard, it leads to mixed feelings amongst both the families. His mother, notwithstanding his claims of being a hardcore non-believer, proudly announces that he is finally on the road to becoming a good Muslim, while Mala's mother is uncomfortable as a beard makes his religion conspicuous. These incidents point out to the precariousness of the Muslim figure as well as foreground the myriad ways in which the menacing exercises of institutionalizing social prejudices continue.

Thus, the "Good Muslim–Bad Muslim" debate that currently rages in the world lies at the heart of *Fugitive Histories*. Hariharan's narrative underscores the confusion and the anguish of a community that finds itself at the crossroads of religious identity. As a character confesses: "I get angry when people think I'm a Muslim, I get angry when they assume I'm too modern to be a Muslim" (*FH* 201). The protagonist

Asad, a proud Marxist, withdraws into a shell, bewildered and exasperated by the politics of identity in the post-2002 nation that has no place for a Muslim other than the one who professes to be a "secular Muslim" (*FH* 237). He is unable to reconcile the past and the present, and is overwhelmed by the nasty propaganda underlining the existence and dominance of religion in Muslims' lives. Asad points out:

> All the days we never used the word "secular" to describe ourselves, all the days when the world was only divided into the progressive and the backward, were we right then? Or just innocent? (*FH* 237)

As an atheist, Asad's Muslim background had never been a matter of concern to him. However, Islamophobia following 9/11 and 2002 awaken him to the reality that his personal beliefs notwithstanding, he cannot escape the implications of being a Muslim. He bitterly remarks:

> Don't you see there is no room for an ex-Muslim anymore? Whatever I am, whatever I believe and however I live, I am an M. Samar too is just another Muslim, a potential terrorist. (*FH* 206)

Asad realizes, too late, the futility of his efforts to transcend his religious identity. This stark realization that his life is defined and circumscribed by the word "Muslim" brings his life to a standstill and elucidates the extent of his precariousness. Through the figure of Asad, Hariharan brings out the desperation with which individuals/communities attempt to rise above and break out of the chain of the pervading precarity in their lives. In the end, Asad's death symbolizes his failure to negotiate the difference between his values and the perception that the world has of him.

These novels foreground varied modes of resistance that individuals/communities adopt in the face of such unwarranted subjugation. To counter their marginalization within the socio-political discourse, Nur and his friends draw solace by adopting an anti-state stance, wherein they stridently critique the policies of the government. In *In Custody*, Nur's *haveli* emerges as a space where he and his friends recreate the past and mourn the loss of their erstwhile glory. In sharp contrast, Asad gives up his faith and identifies himself only as secular and a Marxist. In order to counter the overt and covert strategies of their exclusion, Muslims have also taken to asserting and reiterating their traditional, orthodox religious identities of precept and practice. *Fugitive Histories* parallels reality in reflecting this trend through the figure of Samar, Asad's son. Asad never intended his children to be either Muslim or Hindu. However, polarising debates in the world around Muslim identity push his son Samar to "resurrect his comatose Muslim half" (*FH* 205), and "become a Muslim almost out of spite, a Muslim given to gesture" (*FH* 180). This return to Islam constitutes an act of defiance where Muslims deliberately choose to unite and celebrate their much-reviled faith, its symbols and practices. This need to come together is also reflected in Raj Kamal Jha's *Fireproof*. The dead people – victims of the Gujarat violence – who appear in the footnotes and relive their last moments, fervently hope that their families would relocate to "safe" places where "there are many more people there like us, [for] there is strength in numbers when they single you out" (*F* 49). At the same time, the narratives also point out to how these covert and overt attempts at resisting the precariousness of their existence eventually prove to be exercises in futility.

The novels do not just trace the responses of minority communities but also use a series of images to symbolically delineate their "othered" status in the contemporary socio-political scenario. Borrowing heavily from the majoritarian communal discourse that has consolidated a distorted view of the minority communities rendering them "abnormal," strange, dangerous, and extraneous in the nation, these narratives also construct the minority figures as grotesque entities. Therefore, in some of the novels, the body of the minority figure emerges as a site of ridicule. It is almost uncanny that narratives such as *Beethoven Among the Cows* and *Fireproof*, separated by a gap of almost fifteen years, use identical imagery to comment and reflect on the position of minorities in the nation. Dwarves, clowns, jugglers, and circus acts dominate these narratives. Both Nasterji, a tailor in *Beethoven Among the Cows* and Bright Shirt in *Fireproof* are dwarves. An uncharacteristic figure, dressed in a shirt of "wild colour and twisted asymmetry" (*F* 282), he admits that he can be addressed in any manner:

> You can call me Shirt, you can call me Bright, you can call me Joker, Clown, anything that suits you, depending on the time of the day or night, use Hindi, use English, sometimes Hindi sometimes English, mix it up. Call me names. (Ibid)

These writers use the physically deformed/abnormal body of the minority figures to unveil their emotional and psychological isolation, and thereby draw attention to their inferior and diminished status in the nation. The bear-baiting incident in Rukun Advani's novel establishes how the minority figure exists as a source of entertainment – a spectacle in the nation. Taking place in the early 1960s, in the immediate post-Nehruvian era, the scene is highly symbolic and prophetic in nature in so far as it offers an insight into the psyche of the common man of a new and young India. Nasterji's heroic efforts to save the bear from the unruly crowd are ironic, as in their eyes he is no different from the animal. Satirically referred to as *Chotte*, *Kaddu*, *Baune*, or *Thigne*, Nasterji's physical stature, in the eyes of the crowd, lend to his efforts a singularly comical tinge.

> The leaders in the crowd swaggered with laughter at the dwarf's comic incoherence. Such a huge agitation in such a diminutive figure had all the proportion of clowns in the Gemini Circus. It was fun. It provided good entertainment free of cost. What more could one ask for on a summer afternoon? (*BAC* 62)

Through this setting, the narrator draws a remarkable parallel between the world of the bear and that of the dwarf. The shared precariousness of their existence is reflected in their inherent vulnerability and powerlessness and their consequent inability to articulate their feelings. The bear is unable to defend itself in the face of human authority; the tailor's pleas also fall on the deaf ears of his fellow beings. As the narrative reveals:

> Dwarfs didn't really have names and animals didn't really have feelings … The dwarf neither possesses physical height nor social weight [sic]. He had neither significance nor authority. He was probably circumcised. He was comically incoherent. How could he be anything except a figure of fun? (*BAC* 63)

The evocative scene brings out the cultural and religious prejudices of the people: "Don't you know … dwarfs and bears are all circumcised. Why don't we make them both dance? Don't they look alike?" (*BAC* 61) Moreover, in sharing this fundamental condition of precarity, the bear and the dwarf also symbolize a care community that simultaneously acknowledges as well as resists this state of powerlessness.

By juxtaposing the bear and the tailor, Advani's novel succinctly explores the dilemma of belonging to a minority community in the nation. Nasterji, being a dwarf, is a ludicrous figure, a clown, in the eyes of others, but an inherent awareness of his religious identity lends the attacks an air of greater viciousness. In many ways, his shrunken physicality is symbolic of his relatively disadvantaged situation in the nation. Moreover, this scene does not just seek to underscore the subordinate position of minorities. It also signals the collapse of the Nehruvian ideal of composite India. The novel previews the future to portend how the roots of intolerance and exclusion would strengthen and grow manifold to represent a nation that would be paralyzed by religious hatred and violence.

Clowns constitute an important part of *Fireproof* as well. The circus acts in the novel parody the orgies of violence that shook Gujarat in 2002. As the novel proceeds to its denouement, an interlude in the form of a performance by the Clowns and the Juggler is held in The Tent – a setting eerily similar to a circus with rows of chairs and a gallery. Like Bright Shirt, the clowns are also dwarves. They present a fire act, where a Clown sets the Juggler on fire, amidst a wildly rapturous audience:

> One by one, the balls fell to the floor, as did the steel rings, with a clatter, and Juggler was now running from one end of the stage to the other, blazing, still shuffling his feet, performing his trot and his jig as if the flames weren't there. There was a smell of burnt rubber in the air as Juggler fell down, playing dead, the clowns began crying, their tears mixing with the paint on their faces as they lifted one of his hands still burning, and then let it fall as if it belonged to a corpse. (*F* 329)

This act immediately brings back memories of 2002 and can be regarded as a reconstruction of how fire was used to snuff out innocent lives. Jha's ingenuity lies in using the circus act to comment and reflect on a tragedy that had unfolded in recent times. The antics of clowns and the juggler and their physical incongruity underscore the predicament of the victims. The responses of the audience, ranging from abject apathy, unabated enjoyment to downright hostility brilliantly sums up the response of the unconcerned fellow citizens of the nation who either remained mute to the suffering of victims or positively enjoyed their discomfiture, or worse still, actively connived to carry out such acts.

Perpetrators of the most horrific crimes in the name of religion are seldom brought to justice. For the victims of communal violence, the path to justice also remains torturous and skewed. *Fireproof* mirrors this and highlights the subversion of justice by creating an alternative space that interrogates notions of justice and equality. It is a strange tale that unfolds in the mind of a man guilty of unspeakable horror. The narrator-protagonist Jay symbolises the young man next-door, happily married and eagerly waiting for the birth of his first child. The narrative presents Jay as a quintessential family man whose concern for the well being of his child borders on paranoia. Yet Jay, a commonplace "everyman," also hides a secret that is gradually revealed by the end of the novel. Jay is also B, a part of the leading mob A, B, C, D. Jay is the one who remains a silent spectator when Tariq's mother is gang raped and burnt, he also watches the burning of the auto rickshaw of Shabnam's father, he also dispassionately watches when A, C and D cut off her parents tongues, force them to undress, and set them on fire within a locked house. He is again a part of the same mob that rapes and strangles Abba's pregnant daughter-in-law, slashes her and throws her unborn baby into fire.

Thus, in the novel, it is not human beings but objects such as a book, a watch and a towel that emerge as "eyewitnesses," "earwitnesses" and the only "objective" witnesses to the gruesome murders of Tariq's mother, Shabnam's parents and Abba's daughter-in-law (F 333). The book called *Learning to Communicate* belonged to Tariq. Shabnam's father's watch was torn and flung out of the window during the attack. And lastly, the towel in Abba's kitchen was used to gag and then strangle his daughter-in-law. The highpoint of Jha's narrative is borne out of a unique situation where dead victims and inanimate objects set out to seek justice for the victims as they realize that "death should not be an excuse for inaction … grief should not become a substitute for sloth" (F 6). Therefore, imitating the legal jargon and the highly formal atmosphere of a court room, "witnesses" first identify themselves, explain their presence at the site of the crimes and finally identify the killers, that is, A, B, C and D. It is their testimony that ultimately exposes Jay's complicity and the bizarre appearance of the baby Ithim. Ithim is not Jay's "malformed son" but the unborn child ripped out of Abba's daughter-in-law.

The trial conducted by the dead symbolizes an act of resistance that mocks as it painfully underscores the shortcomings and the insincerity of the state. The lack of collective will and empathy, and the sheer passivity on the part of state either in stemming the tide of violence or bringing the perpetrators to justice is in ironic contrast to the promptness, the single-minded dedication and solidarity displayed by the dead in ensuring that justice, of a unique kind, is administered to the guilty.

Survivors of violence have of late been receiving attention from various academic quarters that seek to understand the event as refracted through the consciousness of the witness/survivor. Testimony has, therefore, emerged as a viable mode of exploring the consciousness of the survivor/victim. The articulation and reconstruction of trauma suffered by the survivor/victim in catastrophic events such as the Holocaust and, closer home, of the Partition of 1947, have not only allowed for the voicing of alternative perspectives but they have also led to the reconfiguration of the historical archives which largely privilege the political aspects of events. Testimonies, either oral or literary, in the form of memoirs, diaries, or letters, by focusing on the human dimension, "articulate the inarticulatable" and emerge as counter narratives bringing to the surface the "inexplicable, ambivalent and paradoxical horrors of violence" (Saint 2010, 23).

In brief, Jha pushes the boundaries of testimony and imagination in *Fireproof* to centralize the experiences of citizens who were killed in 2002. By including the voices of the dead in his novel, Jha brings to life the forgotten citizens of this nation who end up as mere statistics in government records. Thus, in a marked departure from literary representations that use the voice of the survivor to reconstruct traumatic events, Jha challenges the erasure, the silence and the aporia that engulfs the dead. In a single stroke, he symbolically resurrects countless lives that have been lost in successive waves of communal frenzy that grip the nation from time to time. Therefore, cutting across barriers of class, education and profession, Muslims who had been indiscriminately killed in the aftermath of Godhra interrupt the narrative by appearing in the footnotes to describe the story of their daily lives, their small unfulfilled dreams, and their fears for the future of their families. Jha's use of footnotes mirrors the marginal/peripheral status accorded them within the national space. Choosing to remain anonymous, which is extremely ironic (and fitting too) in the light of the fact that they are already dead, they introduce themselves as the Ward Guard, Doctors 1 and 2, the sweeper of Holy Angel Hospital who calls herself Old Bird, the Taxidriver, Ms. Glass, Fruitseller, the Head nurse, the Floor body, and the screaming woman from the TV news. They allow the reader a peek into their ordinary lives and the manner in which death struck them.

Manifest in Jha's footnotes is a compelling analysis of what Hannah Arendt calls the "banality of evil" (2006). The footnotes encapsulate the irrationality, inevitability and the essential meaninglessness of their lives and also reflect their stoic belief that their grieving families would somehow learn to carry on with their lives. In sharp contrast to the survivors, who may be reluctant to speak about their experiences, the anonymous casualties, singularly free from any fear of retribution uninhibitedly voice their thoughts. The last thoughts of a nineteen year old boy stabbed to death in retaliation of the burning of the train at Godhra, amply bear this out:

> I think I should have told them yes, yes, yes, I burnt the train, I was so happy when I heard the news that I told my mother, I will get not only flour but also milk and honey as well, I should have told them that my family attacked the train, my mother was there, my father, my two sisters, my uncle, my cousin, my aunt, my grandmother, all of them were there, even my future wife and my future children, and all of them lit the fire, one by one, and that we should do it again if we got the chance, I should have told them that, if only to see what would they have done different, would they have killed me still?
> (F 103)

The boy's scathing words bring to the fore a panorama of emotions that engulfed the "casualties" of 2002 in their last moments. These testimonies are a reflection of their innermost fears, their helplessness, anger and the amazement at being caught unawares in the communal inferno. Jha's narrative can be viewed as a study in resistance, as it attempts to reclaim those citizens and communities that have been thrust into oblivion. In doing so, the novel also interrogates the secular and democratic underpinnings of the Indian nation-state that prove to be ineffectual in protecting its citizens in moments of barbarity.

Meandering through obscure villages, dusty little towns and fast-paced metropolises, these novels explore the nation's vast terrain offering glimpses of myriad tales of subjugation, injustice and prejudice. They imaginatively and deeply probe the socio-political matrix of the nation to reveal the ugly truth that though numerous religions, sects, communities, and languages, might exist in the nation, in reality India's image as a "home" to all its citizens remains deeply contested and problematized. In addition, these literary narratives should not be construed merely as a significant comment on contemporary India, for they also bring alive the nation's past. In highlighting the forms and extent of precarity that marks the existence of a minority community, the novels reveal the crucial role that the socio-political history of the subcontinent has played in institutionalizing the precariousness of their lives by tracing strong continuities that bind the past with the present. Hence, at one level, these novels are not just about 1984, 1992 or 2002; indeed, they reenact the writers' critical engagement with their nation, as from times immemorial.

Curiously, one senses that the writers, in delineating the minority figures and their responses, tread a cautious path as if they are fully aware that these constructions will undoubtedly have deep implications. Unlike reality, where unbridled hatred and violence have pushed several Muslims to pick up arms against the state, none of the characters in the novels are either overtly critical of the state or the majority community, or take recourse to violence. It is only Murad in Desai's novel who uninhibitedly expresses his anger and is blatantly communal in his interactions with Deven. However, he largely corresponds to a comic figure within the framework of the novel. In *In Custody* Hindu-Muslim friction, though very pronounced, did not attain the singularly virulent form that came to characterize the 1990s and reached a crescendo after the Gujarat riots. Therefore, viewed chronologically, as the communal atmosphere of the nation worsened, the writers too, have been more conscious in their delineation of the beleaguered Muslim identity. While creating the character of the protagonist Asad, Githa Hariharan revealed in an interview that she feared that he would be termed as "liberal, secular, broadminded and the rest, for as we define Muslims we like to make them more palatable" (Zaheer 2012). Thus, in a nation where even fiction has the power to ruffle the feathers of radical groups and communities, it can be said that these writers have sensitively attempted to highlight the troubled psyche of a community that has been universally demonized.

As responses to threats posed to the secular and pluralist ethos of the nation, these novels emerge as narratives of resistance/counter narratives at two levels. First, by resurrecting and memorializing events that challenge the nation's pluralist ethos, these novels unravel and resist the politics of silence embedded in contemporary socio-political discourse. This silence speaks of suppression, a sense of evasion, an absence of guilt, or a lack of repentance, on the part of the state and the non-state actors to acknowledge the gross miscarriages of justice that accompanied these times. Secondly, by highlighting the predicament/perspective of the minority figure, these narratives create alternative spaces to mirror, interrogate and challenge the rampant subversion of justice that prevails in the present socio-political scenario. Thus, in foregrounding the precariousness of the minority figure, these novels ruthlessly critique the nation and its institutions. These writers also symbolize a care community that attempts to create an atmosphere conducive to question and debate and presents a significant perspective on discourses of law and justice, minoritarian identities, and the notion of secularism, nationality and citizenship as propagated in the nation. These writers do not just envision an inclusive and hybrid India; their works mark an eloquent plea for a world without hatred and violence. Literary writing comes, thus, to assume the dimensions of historiography by giving a fictional opportunity to the "other."

Notes

1. A well known example is of the Meos of South-east Punjab—a small syncretic community which defies taxonomic labeling as either Hindu or Muslim as its beliefs and practices draw upon both religions. For more details, see Shail Mayaram's work (1997).

2. All future references to the page numbers in the novels will be preceded by the acronyms of their titles. For example *IC* for *In Custody*, *BAC* for *Beethoven Among the Cows*, *ITS* for *In Times of Siege*, *FH* for *Fugitive Histories*, and *F* for *Fireproof.*

Disclosure Statement

No potential conflict of interest was reported by the author.

References

Advani, Rukun. 1994. *Beethoven Among the Cows*. Delhi: Ravi Dayal.

Amanullah, Arshad. 2009. "Is Urdu Journalism a Lost Battle?" In *Muslims and Media Images: News Versus Views*, edited by Ather Farouqui. New Delhi: Oxford University Press.

Arendt, Hannah. 2006. *Eichmann in Jerusalem: A Report on the Banality of Evil*. New York: Penguin Books.

Basant, Rakesh, and Abusaleh Shariff, eds. 2010. *Handbook of Muslims in India: Empirical and Policy Perspectives*. New Delhi: Oxford University Press.

Desai, Anita. 1984. *In Custody*. New Delhi: Penguin.

Hariharan, Githa. 2003. *In Times of Siege*. New Delhi: Penguin.

Hariharan, Githa. 2009. *Fugitive Histories*. New Delhi: Penguin.

Hasan, Mushirul. 2000. "'Majorities' and 'Minorities' in Modern South Asian Islam: A Historian's Perspective." In *Pluralism and Equality: Values in Indian Society and Politics*, edited by Imtiaz Ahmad, Partha S. Ghosh, Helmut Reifeld. New Delhi: Sage Publications.

Jha, Raj Kamal. 2007. *Fireproof*. London: Picador.

Kalin, Ibrahim. 2005. "Roots of Misconception: Euro-American Perceptions of Islam Before and After September 11." In *Islam, Fundamentalism and the Betrayal of Tradition*, edited by Joseph E.B. Lumbard. New Delhi: Pentagon Press.

Mander, Harsh. 2002. "Passing The Buck." In *Lest We Forget: Gujarat*, edited by Amrita Kumar and Prashun Bhaumik. Delhi: World Report and Rupa and Co.

Mayaram, Shail. 1997. *Resisting Regimes: Myth, Memory and the Shaping of Muslim Identity*. New Delhi: Oxford University Press.

Raychaudhari, Tapan. 1999. *Perceptions, Emotions, Sensibilities: Essays on India's Colonial and Postcolonial Experiences*. New Delhi: Oxford University Press.

Saberwal, Satish. 2010. "On the Making of Muslims in India Historically." In *Handbook of Muslims in India: Empirical and Policy Perspectives*, edited by Rakesh Basant and Abdullah Sharif. New Delhi: Oxford University Press.

Saint, Tarun K. 2010. *Witnessing Partition: Memory, History, Fiction*. New Delhi: Routledge.

Yaqin, Amina. 2006. "The Communalization and Disintegration of Urdu in Anita Desai's *In Custody*." In *Redefining Urdu Politics in India*, edited by Ather Farouqui. New Delhi: Oxford University Press.

Zaheer, Noor. 2012. "Fugitive Histories as Fiction." *Infochange*, April 18. http://infochangeindia.org/index2php3option=com_pdf=7369

Teaching Precarity, Resistance, and Community: Rohini Mohan's *The Seasons of Trouble* and Genocide Pedagogy

Colleen Lutz Clemens

ABSTRACT

Testimonials of the Sri Lankan war are just coming to light as people begin to feel like they can tell their stories of being kidnapped into forced military service, fleeing bombings, searching for loved ones, and being displaced in their own nation. This paper argues for the importance of studying the Sri Lankan civil war and its aftermath in the context of genocide pedagogy where students can be given the opportunity to ask critical questions: Why do wars start? How do people that see each other as friendly neighbors come to believe those same neighbors are the enemy in a short period of time? How does genocide start and end? Who controls the narrative during wartime? What does it mean for children to grow up during a war? What does it mean to be a displaced person on the same soil one used to cultivate? How does a nation come back together and heal while simultaneously learning the stories that were kept silent during the decades of war? If we as teachers can get students to consider these challenging questions early in their academic career, our students will be well-positioned to tangle with these issues when it is up to them to work within geopolitical conflicts that arise during their adult lives. Teachers who are interested in learning about the historical, political, and cultural foundations of the war will find Rohini Mohan's *The Seasons of Trouble: Life Amid the Ruins of Sri Lanka's Civil War* an invaluable pedagogical tool.

The train ride from seaside Colombo to Anuradhapura in central Sri Lanka is so bumpy I cannot read the book sitting on my lap. I pass verdant landscapes marked only by thin, dusty walking trails. A lone motorcycle kicks up dirt through my peripheral vision.[1]

But the ride the next day from Anuradhapura to northern Jaffna suddenly turns from bumpy to smooth. And I know that I have transitioned to the new tracks, ones that delineate the past from the future. This ride is a new luxury for Sri Lankans wanting to go to the northern part of the island nation, for until 2014 the Jaffna Peninsula was unreachable by train (Victor 2014). The nation's civil war between a Buddhist Sinhala majority and a Hindu Tamil minority meant the tracks were bombed out, family members in the north unreachable, goods from the south impossible to obtain. During parts of the Eelam Wars (1983–2009), the smooth highways I rode earlier in my trip to Galle did not exist either. The country was divided, its people unable to move around in their own country.

I came of age in the 1980s, when MTV was showing videos about a man named Biko and artists were boycotting Sun City. Part of my deep commitment to social justice pedagogies today stems from learning about apartheid in South Africa from cultural texts such as music, watching apartheid crumble, and then – as a scholar – watching the South African population try to heal through, among other things, literature, public hearings, and music. As someone who has studied, taken students to, and taught about South Africa with a specific eye toward the Truth and Reconciliation Commission and how the nation works toward healing after apartheid, I would argue that students today would benefit from learning about Sri Lanka during their secondary education – just as I learned about South Africa during mine – because during their lifetime they will be witnessing this nation attempt to recover from a 26-year-old civil war and the tsunami of 2004. As a scholar, I see the parallels between the South African and Sri Lankan situations. As a secondary and higher education teacher, I believe that introducing students at those levels to the politics, history, and literature of Sri Lanka will provide them with the foundation for considering how other nations are doing the hard work of remembering and recovering from loss.

Testimonials of the war are just coming to light as people begin to tell their stories of forced military service, escape from bombings, hazardous search for loved ones, and of cruel displacement in their own nation.[2] Such terrors exemplify Judith Butler's definition of precarity, a term that "characterizes that politically induced condition of maximized vulnerability and exposure for populations exposed to arbitrary state violence and to other forms of aggression that are not enacted by states and against which states do not offer adequate protection" (Butler 2009, ii). Studying the Sri Lankan civil war and the stories told in its aftermath can give students the opportunity to ask critical questions and use precarity as a lens for their own understanding of war and genocide: Why do wars start? How do people that see each other as friendly neighbors come, in a short period, to believe those same neighbors are the enemy? How does genocide–more to come on the use of that term soon–start and end? Who controls the narrative during wartime? By focusing on precarity, students can consider what it means for children to grow up during a war. What does it mean to be a displaced person on the same soil one used to cultivate? How does one perform resistance when living through conflict? How does a nation come back together and reform "care communities" while simultaneously learning the stories that were kept silent during the decades of war? If we as teachers can encourage students to consider these challenging questions early in their academic careers, our students will have the tools to wrestle with these issues when they find themselves called to work or live within conflicts that arise during their adult lives.

Secondary and higher education teachers who are interested in learning about the historical, political, and cultural foundations of the war will find Rohini Mohan's 2015 nonfiction book *The Seasons of Trouble: Life Amid the Ruins of Sri Lanka's Civil War* invaluable for introducing genocide pedagogy into the classroom and specifically showing the intersections of precarity, resistance, and community in the context of genocide. Mohan uses the narratives of three people – Sarva, Indra, and Mugil – to tell the story of the Sri Lankan civil war and the nation's ongoing recovery. As I read this book on the smooth train ride back from Jaffna, I told my travel companion that history will look back on this text as a seminal work in the literature of war and recovery because of its depth and focus on several facets of war, its focus on not only what happened, but *how* and *why* it happened.

Because Mohan's text is a versatile tool to expose students to the many elements of genocide and recovery, I ask that educators consider adding Mohan's work to their genocide curriculum. This essay first argues for using the term "genocide" when discussing Sri Lanka's "seasons of trouble" and call for teachers to go beyond only Holocaust literature when teaching genocide. Second, this essay suggests ways to use Mohan's text as a model for secondary and higher education students to learn about the Sri Lankan civil war, the people's resistance to the war, and the recreation of community after genocide.

While this essay is not intended to further the ongoing and contested discussion of the use of the word "genocide" when talking about the deaths of thousands of people during Sri Lanka's civil war, a rationale for the use of genocide pedagogies is appropriate before considering Mohan's text and its use in the classroom. Perhaps, the ongoing debate about the term's usage in reference to Sri Lanka is the most telling and compelling argument for the use of the term "genocide." But an overview of the debate shall suffice for this essay's purposes.

In more than twenty years of debate over the issue of calling the deaths of civilians in Sri Lanka a "genocide," perhaps the loudest voice at the forefront of the discussion is that of Francis A. Boyle's, who from the late 2000s was arguing that the Sri Lankan government was enacting genocide on its Tamil citizens. His book, *The Tamil Genocide by Sri Lanka: The Global Failure to Protect Tamil Rights Under International Law*, collects his writings from this time period where he made a case for using the term "genocide" when discussing the civil war in Sri Lanka. Boyle, Professor of International Law at the University of Illinois College of Law, argued along with Bruce Fein, an American attorney, at a seminar in Chennai in 2009, organized by the International Tamil Center that "the Tamils living on Sri Lanka have been victims of genocide" (Boyle 2016).

In 2010, the Permanent Peoples' Tribunal (PPT), "an international opinion tribunal, independent from any State authority," held the People's Tribunal on Sri Lanka at Trinity College in Dublin. In the final paragraph of their review of the last weeks of the war, they concluded "[i]t is not surprising that charges of atrocities, ethnic cleansing and indeed genocide have been levelled at Colombo" after asserting that "[t]he impression held by most experts and witnesses is that this was a civil war, and an exercise in ethnic cleansing, perhaps even genocide, and that the Government did not wish to share this with the media" (Feierstein 2010).[3] Critics and legal scholars continued to make the argument for Sri Lanka to be tried for the crime of genocide through the 2010s. In the *Colombo Telegraph*, Usha S. Sri-Skanda-Rajah of the Transnational Government of Tamil Eelam's (TGTE) Senate, has made similar calls over the past decade. In her article "Sri Lanka's Genocide: Major Cover-Up Must Be Exposed," she argues that "it is the Indian government's duty to heed the people of Tamil Nadu and not shy away from the 'G' word" and concludes that "[t]he higher standard of proof needed for genocide is there to be discovered" (Sri-Skanda-Rajah 2013).[4]

During the same time period, the Unrow Human Rights Impact Litigation Clinic, an "impact litigation clinic" of the American University Washington College of Law, made a legal case for the "Tamil Genocide" and in 2010 filed the lawsuit Devi v. Silva. Using the United Nations' Genocide Convention (1948) – to which Sri Lanka acceded in 1950 – as its framework, the group argues that "there is also support to conclude that an extreme and inhuman form of persecution against Sri Lankan Tamils occurred, amounting to genocide" (UNROW Human Rights Impact 2015).[5] After reviewing extensive evidence, they conclude that there is proof "available that satisfies four of the five enumerated genocidal acts in the Genocide Convention," noting that several governments and international human rights organizations have called for independent investigations to consider this time period of Sri Lankan history a genocide.[6] All of these outside entities, naming the devastation wrought upon civilians in Sri Lanka "genocide," validate what Mohan presents in *Seasons of Trouble*: the Sri Lankan government perpetrated "extreme" and "inhuman" persecution against civilians, thereby forcing them to live in a constant state of precarity.

Teaching Beyond the Holocaust: Considering the Sri Lankan War in the Classroom

Within the field of genocide education, most scholarship focuses on teaching the Holocaust specifically. While teaching the Holocaust is of great importance, the teaching of other genocides often falls into the margins. Samuel Totten borrows Elliot Eisner's phrase the "null curriculum" to describe the silences in what is *not* taught – in Totten's case specifically, other genocides besides the Holocaust – as detrimental to curricula and student education. Totten argues that "[i]gnoring 'other genocides,' either by excluding them from the curriculum or by simply mentioning them in passing, sends an implicit message that such historical events and their victims are not as important as the Holocaust" (Totten 2001). Promoting the null curriculum, Totten summarizes, can have negative ramifications for the education of students by teaching them to "assume that the Holocaust was simply an aberration of history," rendering them unable to "appreciate that genocide is not simply a curse of the past, but one that haunts contemporary society," and to not understand "the role that the international community has played in regard to 'allowing' genocide to take place." It is, truly, to make them incapable of understanding that "genocide is not inevitable, but that what impedes the intervention and prevention of genocide is largely the will of the international community" (Totten 2001).

If we acknowledge that Sri Lanka's conflict even danced at the edges of what would constitute a genocide, we as educators should take seriously Totten's call to incorporate a discussion of its war and mass civilian deaths into curricula.[7] Totten's concern that the Holocaust solidifies genocide as a problem of the past, suppressing the precarity that menaces contemporary society. He notes that the development of materials to support already overworked teachers to add another element to their curriculum is slow. Remember, those teachers were raised on the "null" curriculum as well, so there may very well be a sharp learning curve for the educators as well, one that requires time for study that puts an additional burden on often time-starved teachers. Only three states have officially generated changes in the curricula. The null curriculum seems to intimate that only the Holocaust is worthy of study, and while,

> such a frame of mind is understandable … it is also extremely parochial and not a little insensitive to the tragic dimensions of so many other genocides that have been perpetrated in recent memory across the globe. Indeed, if educators are truly concerned about contemporary human rights violations (including genocide) and want their students to understand that genocide is something that has plagued humanity for centuries right up to today, then they would want to teach about various genocidal acts.

As a former high school teacher, I want to note the already colossal challenge of designing curriculum that fits district and state mandates. Adding to an already packed curriculum should not become the responsibility solely of classroom teachers but must instead stem from the will – and support – of the community. One goal of this essay is to help educators begin conversations that will move the Sri Lankan conflict out of the null curriculum and bring it to the attention of scholars and educators that want to expand their textual choices beyond the Holocaust by using Mohan's text.

Genocide Pedagogy and *The Seasons of Trouble*: Teaching About Precarity, Resistance, and Caring Communities

Within genocide scholarship, a general feeling that more needs to be done – that clearly something is missing from the pedagogy as genocides continue to happen – susurrates beneath the surface. In "Redefining Genocide Education," Ellen Kennedy, Executive Director of World Without Genocide, summarizes this feeling of the inadequacy in genocide education: "Something is wrong. There is a disjuncture between what we assume genocide education is doing – and what is actually happening. What form should genocide education take if our goal is to make a difference, somehow, in the world?" (Kennedy 2008). "Never forget" is not working. Kennedy argues that the underlying assumption of genocide education has been that "learning **about** genocide will prevent its recurrence" but that this strategy on its own has proven ineffective. Kennedy seeks to add two other approaches to genocide pedagogy: educating against genocide and educating to prevent genocide. Using the concepts of precarity, resistance, and community as themes for teaching Mohan's nonfiction historical work gives students insight into all three elements required of Kennedy's genocide pedagogy framework.

When teaching about genocide, Kennedy emphasizes that educators "must teach about genocide from the *individual and the personal perspectives* … [w]e must bring the picture into sharp focus by looking at the people, at the faces of husbands, fathers, brothers, and sons; wives, mothers, sisters, and daughters, to feel the human tragedy deeply and to grieve for the loss."[8] Here is the most obvious argument for considering Mohan's text as a cornerstone for teaching the Sri Lankan genocide, as the text has a clear and distinct focus of showing the precarity the three main characters face due to ethnic conflict and genocide. *The Seasons of Trouble* offers the perspective of three people, each connected to the war and its aftermath from different subject positions but all in a place of precarity. In a 2014 interview, Mohan talks about her choice to write from these perspectives and how her book differs from other books about war: "I tried to bring a lot of interiority into every narrative. I wanted to get into details about how my characters thought about their children, what they ate, the kind of routine they had in the day; things that make people full" (Sriram 2014). Mohan's work to develop empathy for participants from a variety of spaces in the war – and for people who often commit reprehensible acts – gives students the opportunity to see the actors in "sharp focus."

Mohan's choice to amplify women's voices adds a perspective not included in many other narratives of war. After describing most war narratives as "very masculine," in the same interview she remarks that "I wanted to hear more women's voices; two [out of the three] of my characters are women." Their inclusion can help the student see the gendered nature of war, specifically the use of sexual assault and the threat of it as a tool of war. When the women Mohan interviewed spoke about sexual assault and rape, they would never use the Tamil word for rape. Instead, they changed the word into the phrase "they ruined her" because, Mohan notes, "It was too harsh to say the other thing" (Sriram 2014). Mugil and Sanjeevan's lengthy conversation about rape and war crimes can teach students how war impacts women differently than it does men. In their discussion, Mugil thinks, "It irritated her every time, this dancing around the act, as if it were not a crime but just an embarrassing secret … Emboldened and somewhat proud of herself, she prepared to come clean to Sanjeevan about the rapes she had witnessed." But his response catches her off guard when he dismisses rape as a consequence of having "women in our militia," a "weakness" that distracts from "the real issues" (172). When students read closely this lengthy conversation, they realize that the precariousness of war often impacts people differently along gender lines.

Specific discussion questions about this section could include: Why does Sanjeevan not include rape in his explanation of war crimes? Why does Mohan spend a paragraph focusing on the word "rape"? What rationale does Sanjeevan give to explain away the concept of rape as a war crime? Why is this conversation about rape the catalyst for Mugil's epiphany that all she "wanted was certainty" (173)? Mohan's focus on the gendered nature of war, and the precarity it creates for women specifically, will provide students with an insight into an element of genocide they may not have considered: the vulnerability of women's bodies in sites of conflict.

But precarity is not the only theme Mohan emphasizes. The text can also teach students about the role care communities play during genocide, thanks to its continued emphasis on connection and community throughout the text. For example, in a scene between a secondary figure, the schoolmaster Sanjeevan, and one of the three protagonists, Mugil, she contemplates the challenges of finding empathy and connection in the space of war and ruins:

It was Sanjeevan who had once said, "I know now how the Muslims must have felt when the Tigers forced them out of the north." He had called them the oldest displaced community in the country, expelled entirely from Jaffna... It was unusual for a Tamil man to mention this, especially one who grew up in the Vanni. Mugil had wondered how Sanjeevan was able to acknowledge the suffering of the smaller minority group at the hands of his leaders when his own community was wrapped up in its victimhood. How had he held onto that unselfish thought? How did he preserve his empathy? (173)

An overt writing of an interiority not often seen in similar literature, this scene offers rich fodder for discussion: the feeling of empathy for someone on the other side of a conflict. Mugil's thoughts mirror the questions a reader may have: how does someone who has suffered so much at the hands of a group still see the oppressor as human? Mugil wonders right along with us, even amidst her displacement, yearning to return to her original community that may now be in ruins. If we were to push students even further with their consideration of this scene, we could discuss how gender affects the experience of these two figures, for Mugil's story forces readers to consider gender norms and their subversion in this conflict. She points out how unusual it is for a man to express such empathy aloud. Students can discuss this statement from different angles. Why might it be unusual for a man to express an empathetic state-ment? What could be the implications for a man to express sympathy for those beyond his own gender and religious communities? Why is Mugil so surprised? And what effect does his comment have on her?

If teachers have the time and space to go beyond the most common form of teach-ing pedagogy–teaching about what happened– they can move into other levels of Kennedy's framework for using texts to situate students in the contemporary world in which genocides continue to occur. While teaching about genocide has been the major focus in classrooms, Kennedy argues for the addition of "educating *against* genocide" (2008): "Teaching *against* means creating awareness of ways in which we separate, isolate, and segment people based on any number of classificatory variables such as race, religion, ethnicity, etc. Teaching *against* means understanding manipula-tion, propaganda, and 'othering' of various groups and the many sources from which these influences may arise." Mohan's novel lends itself to this second aspect of geno-cide pedagogy and can show students how othering – in the Sri Lankan case, those of religious practices, language, and culture – renders individuals vulnerable, and has devastating consequences for the entire nation.

For example, Indra's story recounted in the June 1980 section of the book shows the seeds of othering being sown. A Hindu and a Jaffna Tamil, she enters a love mar-riage and ends up living with her brother in Negombo, where "Tamils lived among Sinhalese, Muslims, and English-speaking Burghers" (Mohan 2015, 12). Feeling uncomfortable and othered – "nevertheless she tried to fit in" – she cannot trust her instincts about the danger she may be in as stories of unrest filter down to her. After a slow and methodical study of the devolution of relations among ethnic groups, the book flashes back to July 1983 when Indra hears screams of "They're coming!" alert-ing her to the fact that Sinhala attacks on Tamils had begun. Indra only needs one sentence to encapsulate her certainty that the consequences of this othering were coming to their inevitable fruition: "It was finally happening" (17). She finds no help from her Sinhala neighbors among whom she had lived, so "[b]etween the tea shrubs, she put baby Sarva on the ground and lay on top of him, holding her torso up slightly, lizard-like, with one arm. With her free hand, she covered his mouth" (20). When the attack ends, Indra is surrounded by dead Tamil neighbors.

Indra's June 1980 section is just one example in the text where students can witness the rapid progression from ethnic tension to genocide: that day 3000 Tamils were killed and many of the survivors subsequently fled for fear of more attacks. These sections of *The Seasons of Trouble* give students more than just knowledge *about* the genocide; they are also given the tools to educate themselves *against* genocide. Kennedy outlines the areas of education required to teach against genocide:

1. teaching students to *recognize* when manipulation and othering are present;
2. teaching students to have the strength of their own ethical and moral convictions to *identify* manipulation for what it is; and
3. teaching students to have the personal courage to **resist** their own acts of classification, symbolization, and dehumanization of others despite strong pressure and propaganda.

The sections that articulate the development of hatred can give students the tools they need to identify othering in their daily lives. This skill is different from knowing that a genocide happened and that living through it created precarity; with this new skill, students can situate themselves within contemporary discourses of otherness instead of distancing themselves from history with only historical knowledge *about* genocide.[9]

At a time when politicians deploy colonialist language to marginalize communities (for example, Donald Trump calling African nations "shithole countries"), educators must be vigilant and use texts that teach students how to work against genocide in its early stages before we lose the opportunity to reel back the hate. Though Kennedy does not mention the Sri Lankan conflict in her list of examples (Nazis, Hutus, and the Khmer Rouge), she would no doubt see the othering of Tamils by the Sinhalese as emblematic of what she wants teachers to inoculate students against: "These efforts at manipulation were very powerful and very successful at engendering hate between people who had been friends, neighbors, and even intimates. We need to raise awareness of how this happens and how to resist becoming influenced by potentially lethal propaganda."

The final pages of *Seasons of Trouble* will teach students about the need for vigilance and resistance as the text's ending intimates that Sri Lanka has not learned enough from sectarian violence, and is on the cusp of falling into another pattern of genocide instead of recovering from its genocidal past. In the final scene of the April 2013 section, Divyan "knew the Sinhala Buddhist extremists were now attacking mosques and turning on the Muslims. He had not seen this new hate until this moment" (350). The final image of the text warns readers of the dangers of failing to learn about and against genocide. The nation has disavowed the narratives, and Mohan's parting scene is a reminder of the dire nature of forgetting the experiences she just spent hundreds of pages recounting. In her interview with *Guernica*, Mohan discusses the ending and her fears of a renewed season of trouble in Sri Lanka:

The last scene in the book is set in Colombo. Mugil's husband has just returned from visiting Mugil (who has been detained by the Terrorist Investigation Department in Colombo), and he sees Muslims being attacked by monks and other Sinhalese on the streets. I didn't address the Muslim issue in my book much – it lived in conversations through the book – but in this scene I realized that all of this ethnic war has polarized communities so much that the country will see a repeat of what happened in the '80s against the Tamils. Only now it will be against Muslims.

Educators should take advantage of Mohan's choice of the ending that amplifies precarity instead of safety and community. This analysis will show students that only continuous resistance against othering and hate will function as a safeguard against a new cycle of precarity; as the open-ended nature of the violent conclusion demonstrates genocide can occur during their lifetimes and that these terrors do not belong to only the past.

To come to this understanding, students can analyze Mohan's rhetorical strategy of ending with a warning instead of a neat conclusion. To engage students directly with this final section, teachers could ask a seemingly simple but, in fact, a complex question: How would the text be different if it ended with the March 2013 section, instead of the April 2013 passage? How would the experience of reading alter if the text ended with "Sarva felt a rush of belonging," instead of with an image of stillness and fear before life returns after a mob attack? (342) Students could even read Mohan's explanation for her aesthetic choice and discuss ways they themselves could work against the repeated perpetuation of genocide. The text's conclusion thus emphasizes that precarity lurks under the surface in Sri Lanka, even if the war ended officially in 2009.

Finally, teachers should not forget the book's subtitle, "Life Amid the Ruins of Sri Lanka's Civil War," which reminds students that the work of moving into a new post-war space is ongoing and that learning about genocides is not a linear process with a clear endpoint. Maryse Jayasuriya argues that "true reconciliation cannot happen until the loss and destruction are acknowledged and the perpetrators held accountable … literature provides a powerful alternative means of developing this essential memorialization" (Jayasuriya 2016, 26). Mohan's book details the emotions, movements, and struggles of the three lives affected in seemingly different yet intersecting ways by the conflict and contributes to the resources available to teachers considering genocide pedagogies. Mohan also explicitly states her efforts to create this effect: "*Seasons of Trouble* is similar to others in that they're [war narratives] all searching for the answer to how people in a post-war country live, and what it really means to come out of such a long conflict" (Sriram 2014). While the book will not answer all the questions students may have, it will invite discussions of not only what happened during the genocide in Sri Lanka but also provide an insight into how communities resist and recover from such seasons of trouble.

Notes

1. Parts of this introduction originally appeared in Clemens (2016).
2. Though all the testimonials that come to light in the next years deserve attention, some may be too graphic for a secondary education classroom, though appropriate for a higher education setting.

3. However, the PPT, in a rhetorical gesture similar to that of other organizations', does not go as far as definitively using the word "genocide": "The attempt to annihilate the Tamil population with or without the use of illegal weapons certainly constitutes one form of war crime. The question remains if the government intended genocide in respect of the Tamil people in brutally suppressing armed and political resistance." In its discussion of the "possible commission of the crime of genocide," the PPT writes, "There was not enough evidence presented before the Tribunal to determine that the crime of genocide be added to the charges of war crimes and crimes against humanity. Some of the facts presented should be investigated thoroughly, as possible acts of genocide."
4. For more commentary see Pararajasingham (2017) and Ramakrishnan (2005).
5. In their legal argument, they put forth proof that "Sri Lankan government officials' statements and actions provide sufficient evidence to show that there are reasonable grounds to believe that government officials acted with the specific intent to destroy the Tamils in Vanni" (2015).
6. While the United Nations has not charged Sri Lanka with genocide, to the dismay of much of the Tamil diaspora and civilians, in 2011 it published the Report of The Secretary-General's Panel Of Experts On Accountability In Sri Lanka in which it does not mention the word "genocide" in relation to charges against Sri Lanka. However, the panel found credible "allegations that comprise five core categories of potential serious violations committed by the Government of Sri Lanka: (i) killing of civilians through widespread shelling; (ii) shelling of hospitals and humanitarian objects; (iii) denial of humanitarian assistance; (iv) human rights violations suffered by victims and survivors of the conflict, including both IDPs and suspected LTTE cadre; and (v) human rights violations outside the conflict zone, including against the media and other critics of the Government." (Darusman, Ratner, and Sooka 2011). In Geneva in 2018, at the 37th session of the Human Rights Council, Kate Gilmore, United Nations Deputy High Commissioner for Human Rights, addressed serious concerns about Sri Lanka's lack of follow-through with the ongoing recommendations for the nation that came out of a 2015 United Nations Human Rights Commission consensus resolution: "Yet, it is with much regret that we must report *slow progress in establishing transitional justice mechanisms* … Furthermore, the Authorities have yet to demonstrate with the willingness or the capacity to *address impunity* for gross violations of international human rights and international humanitarian law. This strengthens the argument for the establishment of a specialized court to deal with serious crimes, supported by international practitioners" (Gilmore 2018). Human Rights Watch's 2017 report on Sri Lanka echoes the United Nations' concerns, stating that in response to a 2017 report compiled by civil society leaders and handed to the government, "neither the president not the prime minister received the report publicly and it has since languished, with scant government attention."
7. Based on other examples Totten uses in his urgent call to action to add a discussion of "other genocides" into classrooms, he would surely see the Sri Lankan conflict as an important lesson for students. He stresses that even without an advocacy group (e.g., the Armenian community), all genocides should be incorporated into genocide education: "Yet the lack of an advocacy group should not assign the history of any genocide to the equivalent of educational oblivion. This is where both scholars and concerned educators need to make a concerted effort to develop curricula on various genocides and to call for the inclusion of such subject matter in school textbooks."
8. A clear number of deaths is elusive. In 2012, Sri Lankan officials claimed the number of deaths in the North at 9,000, a number that conflicts with a United Nations report that put the number at 40,000 (Haviland 2012).
9. James Frusetta writes about implementing this shift in focus in his narrative of teaching a comparative course on genocide to a diverse classroom in Eastern Europe. Quickly his "rosy picture" of his classroom that was agreed that ethnic cleansing was wrong is shattered when he encounters a student beyond the classroom. This student "others"

another ethnicity and says he would "shoot the first one of them that came to his house." The disconnect between what was happening in the classroom and what students were saying in their lives jarred Frusetta and forced him to consider his approach. When asked about that disconnect, students responded that in class they say "what Americans wanted to hear" and the classroom space was not the place for controversy (especially controversy that might affect their final grade). Frusetta realized that he needed to shift his focus to the "*logic*" of genocide and started using why questions and to consider the roles of power and people. He was moving students through Kennedy's steps of educating against genocide instead of stopping at educating about genocide. Such an approach, Frusetta came to find, "encourages students to consider the narratives of history they bring with them" (Frusetta 2010).

Disclosure Statement

No potential conflict of interest was reported by the author.

References

Boyle, Francis. 2016. *The Tamil Genocide by Sri Lanka: The Global Failure to Protect Tamil Rights Under International Law.* 2nd ed. Atlanta, GA: Clarity Press.
Butler, Judith. 2009. "Performativity, Precarity and Sexual Politics." *Journal of Iberoamerican Anthropology* 3 (3): i–xiii.
Clemens, Colleen Lutz. 2016. "Sri Lankan History and Literature Deserve a Place in Our Classrooms." *World Literature Today.* https://www.worldliteraturetoday.org/blog/cultural-cross-sections/sri-lankan-history-and-literature-deserve-place-our-classrooms-colleen
Darusman, Marzuki, Steven Ratner, and Yasmin Sooka. 2011. "Report of the Secretary-General's Panel of Experts on Accountability in Sri Lanka." *United Nations.*
Feierstein, Daniel, Denis Halliday, François Houtart, Mary Lawlor, Francesco Martone, Nawal al Saadawi, and Rajindar Sachar. et al. 2010. "People's Tribunal on Sri Lanka." *Permanent People's Tribunal.*
Frusetta, James. 2010. "Beyond Morality: Teaching about Ethnic Cleansing and Genocide." *Perspectives on History: The News Magazine of the American Historical Association.* https://www.historians.org/publications-and-directories/perspectives-on-history/may-2010/beyond-morality-teaching-about-ethnic-cleansing-and-genocide
Gilmore, Kate. 2018. "Introduction to Country Reports/briefings/updates of the Secretary-General and the High Commissioner under Item 2." United Nations Human Rights Office of the High Commissioner. https://www.ohchr.org/EN/NewsEvents/Pages/DisplayNews.aspx?NewsID=22875&LangID=E
Jayasuriya, Maryse. 2016. "Bricks, Mortar, Words: Memorializing Public Spaces Destroyed in the Sri Lankan Ethnic Conflict." *South Asian Review* 37 (3): 25–36. doi:10.1080/02759527.2016.11978317.
Haviland, Charles. 2012. "Sri Lanka Government Publishes War Death Toll Statistics." *BBC News.* Accessed 30 August 2018. https://www.bbc.com/news/world-asia-17156686

Kennedy, Ellen J. 2008. "Redefining Genocide Education." *Genocide Watch*. Accessed 9 July 2018. http://www.genocidewatch.org/images/Genocide_Redefining_Genocide_Education.doc

Mohan, Rohini. 2015. *The Seasons of Trouble: Life Amid the Ruins of Sri Lanka's Civil War*. Verso Books.

Pararajasingham, Ana. 2017. "Why is Sri Lanka Defying the United Nations?" *The Diplomat*. https://thediplomat.com/2017/12/why-is-sri-lanka-defying-the-united-nations/

Ramakrishnan, T. 2005. "UN Defends 'Silence on Genocide' in Sri Lanka War Crimes Report." *The Hindu*. https://www.thehindu.com/news/international/south-asia/un-defends-silence-on-genocide-in-sri-lanka-war-crimes-report/article7674861.ece

Sri-Skanda-Rajah, Usha S. 2013. "Sri Lanka's Genocide: Major Cover-Up Must Be Exposed." *Colombo Telegraph*. https://www.colombotelegraph.com/index.php/sri-lankas-genocide-major-cover-up-must-be-exposed/

Sriram, Aditi. 2014. "Rohini Mohan: 'Prachanai' (Trouble) in Sri Lanka, Past and Present." *Guernica*. https://www.guernicamag.com/aditi-sriram-prachanai-trouble-in-sri-lanka-past-and-present/

Totten, Samuel. 2001. "Addressing the 'Null Curriculum': Teaching about Genocides Other than the Holocaust." *Social Education* 65 (5): 309–313. https://search.proquest.com/docview/210639022.

UNROW Human Rights Impact. 2015. "The Legal Case of the Tamil Genocide - Human Rights Brief." *Human Rights Brief*. http://hrbrief.org/2015/01/the-legal-case-of-the-tamil-genocide/

Victor, Anucyia. 2014. "The Queen of Jaffna Rides Again 24 Years after it Was Suspended." *Daily Mail Online*. http://www.dailymail.co.uk/travel/travel_news/article-2790750/the-queen-jaffna-train-rides-24-years-suspended-sri-lankan-civil-war.html

"World Report 2018: Rights Trends in Sri Lanka." *Human Rights Watch*, January 5, 2018. https://www.hrw.org/world-report/2018/country-chapters/sri-lanka

Teaching Beyond Empathy: The Classroom As Care Community

Matthew Dischinger

ABSTRACT

This essay argues for a pedagogy of care, which I frame against discourses surrounding both empathy in the classroom and civility in public discourse. Many scholars and critics have identified the problems with civility, most notably that it urges polite behavior at the expense of difficult change. My essay suggests that organizing the humanities around empathy likewise proffers behavioral solutions to systemic problems. Furthermore, a pedagogy of empathy teaches students to project the self forward in every situation – an act that is particularly harmful when teaching students about coloniality. My essay puts forth a pedagogy of care as an alternative to these frameworks. Organizing classrooms to mimic what Isabell Lorey describes as a "care community" places relationality and mutuality at the center of learning and civic engagement. As a case study for examining how such a community might be installed and function, I discuss how Mohsin Hamid's *Exit West* (2017) elucidates the concept of care communities. Additionally, I outline how my classroom dynamics helped students reinforce and locate care as a central value not just of the novel, but of our class as a whole.

This essay argues for a pedagogy of care, which I see as an essential alternative to current conversations, both in the humanities and the mass media, about the roles of civility and empathy. The issues with civility in political discourse and journalism are, by now, well established. Questions about civility in academia are also becoming increasingly common. In the first section of this essay I will, however, question the projection of empathy as a frequently unchallenged platitude used to defend the study of literature specifically and of the humanities generally. As others have noted regarding civility, I read empathy as a contextual value that is invoked in an effort to bridge positions that may simply be incompatible. Because empathy involves the recurring projection of the self, a pedagogy of care better serves the particular values of anti-colonial pedagogy that faculty teaching in South Asian literary studies employ. Indeed, if learning about postcolonial and Global Anglophone literature is predicated on a constant projection of the self, that very practice can subvert much of the anti-colonial work these courses ask students to undertake. A pedagogy of care, alternatively, prepares students to understand political engagement through relational frameworks that highlight the mutually determining effects of political action. Organizing the classroom through what Isabell Lorey describes as a "care community" models relational thinking and collaboration rather than self-projection. Focusing on a course examining speculative postcolonial fiction, the second section of the essay explores how South Asian literature aides in this installation of pedagogies of care and is, at once, better understood through close attention to relationality and precarity. In that section, I discuss how Mohsin Hamid's *Exit West* (2017) can help students envision a model for civic and geopolitical engagement beyond the classroom.

Civility, Empathy, and Care

As I write this essay, two unfolding events dominate the news in the United States.[1] The first is perhaps the most troubling set of policies the Trump administration has carried out: the separation of families at America's southern border. The images, testimonies, and recorded sounds of families being pulled apart are, in a word, horrifying. Forged in the crucible of the post-2016 election cycle is another narrative: a seemingly unending debate about *civility* in public discourse. Fervent calls for civility surge across the political spectrum with renewed vitality in response to the human rights crisis at the Mexican–American border. Amid a growing trend of heckling Trump administration staffers as they go out to dinner – often choosing Mexican cuisine, devoid of any sense of irony or decency (Rosner 2018) – *The Washington Post*'s editorial board penned an op-ed entitled, "Let the Trump Team Eat in Peace" (2018). To focus on civility amid these circumstances exposes how valuing polite service over difficult confrontation serves only to make the powerful more comfortable.

This foundational problem with installing civility as a point of departure for political action depends upon a modern understanding of the term itself, which derives from the Latin "civitas" ("city") and, later, "civilitas," or "the conduct becoming citizens in good standing, willing to give of themselves for the good of the city" (Forni 2010). This understanding of civility as sacrificing the self for the good of others is clearly at odds with civility as mannerly political behavior, which privileges order over social justice. Keith J. Bybee traces the term's mutation from its civic and relational origins to one focused on upper-class manners, locating this transformation in the sixteenth century, when modern Western notions of civility became entrenched: "After being adopted by the upper classes (and connected with politeness), civility gradually spread throughout society, developing into a standard of conduct for all citizens in the polity" (Bybee 2016, 9). The issues with enjoining citizens to display civility in public discourse became, from this point onward, entangled with the customs of the powerful.

Demands for civility share some of their rhetorical foundation with an affective displacement that, much less controversially, faculty in the humanities are likewise strongly encouraged to centralize in their classrooms: empathy. In a moment in which faculty in the humanities frequently find their disciplines under threat, empathy has been heralded as an interdisciplinary triumph. Carol Scheidenhelm writes that studying literature, in particular, should be done in the service of learning how others think and how the many differences of birth generate those perspectives, claiming that "reading about others" ultimately allows us to "see the worst sides of ourselves – and the best" (Scheidenhelm 2018). Likewise, in an essay broadly against "speed and conclusive answers" as alternatives to the humanities' valuing of "leisurely thought and complex questions," Sophie Gilbert expands upon Harvard University president Drew Gilpin Faust's claim that the humanities "widen the world" for students by teaching them to cultivate "empathy for people outside" themselves (Gilbert 2016).

Without dismissing these impassioned defenses of reading and expanding one's cultural horizon, we must acknowledge how the privileging of personal behavior and individual experience above all else elides the structural and historical systems that produce our thoughts, feelings, experiences, and language. Mohsin Hamid's *Exit West* (2017) investigates the intersection of national identities and resulting antagonisms toward geopolitical refugees. As a result, it offers a unique pedagogical opportunity to examine how the individual act of empathy is overmatched – indeed, nearly irrelevant – in the face of cascading global crises that relate to what critics have described through the term precarity. Lauren Berlant's definition of precarity is especially instructive in helping us think through the xenophobic resentment that global refugees face the world over. Berlant describes the precarity that these movements attempt to claim as a "way to recognize and organize the ongoing class/group antagonisms/nostalgias/demands that symbolize the causes, effects, and future of the postwar good life fantasy" (Jasbir 2012, 166). These sorts of "precarity movements" hover at the margins of Hamid's novel, which features named and unnamed characters believing themselves to be participating "in a structure of feeling, a desperation about losing traction that is now becoming explicit and distorted politically" (Jasbir 2012, 166). Positioning empathy as a first offered and reciprocally received path to redress these political distortions is never an option in the novel, and, therefore, it never posits that the individual work of empathy can cure the structural conflicts imbricated into various states of precarity.

Attention to these dynamics in *Exit West* can enrich our understanding of the important differences between pedagogies of care and those that centralize empathy. For now, I will say that while organizing humanities pedagogy around empathy risks obscuring structural conflict, I do not want to suggest that such an approach is without any value. Given that a pedagogy of empathy is, at its root, devoted to helping students arrive at a higher level of self-awareness, it may well help students achieve what Paolo Freire famously termed "conscientization" (translated from "conscientização"), or the critical consciousness that allows students to see their own oppression and begin a "fight for their own freedom" (Freire 2005, 67). More generally, an attention to emotion may allow faculty to help students see "the tight braid of affect and judgment, socially constructed and historically constructed and bodily lived, through which the symbolic takes hold and binds the individual, in complex and contradictory ways, to the social order and its structure of meaning" (Worsham 1998, 16). Most teachers working in institutions of higher education in the United States share these foundational goals: to help students see their own position in the world as contingent and, thus, changeable.

A pedagogy of care shares these goals without the added risk of transforming learning into a colonial mission. Rather than solely achieving radical self-awareness, teaching empathy treats the other as a mere self-in-waiting, a convert requiring only convincing. That is, by collapsing the desires of self and other, the potentially consciousness-raising work of empathy can just as likely slide into a hollow rhetorical appeal. As opposed to empathy – the notion that great change can arrive by imagining the self as the other and vice versa – care does not attempt to remove vast differences between the self and the other.[2] To establish care communities in the spirit of Isabell Lorey, furthermore, is to first "acknowledge our relationality with others" through spaces in which the self is unfinished, vulnerable, and dependent (Lorey 2015, 95). Empathetic thinking maintains the boundaries of self and other by encouraging the self to project forward into the conditions of the other as a means – in fact, the only means – of understanding those conditions. At its core, empathy is ultimately about the self's conception of the self. When the ideal self is carried forth into the other, the work itself lands continually on the self's experience. In this way, empathetic thinking focuses on self-improvement.

At its best, placing empathy at the center of our pedagogy helps our students expand their narrow parameters for everyday life at a time when they are examining, perhaps for the first time, the political worlds they have always occupied. At its worst, resorting to empathy teaches students that the most complex systemic problems can be fixed with behavioral solutions.

The long-term effect of this sort of thinking might be that students see civic engagement as a set of object choices through which they can define themselves rather than a lifetime mission of establishing communities that begin and end with relational care. In such a vision, our classrooms are better off if they resemble Lorey's care communities, or spaces in which "care work" becomes "the starting-point for political-economic considerations" (Lorey 2015, 94).

Transforming the classroom into a pedagogical care community differs from pedagogies of empathy in that the former emphasizes the role of the self and other in mutually beneficial interaction in an increasingly precarious world. I define pedagogical care through a juxtaposition of two frameworks. First, I build from the student-centered approaches that teach relational care through what Sara C. Motta and Anna Bennett call "affective and embodied praxis" (Motta and Bennett 2018, 632). I also build toward the installation of a classroom *ciudadanía*, or a care community as defined by the group of feminist activists from Madrid, Precarias a la deriva. Lorey explains that the *ciudadanía* establishes community as a space "in which our relationality with others is not interrupted but is regarded as fundamental" (Lorey 2015, 99). Combining these frameworks leads to pedagogical practices that move beyond just student-centered learning and requiring, instead, that teachers embrace the whole of a student's experiences in a dialogue that serves as a foundation for student work. Indeed, the goal of such an approach is that classroom itself becomes a model for civic and political engagement beyond each student's education, so that the transformative work that happens in the classroom can be carried out successfully in the world beyond higher education.

While Motta and Bennett state that their advocacy of pedagogies of care "constitute(s) an emergent philosophy of education" meant to guide programmatic approaches to pedagogy rather than a prescriptive approach to classroom dynamics, much of their work is relevant to the individual classroom, as well. For instance, they argue that "the complexities and wisdoms of students … often (follow) on from experiences of exclusion and misrecognitions," that the structural forms of oppression many teachers devotedly attempt to help students overcome must also be recognized as foundations upon which intellectually rigorous work can be constructed (2018, 636). Through the modeling of recognition as a real value between students and teachers, students begin to see relational and reciprocal collaboration as fundamental to successful learning. Furthermore, rather than having to disavow teachers of their hard-earned knowledge (a common misconception about student-centered learning), moving from recognition to collaboration instead acknowledges that the experiences of students and teachers are not simply valuable but, in fact, essential to a successful work in the classroom. The work of caring, therefore, can be established as more than a rule-dictating behavior and discourse; relational dialogue and collaboratively established knowledge "enhance the status of care work" by making it "the starting-point for political-economic considerations" in and beyond the classroom (Lorey 2015, 94). As opposed to empathy's centering of the self as the site of projection and improvement, pedagogies of care are first and fundamentally both relational and collaborative. Indeed, care illuminates through parallax the structures of empathy that create impasse.

The conflict between empathy and care can be difficult for students to understand, but Hamid's novel helps illustrate this conflict by staging it through the relationship of its two central characters, Nadia and Saeed. The two characters are brought together through a series of personal and political tragedies. They live in a failing state that loosely resembles contemporary Syria and are faced with the political realities of living in a war zone. Saeed's mother is killed by "a stray heavy-caliber round passing through the windshield of her family's car" while she searched for a lost earring (Hamid 2017, 74). Her death brings Nadia and Saeed together, and as they later leave the country and try to make a home in refugee communities abroad, they are only successful insofar as they are able to connect with communities of refugees from a variety of places brought together by similar circumstances. Rather than attempting to erode the xenophobic resentment of the communities they travel to, they rely upon collective action, such as banding together with other refugees and refusing to leave a home in London that they have occupied. They never request empathy, and the communities they form are based on relational care rather than empathy.

Given that the very concept of a *ciudadanía* is somewhat utopian and speculative, it might seem impossible to install the notion of care in such a way that the classroom could function as a relational care community. Treating the classroom as a space of (un)becoming embraces the possibility of failure – or at least the incompleteness of knowledge. However, if it is true that the transformative teaching works to reorient students' understanding of past educational experiences then the classroom space presents an exceptional opportunity to reinvent the praxis of learning in such a way that it is tied to a communal and relational becoming. The classroom is always a space of possibility that has the potential to reframe not just learning but also what students begin to see as the links between academic work and civic engagement.

The classroom space, however, can just as frequently work through firm hierarchies that reinforce the idea that students bring little of value to their own education and, thus, need not rely upon one another at all. Reflecting on her own education in her germinal book, *Teaching to Transgress: Education as the Practice of Freedom*, bell hooks argues that such a setting can often feel like an "exercise of power and authority within [a teacher's] mini-kingdom, the classroom" and allow students to "slowly [become] estranged from education" (hooks 1994, 17). While "the sage on the stage" has largely fallen out of pedagogical vogue, the lesson hooks provides is important: this pedagogical model is not just (potentially) boring, it enacts and continually reinscribes a dictatorial hierarchy as the model for learning. In such a setting, the making of knowledge is mysterious; the student only needs to access knowledge that has already been made – even then only at the teacher's discretion. It is fair to call this pedagogical method transactional. It may pass along information to interested students, but the process constructs a firm boundary between teaching and learning. This lesson undermines critical thinking, active citizenship, and pedagogical collaboration.

Not only can the classroom be a space to model our best practices for civic engagement and community building beyond higher education, in fact it must be such a space. Creating a class environment structured around care is an opportunity most available in humanities courses – particularly those that deal with concepts such as colonialism and precarity.

The postcolonial studies classroom can be an ideal space to teach students how to engage with complex geopolitical issues with care and generosity, in part because these courses often encourage students to think about politics outside the trenchant and inflexible environment of American politics. The course I discuss in the following section is a multimodal composition and literature course taught to first-year students entitled "Speculative Postcolonial Fictions: Alternative Realities Around the Globe." Our focus on the genre of speculative fiction offers a way to further explore the meanings and uses of postcolonial frameworks in the twenty-first century. I chose contemporary speculative fiction because of what Ramón Saldívar has described as its "utopian desire" to project symbolic measures as a form of historical, corrective justice (Saldívar 2013, 12). Exploring the utopian drive of contemporary U.S. Multi-Ethnic speculative fiction, Saldívar argues that the speculative fiction he investigates "perform the critical work of *symbolic action*, denoting the public work of the private imagination" (Saldívar 2011, 595). This symbolic work should be understood as the tentative "construction of the new political destinies" that "transcend and exceed the boundaries of nation-states" (Saldívar 2011, 595). Similarly, care communities attempt not primarily to literally disintegrate from the state but to emphasize mobility, movement, and exodus from the injunction to "govern oneself" through the seemingly immutable logics of precarity (Lorey 2015, 101–102).

A Door to Another World: Teaching with Mohsin Hamid's *Exit West* (2017)

Few texts embody these frameworks more profoundly than Mohsin Hamid's 2017 novel, *Exit West*. The novel is two things: on the one hand, an intimate portrait of two young people in love, Saeed and Nadia, who flee an unnamed city as religious fundamentalism and violence push it to near ruin; on the other, it is a text that operates through a speculative premise that heightens a global refugee crisis, as doors begin to mysteriously and inexplicably allow people to instantly travel across regional and national boundaries. These two narrative lines work hand-in-hand, and a premise that might sound spectacularly far-fetched becomes quickly enmeshed in a familiar politics of nativism that typifies the current state of politics in America and across Europe. The unnamed country that Nadia and Saeed are born into seems to easily reflect recent events in Syria. By leaving the location unnamed, however, the novel more easily connects the journey of Nadia and Saeed to others originating from nations across South Asia, Africa, South America – indeed, from the entire Global South.

The novel earned widespread praise upon its publication and was eventually short-listed for the Man Booker Prize. Viet Thanh Nguyen praised it for deepening its Western readers' "empathy for characters who can be, or should be, just like the reader" in the midst of the post-2016 election's sharpening of anti-immigrant discourse across mainstream American culture (Nguyen 2017). Rather than teaching the novel solely as an instructive text about empathy for political refugees and immigrants, I encouraged students to think deeply about the ways the novel explores mis-recognition and reimagines the future of community for a world that will increasingly involve movement, migration, and consequent precarity that must be resisted. Much like Hamid's (2007) *The Reluctant Fundamentalist*, in which a clever usage of the second person places the reader into the narrative perspective of an operative of the American government interrogating the novel's eponymous narrator, *Exit West* anticipates the expectations of its readers and endeavors to subvert them. One example of this narrative trick that we discussed at length was Nadia's choice to wear a robe despite the fact that she is not religious. When Saeed, who grows more religious as the novel unfolds, asks why Nadia wears the "virtually all-concealing black robe," her explanation anticipates and undermines a typical objection: "'So men don't fuck with me'" (Hamid 2017, 16–17).

Nadia defies what Theresa A. Kulbaga calls the "familiar imperialist construction of the veiled woman awaiting Western empathy and rescue" (Kulbaga 2008, 517). Rather than reading Nadia's robe as an instrument of misogyny, the novel requires that we see how she uses it to gain agency and freedom. In the classroom, the scene occasions a discussion about the politics surrounding hijabs specifically and, more generally, debates about the nexus point between theories of postcolonialism and feminism that students could use to interrogate their understanding of texts and spaces across the Middle East and South Asia. Productive conversations on this subject turn on students' ability to see how the intersection of Western feminism and empathy can lead to a colonialist action: to perform what Kulbaga rightly and ironically calls a "rescue" is to simultaneously remove the agency of a woman wearing a robe (517).

In my class, we built from a robust conversation about Nadia's conception of her own identity and the way characters throughout the novel misinterpret her conception to break out into groups that we assembled earlier in the semester. I asked students to spend a few minutes researching and reading about debates surrounding hijabs, a task that required them to use computers or phones and thus drew clear connections between the subject of the text and ongoing debates they could locate in their own media environment. Students found short news articles about some of the most notable manifestations of this debate – such as those relating to the ban of religious clothing in French schools – and, after taking time to read them, had quick conversations in their groups about what these debates can teach us about broader intersections of community, nationality, and gender.

Such breakout activities achieve a few specific goals. First, they teach students how much they can learn from a quick dive into the broader context of a text. This lesson is self-evident to experienced close readers, but it is often and perhaps surprisingly new to students. Helping them see that they can find this information on their own before beginning to unpack the ideas in groups illustrates the process of knowledge production in real time. By allowing students to locate and read articles they find rather than passing along articles I pre-selected, they see their partial role in the direction of the class discourse. This work is essential to establishing the classroom as a care community in which students can work together to shape not only the direction of the course but also the methodology of their learning. In addition to the metacognitive work this short activity achieves, it is of course helpful in continuing the work of dissecting the novel's investigation into community. A conversation about French schools, for example, engenders student comments about what can be lost to a community when some of its members are either excluded or believed to be in need of rescue. This dichotomy does not account for their individual agency in deciding whether to, in this case, wear a robe. Without much or any knowledge of the ongoing debates in postcolonial studies and in public discourse about robes, my students were able to quickly and effectively understand the sense of invisibility that one might encounter wearing a robe. Rather than linking this sense of invisibility to the self by asking students to think about instances in which they were misunderstood, we discussed how a community based around care and relationality would differ in its response to women wearing robes to those communities organized around coercion, monolithic ideals, and exclusion. The conversation brought us back to the instructive force of "experiences of exclusion and misrecognitions," which is essential to establishing a pedagogy of care in our classroom (Motta and Bennett 2018, 636). Just as importantly, the exercise offers one of many possible points of access to Gayatri Chakravorty Spivak's (1985) "Can the Subaltern Speak?", a foundational and often difficult text for students new to Postcolonial Studies. Once students understand the way Spivak's essay leverages its critique through a language game, the specific example of women wearing religious robes moves Spivak's question out of the realm of deconstruction and into a real set of political problems students can easily explore.

While the previous example required us to ask questions about the novel's many reconfigurations of identity through its central characters, our focus on speculative narrative practices led us toward work that considered deeply the speculative premise that activates much of the plot in *Exit West*. In a more traditional class discussion, we explored the thematic function of doors and windows in the novel. The discussion was inspired by a student's online reflection, which I often use as a jumping-off point for class discussion. The student focused on one particular section from the novel about the precarious feeling produced by a window when one is in a war zone:

> One's relationship to windows now changed in the city. A window was the border through which death was possibly most likely to come. Windows could not stop even the most flagging round of ammunition: any spot indoors with a view of the outside was a spot potentially in the crossfire. Moreover, the pane of a window could itself become shrapnel so easily, shattered by a nearby blast, and everyone had heard of someone or other who had bled out after being lacerated by shards of flying glass. (Hamid 2017, 71)

As we discussed this passage, students were able to navigate the obvious conflict between the way we typically think of windows as connecting us to the outside, letting in light and warmth, and opening up spaces to the precarity experienced by Nadia and Saeed. We then compared the anxiety windows produce to the possibility doors provide the characters:

> Rumors had begun to circulate of doors that could take you elsewhere, often to places far away, well removed from this death trap of a country. … Most people thought these rumors to be nonsense, the superstitions of the feeble-minded. But most people began to gaze at their own doors a little differently nonetheless. Nadia and Saeed, too, discussed these rumors and dismissed them. But every morning, when she woke, Nadia looked over at her front door, and at the doors to her bathroom, her closet, her terrace. Every morning, in his room, Saeed did much the same. All their doors remained simple doors, on/off switches in the flow between two adjacent places, binarily either open or closed, but each of their doors, regarded thus with a twinge of irrational possibility, became partially animate as well … (2017, 72–73)

These two passages helped us have a fairly straightforward conversation about the novel's positioning of windows and doors, the former as an object of fear and the latter as an object of hope. Students discussed how doors might normally be seen as objects that provide access and opportunity only to those who can pass through them – with a key or invitation. One student insightfully noted that the absence of this control would destabilize those with power; in one example in the novel, a woman's closet door becomes "a special door" (72). That example showed the way the novel's speculative premise, the student noted, shifted private spaces to public spaces, national spaces guarded by borders to globally shared spaces. Even this quick conversation about how the novel renegotiates spaces pushed us to think about what sort of community can and should emerge in such an environment, returning us to a conversation about care communities in the novel.

Indeed, the fact that Hamid leaves many spaces in the novel unnamed further abstracts the ideas of solid borders and even nationhood. The "West" is one of the few named, meaningful spaces, and the novel's title suggests that one must leave that legible space behind in order to join an emerging refugee community. The last space that Nadia and Saeed live in together is one such place, the "new city" of Marin, which is a shanty town located just out of the reach of San Francisco's city services (193). Most of the occupants of Marin are from elsewhere. Even the idea of "nativeness" to Marin is described as "a relative matter," as the old bonds that tether Americans to the idea of the nation, for instance, are starting to break (197).

In the course of discussing these shifts, I want the form of our dialogue to echo the content of our conversation and, at once, allow the knowledge the text provides about these emerging communities to affect the way we position ourselves in the classroom. For that reason, I move through the room and relinquish the front of the class so that students can map out ideas on the board or in small groups, a practice that inevitably leads to vastly different representational practices. Some students draw, others produce word maps, others simply note ideas in lists. These differences may seem small, but the practice of giving students the power to record class conversation shows them, yet once more, that we are building ideas together, using the strengths and styles we each bring to the group. Students give one another feedback in real time; while most of this feedback is positive, even questions and problems with the methods or findings of our discussion help students understand how they must be responsible to the community of the classroom. In such a method, the subject of our conversation is complemented by the style in which we carry out our dialogue. The learning outcomes from a conversation like this stretch to include not principally specific information but a critical practice of care for the group as a whole. As many pedagogy scholars have noted, such a praxis views the distinction between cognition and emotion as a false dichotomy (see Walker and Gleaves 2016). In fact, the emotional work of establishing a care community is at the root of what I hope my students will take from a discussion like this. In the case of *Exit West*, in particular, a conversation that allows students to move freely through the classroom and take up and relinquish control of our conversation is also an appropriate style to better understand the possibilities the novel imagines. We frame these possibilities as a type of care and relationality that the novel's speculative premise makes it impossible for characters to avoid. The fact that Westerners and global refugee communities must come into contact with one another in *Exit West* opens up the possibility of rethinking our relationship with the ideas and political structures that typically prevent this sort of speculative commons from taking shape.

Outside of class discussion, our work followed a similar trajectory. Students worked in groups on class presentations that opened up previously undiscussed linkages between our reading and the wider context of speculative postcolonial fiction. In those projects, I encourage students to take a creative approach that fit the skills and ideas of the group rather than mimic me or their classmates. The final project at the end of the semester was a short podcast that could help a wide, public audience understand the work that speculative postcolonial fiction carries out. The project mirrors both the forms our class has taken and the content of *Exit West*; we work in groups to produce a text in a genre that can be widely disseminated and used to connect people and stories from across the world. Just as Nadia and Saeed are able to use their phones to access news and thus put themselves in limited contact with many communities, my students produce work that is accessible for broad (and somewhat unknown) audiences about the novel, speculative aesthetics, postcolonial feminism, and many other topics. Indeed, the final project takes the methods we had installed in our classroom through the door and out to the world, once again emphasizing that our success is linked with others – in the room and beyond.

Many similar course topics could use *Exit West* to examine and establish care communities in the literature classroom to different ends. My class examines speculative postcolonial fiction from many nations and regions, but other courses might press on the novel as one that importantly departs from the author's South Asian roots. A focus on South Asian precarity would open up exciting opportunities to investigate different care communities than those featured in the novel, such as the longstanding and frequently evolving feminist movement in Hamid's birthplace, Pakistan. While such an approach might appear to run counter to a novel that often evacuates particular histories by focusing on constantly shifting communities of refugees moving from place to place instantaneously, it would show students that care communities and resistance do not require such a speculative premise. In other words, the move between the novel's speculative aesthetics and specific histories could be a productive point of access for students in South Asian literature courses. Examining the novel in this way would allow students and faculty to work together to consider with greater emphasis whether abstracting particular histories and nationalities – such as South Asia in this novel – undercuts the novel's message about twenty-first century refugee communities through abstract representations that are more about routes than roots. These questions need not be purely oppositional to the text; instead, they can open up questions that nearly every course on postcolonial literature may usefully address.

Notes

1. I should say at the outset of this essay that my only point of reference for pedagogy is, unfortunately, institutions of higher education in the United States, which is where I have studied and taught. I hope that scholars working outside of North America will be able to take my essay in exciting and different directions.
2. Exciting and interesting work at the intersection of care work and pedagogy has been carried out in disability studies. For an exploration of these intersections, see the 2015 special issue of *Pedagogy* entitled "Caring From, Caring Through: Pedagogical Approaches to Disability." In the introduction to the special issue, Allison P. Hobgood writes that the special issue "asks scholars to articulate the ways in which living with or caring for (and along with) children, siblings, spouses, parents, and clients with disabilities informs our lives and teaching – beyond, of course, simply making one more sensitive to disability matters" (2015, 415).

Disclosure Statement

No potential conflict of interest was reported by the author.

References

Bybee, K. J. 2016. *How Civility Works*. Stanford, CA: Stanford University Press.

Editorial Board. 2018. "Let the Trump Team Eat in Peace." *Washington Post*, June 24.

Forni, P. M. 2010. "Why Civility is Necessary for Society's Survival." *Dallas Morning News*, July 23.

Freire, P. 2005. *Pedagogy of the Oppressed*. 30th Anniversary edn. New York: Continuum.

Gilbert, S. 2016. "Learning to Be Human." *The Atlantic*, June 30.

Hamid, M. 2017. *Exit West*. New York: Riverhead Books.

hooks, B. 1994. *Teaching to Transgress: Education as the Practice of Freedom*. New York: Routledge.

Jasbir, P. 2012. "Precarity Talk: A Virtual Roundtable with Lauren Berlant, Judith Butler, Bojana Cvejic, Isabell Lorey, Jasbir Puar, and Ana Vujanovic." *TDR: The Drama Review* 56 (4): 163–177.

Kulbaga, T. A. 2008. "Pleasurable Pedagogies: Reading *Lolita in Tehran* and the Rhetoric of Empathy." *College English* 70 (5): 506–521.

Lorey, I. 2015. *State of Insecurity: Government of the Precarious*. New York: Verso.

Motta, S. C. and A. Bennett. 2018. "Pedagogies of Care, Care-Full Epistemological Practice and 'Other' Caring Subjectivities in Enabling Education." *Teaching in Higher Education* 23 (5): 631–646.

Nguyen, V. T. 2017. "March's Book Club Pick: 'Exit West,' by Mohsin Hamid." *New York Times*, March 10.

Rosner, H. 2018. "The Absurdity of Trump Officials Eating at Mexican Restaurants during an Immigration Crisis." *The New Yorker*, June 22.

Saldívar, R. 2011. "Historical Fantasy, Speculative Realism, and Postrace Aesthetics in Contemporary American Fiction." *American Literary History* 23 (3): 574–599.

Saldívar, R. 2013. "The Second Elevation of the Novel: Race, Form, and the Postrace Aesthetic in Contemporary Narrative." *Narrative* 21 (1): 1–18.

Scheidenhelm, C. 2018. "Losing Humanities in Education is Propelling a Deficit of Empathy." *The Hill*, April 9.

Walker, C. and A. Gleaves. 2016. "Constructing the Caring Higher Education Teacher: A Theoretical Framework." *Teaching and Teacher Education* 54: 65–76.

Worsham, L. 1998. "Going Postal: Pedagogic Violence and the Schooling of Emotion." *Journal of Rhetoric, Culture, and Politics* 18 (2): 213–245.

POETIC INTERLUDE

Birds Come After Me

K. Satchidanandan

Birds come after me, as if
I were a walking tree.
I spread my crown for them,
like the mushroom in the a Russian children's tale
growing ever wider to shelter
birds and beasts from rain.
I grow many hands,
from the legs for the parrots,
from the hip for crows,
from the belly and the back
for the cranes, eagles,
kingfishers and owls
and tiny twigs for
sparrows and treepies.
They fruit, my head opens out
like a tree top , and bats hang from them
undefined, between bird-ness and beastliness.
My hairs blossom, butterflies looking for honey
surround my head like a halo.
As I watch, each bird turns into a letter:
an alphabet of birds.
The wind passes between them,
they make many noises,
order themselves into lines,
resound with suggestions,
change places, combine

to become something else,

sing and tell stories.

Vanished hills and forests

crowd their memory,

dried up pools and streams,

roofs and telephone cables

with screams passing through them

and the scalding grammar

of electric current.

A tree is a dictionary of leaves.

My branches fill with poems,

the history of clouds*.

*A *History of Clouds:* the title of a new collection of poems by Hans Magnus
Enzensberger

AFTERWORD

Precarious Futures, Precarious Pasts: Climate, Terror, and Planetarity

Gaurav Desai

ABSTRACT

This is a transcript of the Keynote Lecture delivered at the annual conference of the South Asian Literary Association in Chicago on January 8th, 2018. The talk, opening with the devastation caused in the nineteenth century by the British cultivation of opium in India, closes with a discussion of the current opium production in Afghanistan and its widespread consequences. Both these cases show the ways in which political entities (whether nation-states or non-state actors) and private interests collude, often resulting in harm to vulnerable populations. In this discourse, I am interested in thinking about the human toll of changing ecologies, of climate change and of the impact they have on violence and the attendant migration.

Right now the earth is full of refugees, human and not, without refuge.

Haraway (2015, 160)

In *Sea of Poppies*, the opening novel of Amitav Ghosh's Ibis trilogy, Deeti, a peasant woman from Ghazipur, India, having signed on as an indentured laborer, is on board a ship headed to Mauritius. At one point during the journey, one of the other women in the ship's hold, knowing that her own death is imminent, hands over to Deeti a packet of seeds – among them seeds of ganja, Datura, and Benares poppy: "It's yours, take it, keep it. This, the ganja, the datura: make of them the best use you can … They'll keep for many years. Keep them hidden till you can use them; they are worth more than any treasure" (2008, 438). Examining the poppy seed, Deeti, a believer in astrology and of reading the stars for the signs of human destiny, recognizes instead her destiny in the seed: "She looked at the seed as if she had never seen one before, and suddenly she knew that it was not the planet above that governed her life: it was this miniscule orb – at once bountiful and all-devouring, merciful and destructive, sustaining and vengeful" (2008, 439). Indeed, it is poppy that has hitherto underwritten the main thrust of her life story. She has lost both her husband and her land to poppy, her husband giving way to opium addiction and her land being forcefully transformed by the British from being a field for growing wheat to the cultivation of poppy. Her hut, which in years past would have been re-thatched with wheat straw, is now left without repair. Her husband has left her to pay off his debts and she is reduced to poverty. Not formally schooled and unable to read, Deeti puts her thumb impression on a loan from an unscrupulous money-lender, a transaction which in effect, leads to the physical loss of her land. Resisting her brother in law's unwanted sexual advances, Deeti decides to commit sati on her husband's funeral pyre, an act from which she is dramatically rescued by a fellow subaltern, Kalua, whom she will, later on, marry.

The ecological damage caused by the transition to poppy cultivation and the resultant loss of food security is palpably clear to Deeti not only in her own village but in places that she travels through on her flight from her past. She wonders as she examines the changed landscape what the farmers "would eat in the months ahead: where were the vegetables, the grains? She had only to look around to know that here, as in the village she had left, everyone's land was in hock to the agents of the opium factory: every farmer had been served with a contract, the fulfilling of which left them with no option but to strew their land with poppies. And now, with the harvest over and little grain at home, they would have to plunge still deeper into debt to feed their families" (2008, 189). It is such dire circumstances, resulting directly from the prescriptions of the British East India Company, that led many to sign on to the *girmitiya* contracts – to serve as indentured labor in the plantation societies of Mauritius and the West Indies. The conditions and terms of indenture changed over time, but Indian indentured labor that began in 1833 and ended in 1920 resulted in approximately 3.5 million people moving to various European colonies. The migrations that have followed since, in the latter half of the twentieth century and the twenty-first, have been caused by many factors – both push and pull – as human geographers have noted, amongst them political strife, drought and famine but also the ability to tap into networks of those who have previously migrated and the promise of economic opportunity and upward mobility. Among the many factors that prompt migration, of increasing significance today are environmental pressures, ecology, and climate change and it is to these matters that I would like to pay some attention today.

My remarks, then, may seem at first to be at some remove from the most pressing concerns that have traditionally driven postcolonial studies, but they are made, as you no doubt recognize, both in the aftermath of a devastating hurricane season in the Atlantic and the Gulf, and in the context of the on-going refugee crisis in Europe, a crisis that is variously related to a rise in racism, radical nationalisms, terrorism, infringement of human rights and rising poverty levels. We meet today almost two decades after the signing of the Kyoto protocol – which, despite its challenges in implementation, was at least a preliminary coming to terms with the effects of greenhouse gas emissions and global warming. Though the debates around climate change have continued and though climate change deniers – despite the preponderance of scientific evidence to the contrary otherwise – continue to make themselves heard, the vast majority of observers today are persuaded that climate change is real and is something that needs a concerted reckoning.

To reckon with climate change is to be better able to imagine it and to represent it. Are our art forms, our literary forms, our theoretical frames of reference and indeed the legacy of Enlightenment humanism that continues to inform our debates (at least in the Euro-American academy that we inhabit) adequate to the task? Disasters such as tsunamis, earthquakes, and hurricanes lend themselves to spectacular representations of victims that may interpellate the empathy of viewers. But what about the less spectacular ongoing ecological damage that can lead to equally precarious conditions? In his pioneering study *Slow Violence and the Environmentalism of the Poor*, Rob Nixon (2011) drew our attention to the "slow violence" of environmental and ecological degradation. "By slow violence, I mean," he writes, "a violence that occurs gradually and out of sight, a violence of delayed destruction that is dispersed across time and space, an attritional violence that is typically not viewed as violence at all" (2). Such violence challenges our representational registers and, thus, also our ability to engage with it, to expose it, and to work towards a politics of environmental social justice.

In a similar vein, in his recent study, *The Great Derangement: Climate Change and the Unthinkable*, Amitav Ghosh charts out some of the challenges confronting contemporary writers. Noting that "fiction that deals with climate change is almost by definition not of the kind that is taken seriously by serious literary journals" (7), Ghosh points out that dominant literary forms such as realism emerged "in precisely that period when the accumulation of carbon in the atmosphere was rewriting the destiny of the earth" (7). Furthermore, the desires that such literature inculcated in its readers, were desires for lifestyles that may well be unsustainable on a global scale. For Ghosh, the key frames of reference for understanding our current ecological plight are the history of European empire and the central role of Asia. If the history of European colonialism is the history of uneven global development, the post-WW II history of Asia and the unprecedented speed of its ongoing embrace of modernity have resulted in Asia's becoming both a key agent and a particularly precarious victim of climate change. In contrast to the critics who underscore the role of capitalism in the story of climate change, Ghosh insists that the "imperatives of capital and empire have often pushed in opposite directions, sometimes producing counter-intuitive results" (87). So, for instance, Ghosh shows how the desire to acquire raw materials from the colonies for industrial production in the metropole resulted in colonial policies that actively curtailed early industrialization in the colonies. Empire may, in this sense, have delayed the processes of climate change which after WW II and the movement towards decolonization were unleashed in the East in full force.

In addition to the challenge of representation is the challenge posed by climate change to critical thought itself. In a series of thought-provoking essays Dipesh Chakrabarty (2009) has argued that historically emancipatory thought – whether that be on behalf of women, the racially marginalized, the economically disadvantaged, the former colonies and so on–has assumed a rights bearing subject. The model has been one of ensuring that those who have been left outside the orbit of modernity have the same access to fundamental rights as others. When we consider the agency of humans in climate change, however, we are called to understand our role not as rights-bearing subjects but as a planetary species that has turned into a geological force. It is our collective behavior, our collective actions as a species that we are asked to consider as we think ahead to the challenges that climate change poses for us.

These two ways of imagining the human are not just matters of a difference in scale, they also pull us in different directions. While the first orientation reminds us that we need to continue to pay attention to human inequality, prejudice, and discrimination, the second orientation – imagining ourselves as a species – tends to want to put us all in the same boat – a boat by the way, we now sometimes begrudgingly acknowledge that we share with other species and matter both animate and inanimate. There is perhaps some irony in the fact that the struggle for increasing emancipations occurred at the same time as humanity increasingly polluted the environment. "The mansion of modern freedoms," writes Chakrabarty, "stands on an ever-expanding base of fossil fuel use" (208). But this has serious implications for imagining a planetary politics that does justice both to past inequities and to future sustainability. As Ghosh puts it, "Inasmuch as the fruits of the carbon economy constitute wealth, and inasmuch as the poor of the global south have historically been denied this wealth, it is certainly true, by every available canon of distributive justice, that they are entitled to a greater share of the rewards of that economy" (2017, 110). And yet, the fact that such justice is predicated upon an ecologically precarious future suggests that perhaps the belief in an all-encompassing modernity – a modernity for all – was a false promise to begin with. What we have learned, argues Ghosh, is "that the patterns of life that modernity engenders can only be practiced by a small majority of the world's population. Asia's historical experience demonstrates that our planet will not allow these patterns of living to be adopted by every human being. Every family in the world cannot have two cars, a washing machine and a refrigerator – not because of technical or economic limitations but because humanity would asphyxiate in the process" (2016, 92). Here, then, the emancipatory project of our first orientation finds as its limit the very possibility of species extinction.

How then are we to calibrate our sense of justice to those around us who may find themselves in precarious conditions? What is our responsibility to those who may knock on our doors and seek refuge? How might we imagine unconditional hospitality as a gesture not only towards those who seek political refuge but also those, affected by the climatic changes in their home environments appeal to us as members of the same human species? The recent images of gassed Syrian children, or that of Alan Kurdi, the three year old Syrian boy, whose body surfaced on a beach in Turkey, have compelled our attention to the horrific plight of the victims of the war. But such spectacular violence belies earlier forms of precarity that we might agree at least partially led to the crisis. In a report released in October 2016, the German Climate Diplomacy Group, in collaboration with the Federal Foreign Office of Germany, concluded that while drought was not the only cause of the civil war, it played a significant role in the developing conflict. According to this report, by 2007 Syria's water consumption had exceeded the rate of replenishment by more than 20%:

> Syria's water system was thus vulnerable when a five-year drought hit the country in 2007. It was the worst long-term drought since the beginning of historic records and its impact on the livelihoods of many farmers and herders [was] devastating. Absence of rain, overuse of ground water, and dam projects in Turkey further decreased water availability. In the mostly rain-fed region in the North-East, 1.3 million people dependent on agriculture experienced crop failure and herders lost upto 85% of their livestock. The preceding cut of fuel and food subsidies in 2008/9 and lack of social

safety nets decreased people's ability to cope. Massive loss of livelihoods caused migration from the countryside into the cities… Crime, unemployment, food price hikes and stress on urban infrastructure increased, and grievances from disenfranchised urban and displaced rural people combined, deepening pre-existing ethnic and socio-political divides. (Nett and Ruttinger 2016, 22)

In this chaos and instability, groups such as ISIS could gain territory, recruit fighters with the promise of pay and use the ability to control water as a weapon of war. "Though far from being the only or the primary driver of conflict in Syria, climate change," the report concludes, "did play a catalytic role in accelerating the descent into fragility and facilitating the rise of Non-State Armed Groups" (23).

Indeed, if the underlying message here is that the slow violence of climate change in the form of drought, in concert with other social and political cleavages led to the spectacular violence and violations enacted upon Syrian bodies, this is a message that can be heard in other contemporary contexts as well. The rise of Boko Haram in Nigeria and its spreading influence in the neighboring countries of Chad, Cameroon, and Niger are not unrelated to the continued shrinkage of Lake Chad. "Since the 1970s the number of rainy days in Northern Nigeria has decreased by 53 percent and southward desertification of the Sahara of 1–10 km per year is reducing arable land" (13). This, in addition to the increase in population in the immediate area surrounding the lake as well as excessive irrigation and dam construction have resulted in severe water shortages. As in the case of ISIS in Syria, Boko Haram, at first, capitalized on resource insecurity and political disenfranchisement to recruit followers but later shifted to more violent means of enforcing collaboration. While it would be inaccurate to establish direct causal links between the ecological challenges and the rise of Boko Haram, the Climate Diplomacy Group argues that the conflicts around natural resources in the region "contribute to overall instability and fragility, thus creating more hospitable conditions for Boko Haram to mobilize support, commit acts of violence, and engage in organized criminal activities" (16).

President Obama caused an uproar in some circles when, at the Paris Accord conference taking place in the aftermath of the 2015 Paris terrorist attacks, he suggested a link between climate change and terrorism. "Terrorism is an ideology rooted in religious extremism" proclaimed the critics. "Obama should be fighting ISIS and not climate change" claimed others. What these critics failed to recognize is what the German report has clearly outlined. While climate change is not the singular cause for the rapid rise of non-state sponsored terrorism, it is an important condition of possibility for its rapid expansion. Hunger, poverty, unemployment, lack of safety nets natural to politically weak states are all conditions of precarity in which terror groups can recruit, mobilize and expand their base. The world does not live or die by political ideology alone.

More recently, President Trump has refused to endorse the Paris Accord despite pressure from other leaders at the Group of 7 summit in Sicily. And yet, the security implications of climate change were clearly evident in the U.S. Department of Defense report to the Congress presented in July 2015. Of all the bodies in Washington, the Department of Defense has long recognized, budgeted for, and planned responses to the adverse effects of climate change and in this particular report the department is crystal clear in its findings: "Global climate change will have wide-ranging implications for U.S. national security interests over the foreseeable future because it will aggravate existing problems – such as poverty, social tensions, environmental degradation, ineffectual leadership, and weak political institutions – that threaten domestic stability in a number of countries" (3). The report specifically lists as greatest threats "persistently recurring conditions such as flooding, drought, and higher temperatures" (4), "more frequent and/or more severe weather events" (4), "sea level rise and temperature changes" (5) and "decreases in Arctic ice cover, type and thickness" (5).

In her careful study *Climate Change, Forced Migration and International Law*, Jane McAdam argues for a determined but measured response to the challenges ahead. Not wanting to deny the realities of climate-induced migrations, she is at the same time cautious of the overly crisis-bound rhetoric which, she argues, may tend to hurt migrants more than help. The alarmist tone of many of the discussions may, indeed, feed into the ultra-nationalisms and xenophobias that work to keep migrants at bay – migrants, who we might add, often arrive from developing or underdeveloped nation-states. Currently, no international agreement or treaty protects those displaced by climate related causes. International refugee law provides refuge only to those directly escaping political conflict and those who can establish persecution and vulnerability if they were to return home. Some have argued for an expansion of the category of "climate refugee" to include those displaced by environmental and/or climatic factors. But, as McAdam argues, migration decisions are not always made on one factor alone and it is often difficult to establish direct causality, especially when the factors involve slow-onset disasters.

If we set aside the security and the legal frameworks that prompt the thinking of states and think along with the migrants on the brink of displacement by environmental or climatic factors, we find that they often reject the term "refugee" as applied to them. In Kiribati and Tuvalu, both nation-states threatened by the rise of ocean waters, the term is considered offensive. In an interview with McAdam, here is what the President of Kiribati had to say: "We don't want to lose our dignity. We're sacrificing much by being displaced, in any case. So we don't want to lose that, whatever dignity is left. So the last thing we want to be called is 'refugee.' We're going to be given as a matter of right something that we deserve, because they've taken away what we have" (McAdam 2012, 41). The President's claim here echoes a debate that took place in the aftermath of Hurricane Katrina, my own first-hand experience with a hurricane-induced displacement. Katrina, whose intensity many scientists now believe was augmented because of global warming, led to the displacement of over 400,000 people from the New Orleans metropolitan area alone. As my family and I evacuated from New Orleans and settled into Austin, Texas, we monitored the media reports that flooded us with images of our fellow citizens destitute on rooftops or yet to be evacuated from the New Orleans superdome. The world at large was shocked by these images, images, for the most part – though certainly not exclusively – of lower-income African Americans who, often without prior means of evacuation, had been left to fend for themselves. Media references to the displaced of Katrina as "refugees," angered many in the African American community. "It is racist to call American citizens refugees," said Rev. Jesse Jackson and his sentiments were shared not only by members of the Congressional Black Caucus but by many of the displaced themselves. "I can't stand people calling me a refugee. I am an American and I love America," claimed one such person displaced by the hurricane.

This reluctance to be labeled 'refugees' on both the part of the President of Kiribati and of the displaced of Katrina speak to the associations of helplessness and victimhood that the term 'refugee' invokes. But it also speaks to an insistence that their plight be clearly understood within an already existing social contract and not as a gesture of charity or generosity. In the case of Kiribati, the people, as the President puts it, are "going to be given as a matter of *right*, something that we deserve, because they've taken away what we have." A right for compensation rather than a plea for charity – those responsible for releasing large amounts of greenhouse gasses and for global warming, the logic goes, owe the people of Kiribati reparations in the form, perhaps, of new inhabitable lands. Likewise, the appeal to citizenship as an essential social contract on the part of the displaced of Katrina is a rejection of any suggestion of second- class citizenship. Ironically, some of those who originally used the term 'refugee' to describe the victims of Katrina did so precisely to point to the less than adequate safety nets that the U.S. government at both federal and state levels had provided these inner-city citizens for decades. They had been ignored, left out of the alleged American Dream, as though their lives did not matter, as though they were really not like "us." But there may also have been other reasons why the term 'refugee' came so naturally. For many, both within the United States as well as abroad, the exposure to the stark poverty in the midst of one of the richest countries in the world was a shock. For a country that repeatedly told itself that it takes care of its own – the only way that such individuals could be read was as refugees from a foreign country. In such a context President Bush's statement that "now we're going to try and comfort people in *that part of the world*" to refer to New Orleans and the Gulf Coast would only have bolstered this image of the New Orleanian as foreigner.

Regardless of whether or not Katrina was just an oddity or was, instead, directly affected by the factors that have caused global warming and climate change, the Environmental Protection Agency in August 2016 released a report that warns of the challenges that lie ahead. In recent decades, Louisiana has been losing 25 square miles of land each year due to sinking land and human activities. Because of the elaborate levee system built around the Mississippi, natural land growth through the build-up of sediment has been thwarted. This, along with projected sea level rise will mean significant loss of coastal land. The EPA report also notes that the area is becoming even more vulnerable to both coastal as well as inland flooding. The rising sea level and higher temperatures are a threat not only to human populations but also to fisheries. The Coastal wetlands that are being lost are the breeding grounds for almost 75 percent of the state's fisheries. In addition to lowering levels of oxygen in the water due to higher temperatures a separate concern has been the development of a "dead zone" in the Gulf of Mexico resulting from the nutrients – especially phosphorus and nitrogen – from lawns, sewage treatment plants and farm lands – which come down the Mississippi river. And this is not a problem that is limited to the Gulf of Mexico. The Mississippi Gulf shares these vulnerabilities with the Bay of Bengal. As Sunil Amrith (2013) reminds us, the rivers that flow into the Bay are in 'dire health.' "The excess of nutrients that flows through the rivers – most damaging is the nitrogen from the agricultural fertilizer runoff, and from vehicle and factory exhausts – creates 'dead zones' starved of oxygen" (260). Here too the impact is not only on the human inhabitants of the coastal areas but also on its flora and fauna.

As these ecological changes continue to take place, they will increasingly affect the lives and well-being of those who live in vulnerable environments. Some will be forced to re-locate domestically, others will seek opportunities across national borders. While no current legal regime dictates the plight of such migrants, we must find ethical ways of engaging and embracing them. Those who arrive at our shores in order to escape drought or desertification surely deserve our sympathy as much as those who escape political persecution. Indeed, insofar as their plight is the result of greenhouse-induced global warming, they may have an even larger claim to make upon our obligations to them. Here, as in the case of the Katrina evacuees, we may be better served by casting our obligations as forms of reparative justice than acts of charity. But this is an argument that will need to be persuasively made since it is by no means clear that it is either the current wisdom on the streets or in any ways one of consensus among political thinkers and policy makers. The political theorist Michael Walzer (1984) has argued, for instance, that it is right for any given community or nation-state to decide on who can or cannot be taken into its fold. This is an argument that is increasingly made by those who would enforce closed borders. We cannot let them in because they do not share our values. Or, even more explicitly, we cannot let them in because there may be terrorists among them. It is in the light of such arguments and rhetoric that it is well worth remembering that much of the current anxieties about refugees are continuous with a long-standing fear of racialized, darker bodies. Here again, while the discourse of the Anthropocene invites us to think of ourselves as an agential species, we cannot at the same time forget that the struggle for recognition, for being seen as fully human – continues among those who have been historically racialized as inferior, primitive, not quite human. In case anyone has any doubts about the ongoing rhetorical dehumanization of refugees, we may recall the British columnist Katie Hopkins who, in 2015, suggested using gunships against the migrants in the Mediterranean, calling the migrants cockroaches.

I want to end by going back to the character of Deeti, her dispossession from Ghazipur resulting both from an oppressive patriarchy (as characterized by her brother-in-law) and from the economic destitution caused by the colonially forced production of opium. Two centuries later Fariba Nawa (2011), a journalist of Afghan origin but who was raised in the United States went back to Afghanistan to report on the war in the aftermath of 9/11. In her book, *Opium Nation: Child Brides, Drug Lords, and One Woman's Journey Through Afghanistan*, Nawa presents an intimate picture of the many ways in which the production, distribution, ingestion and eradication of opium affects the lives of a great number of Afghans. "Opium," she writes, "is everywhere – in the addict beggars on the streets, in the poppies planted in home gardens, in the opium widows hidden from drug lords in neighbors' homes, in the hushed conversations of drug dealers in shops, in the unmarked graves in cemeteries, and in the drug lords' garish opium mansions looming among the brick shacks and mounds of dust" (3–4). Once again we see, as the narrative unfolds, how various non-state actors with ties to terrorist networks mobilize the drug trade to finance their operations. Among all the individuals whom Nawa introduces, two figures haunt my own reading of the text. The first is Darya, the twelve-year-old daughter of a narcotics dealer who gives her as a child bride to a drug lord to settle his opium debt. Darya resists going with the man for a few years but ultimately succumbs to family pressure. Around the same age as Deeti when she is herself married, Darya too is caught in an oppressive patriarchal system that is enmeshed in the opium trade. While Darya like Deeti has not gone down the route of self-immolation, based on the life stories of other young girls with similar stories, the author fears that this could, indeed, have been her fate.

The second figure who haunts my imagination is Parween, a poppy farmer and mother of nine who lives in the remote province of Badakhshan. We meet her as she despairs and weeps over the loss of her poppies that have been subjected to the eradication campaign of the Afghan government. The eradication campaigns are erratic and likely affected by which authorities have been paid off. The women who depend on the growth of poppies often farm on rain-fed land. Since poppy is a plant that can withstand drought more than many others, it is a less risky crop than others. Indeed, as one woman told UN surveyors in 2004: "In fact, I should say that it is not an illicit crop but rather a blessing... It is the only means of survival for thousands of women-headed households, women and children in our village whose men are either jobless or were killed during the war" (Nawa 2011, 151). What we recognize in this claim is that eradication schemes must be alert to how the suppression of the drug may also at the same time simultaneously disempower the most vulnerable. "A sustainable, long-term plan to curtail the drug industry" writes Nawa, "should focus on bigger issues of stability and security" (308). "Voluntary eradication should continue, and forced eradication should target the small number of wealthy landowners. Farmers should continue to receive alternative seeds and fertilizer, but they should also have access to a fair and legal banking system" (309).

With the story of Parween and the other women who farm poppies, we return to the scene on the ship where a dying woman hands over to Deeti seeds of ganja, Datura, and poppy telling her that they are an insurance for her future. "Make of them the best use you can... They'll keep for many years. Keep them hidden till you can use them; they are worth more than any treasure" (Ghosh 2008, 438). There is no indication in the novel or in the subsequent two that make up the trilogy that Deeti ever uses the seeds to cultivate poppy or ganja or Datura as she makes a new life on the island of Mauritius. Indeed Deeti's story is meant to be a story of contrast, a story that is a move away from the grasp of poppy and opium, even as the story of the American Zachary Reid, the Englishman Benjamin Burnham and the Parsi Bahram Modi is one of an ever greater embrace of the drug trade.

If the primary victims in that earlier drug trade were the Indians who were displaced by it and the Chinese who became addicted to it, the victims of this more contemporary trade are not only those who suffer its consequences in Afghanistan but also the many across the world who are addicted to heroin. The Opium War was fought by the British in China in the name of free trade. There, a private group of opium traders, some who invoked not just the ideology of free trade but also of the

Christian duty to "emancipate" the Chinese from their alleged mercantile slumber, ultimately sought the power of the British state to secure their interests. The story of Afghanistan can be told somewhat in reverse. Here, Cold War politics, after the Soviet invasion of Afghanistan, prompted the entry of the United States who supported the mujahideen, who brought together a different religious ideology with armed conflict funded by the drug trade. Both the world of Deeti and the world of Parween are worlds in which powerful state actors working in concert with private interests have led to suffering, death, and a general sense of precarity among the many caught between them. Deeti, it seems, was able to break out of this circle, to refrain from planting the poppies. The likes of Parween are, as yet, unable to do so. If in Ghosh's novel, Deeti sees in the poppy seed the signs of her own destiny, the poppy seeds in Afghanistan have many destinies yet to see unfold and many lives yet to risk. There are no easy solutions here – but reading these histories conjunctively and reading them as connected not only to the plight of migrants and refugees but also to our planetary challenges of climate change, is to be alert and vigilant as to who cultivates, what we cultivate, and under what circumstances. In such vigilance will lie the path ahead towards the healthy cultivation of our common humanity and our planetary future.

Disclosure Statement

No potential conflict of interest was reported by the author.

References

Amrith, Sunil. 2013. *Crossing the Bay of Bengal: The Furies of Nature and the Fortunes of Migrants*. Cambridge, MA: Harvard University Press.

Chakrabarty, Dipesh. 2009. "The Climate of History: Four Theses." *Critical Inquiry* 35 (Winter): 197–222. doi:10.1086/596640.

Ghosh, Amitav. 2008. *Sea of Poppies*. New York: Picador.

Ghosh, Amitav. 2016. *The Great Derangement: Climate Change and the Unthinkable*. Chicago, IL: University of Chicago Press.

Haraway, Donna. 2015 "Anthropocene, Capitalocene, Plantationocene, Chthulucene: Making Kin." *Environmental Humanities* 6 (5), 159–165. doi:10.1215/22011919-3615934.

McAdam, Jane. 2012. *Climate Change, Forced Migration and International Law*. New York: Oxford University Press.

Nawa, Fariba. 2011. *Opium Nation: Child Brides, Drug Lords, and One Woman's Journey Through Afghanistan*. New York: Harper Perennial.

Nett, Katarina, and Lukas Ruttinger. 2016. *Insurgency, Terrorism and Organized Crime in a Warming Climate: Analysing the Links Between Climate Change and Non-State Armed Groups*. Berlin: Adelphi Research Group.

Nixon, Rob. 2011. *Slow Violence and the Environmentalism of the Poor.* Cambridge, MA: Harvard University Press.

United States Department of Defense. 2015. "National Security Implications of Climate-Related Risks and a Changing Climate." Report presented to the U.S. Congress on July 23. Accessed 22 December 2017. https://archive.defense.gov/pubs/150724-congressional-report-on-national-implications-of-climate-change.pdf?source=govdelivery

United States Environmental Protection Agency. 2016. *Climate Change Indicators in the United States.* 4th ed. https://www.epa.gov/sites/production/files/2016-08/documents/climate_indicators_2016.pdf

Walzer, Michael. 1984. *Spheres of Justice: A Defense of Pluralism and Equality.* New York: Basic Books.

Index

Abhinavagupta (philosopher) 65
activism, imaginative 46
Adams, Kathleen 84
Adichie, Chimamanda Ngozi: *Half of a Yellow Sun* 84
Adiga, Aravind 72, 84; *White Tiger* 74
Adorno, Theodore 4
Advani, Rukun: *Beethoven Among the Cows* 106, 112
aesthetic pleasure 4
agencies of convergence 17
agency 5, 93; climate change 146; domestic servant invisibility and precarity 75, 79, 83; ethics of representation and the figure of the woman: agency 47; Naxalite movement 30, 34–5, 38, 40, 41; teaching beyond empathy: the classroom as care community 136, 137
Alliance Party (Fiji) 102
Amrith, Sunil 150–1
Anand, Mulk Raj: *Untouchable* 72
animality 49–50, 53
anticolonialism 59, 68
antithetical binaries 68
Arendt, Hannah: 'banality of evil' 115
Aristotle 4
arranged marriages 26
art, value and morality of role of 4
Ashfaq, Saman 6, 105–17
Asif, K.: *Mughal-e-Azam* 18, 24–5, 26–7, 29
autonomy and personhood 81

Bahri, Deepika: *Postcolonial Biology: Psyche and Flesh after Empire* 22
Bandyopadhyay, Bhabani Charan: *Nabababu Bilas* (*Amusements of the Modern Rich*) 58
Bandyopadhyay, Sibaji: 'Latar Din' ('Lata's Day') 46, 51–2
Bandyopadhyay, Srikumar 59
Banerjee, Prathima 20
Bartley, Nancy 30
Bavadra, Timoci 102–3
bell hooks: *Teaching to Transgress: Education as the Practice of Freedom* 135
Bengali language texts 5
Bennett, Anna 133–4

Berlant, Lauren 132
Bhabha, Homi 4, 5; 'Janus-faced discourse of the nation' 19; *Nation and Narration* 8
Bhaduri, Bhubaneswsari 52–4
Bharata (dramaturge) 65
Bharatiya Janata Party (BJP) 22
Bhattacharjee, Anirban 46–54; 'Ethics of Representation and the Figure of the Woman: The Question of Agency' 5
Bidyasagar (social reformer) 60
Biswas, Manohar Mouli: *Amar Bhubane Ami Benche Thaki* ('Surviving My World') 46, 49
#BlackLivesMatter 19
Boko Haram (Nigeria) 7, 148
Bollywood (Hindi cinema) 5, 19, 23, 24
bombogenesis 3
Boyle, Francis A.: *The Tamil Genocide by Sri Lanka: The Global Failure to Protect Tamil Rights Under International Law* 120
Brecht, Bertold 4
British East India Company 145
Brooms of Doom: Notes on Domestic Bodies Gendered to Death in Mughal-e-Azam, Fire *and* Earth 5, 18–30; bodies of evidence 29; domesticity and death in Deepa Mehta's films 25–29; *Earth* (Mehta, Deepa) 18, 24, 28–29; filmic texts and critique of gendered bodies 24–5; *Fire* (Mehta, Deepa) 18, 24, 25–7, 29; matters that embody 22–43; *Mughal-e-Azam* (Asif, K.) 18, 24–5, 26–7, 29; patriarchy 18, 19, 23, 24, 25, 26, 27, 29, 30; prelude: opening minutes 18–20; skin of subalternity 20–2; *Water* (Mehta, Deepa) 24
Bush, George W. 18, 150
Butler, Judith 72; definition of precarity 119; 'Imitation and Gender Insubordination' 27; *Precarious Lives* 92
Bybee, Keith J. 131

capitalism, colonial 91, 94
care communities 1, 3–7, 8; domestic servant invisibility and precarity 72, 77, 81, 84; Fiji: precarity and resistance 91, 101; minority discourse in postcolonial Indian English novel

113, 116; *see also* Sri Lankan civil war: teaching precarity, resistance and community; teaching beyond empathy: the classroom as care community
Certeau, Michel de 22
Chakrabarty, Dipesh 146–7; 'Postcolonial Studies and the Challenge of Climate Change' 19
Chandan, Advait: *Secret Superstar* 22
Chattopadhyay, Bankimchandra: *Anandamath* (*The Alley of Bliss*) 63
citizenship 93, 116, 135, 150
civility 130, 131–5
class 4, 6, 117, 131, 132; *Brooms of Doom: Notes on Domestic Bodies Gendered to Death in Mughal-e-Azam, Fire and Earth* 22, 24–5, 27, 29; domestic servant invisibility and precarity 70–1, 73–87; literary lumpen 56–8, 59–1, 63–4, 66–8; Naxalite Movement: female guerilla fighters 30, 36, 42
Cleaver, Eldridge 56, 57, 68
Clemens, Colleen Lutz 6, 118–28
climate change 3, 7, 17, 18–19, 144–53; climate-induced migration 149; collective behaviour 146–7; drought as contributor to Syrian civil war 7, 147–8; ecological degradation 7, 145–6, 150–1; environmental degradation 7, 145–6; Fiji 92, 93, 101; human damage 7; indentured labour 144–5; Kiribati sea level rise 149–50; refugees/refugee crisis 144, 145, 149, 150, 151, 153; and terrorism link 148
Climate Diplomacy Group 148
collective will and empathy, lack of 114
Colonial Sugar Refining Company (CSR) 94
colonialism 30, 68, 135, 146; biological impacts of 22; British 19, 23; and capitalism 91, 94; Islamic 63; and precarity 93, 94–6; teaching beyond empathy: the classroom as care community 135
communalism 106
Communist Party of India (Maoist) 34
conscientization 132
counter narratives 114
crude humour 59
cultural criticism 4

Dalit life 46, 49–50
Dalitude 53
Dasgupta, Rajarshi 60–1
Dasi, Rassundari: *Ama Jiban* ('My Life') 50–1
death: choice of manner of one's own 34, 40, 52
dehumanization 72, 73, 78, 125, 151
Deleuze, Gilles 20
Deloughrey, Elizabeth 95–6
deprivation 49
Desai, Anita: *In Custody* 106, 107–9, 111, 116
Desai, Gaurav 7, 144–53
Devi, Mahasweta: 'Draupadi' 37–8, 43
Devi v. Silva lawsuit 121
Dickens, Charles: *Sketches of Boz* 58
Dickey, Sara 84

difference 18, 20, 21, 57; class 57; cultural 48; racial 46, 47, 48
digital advertisements 23
Dischinger, Matthew 7, 130–40
disempowerment 71, 84, 152
displacement 6, 97–8, 102
dispossession 106
D'Mello, Bernard 34, 37, 44
domestic servant invisibility and precarity 6, 70–87; abusiveness of employers 73; agency 75, 79, 83; amity 83; autonomy and personhood 81; caste and untouchability 72; culpability 82; deceitfulness and unreliability 79; dehumanization 72, 73, 78; distance and distinction 73; domination, dependency and inequality 84, 86; employer suspicions 82; exploitation 70–2, 76, 85, 86; in-country migrants 72–3; individuality and identity 75, 82; injustice 70, 72, 76, 77–8, 85, 87; learned contempt of employers 84; minimal remuneration 75; obsequiousness and self-abasement 73; oppression 74, 77; pervasive cultural tendency 72; power 71, 75, 76, 79, 84, 85; precarity 70, 72, 76, 80, 85; resistance 71–2, 74, 79, 82, 84; sexual harassment 86; subjectivity 85; subordination 72, 73, 78, 84; trust/distrust 80, 81, 82, 83, 84, 85, 86–7; vilification 77; vulnerability 76, 82; *see also* Narayan, R.K.
Dutta, Saroj 58

ecological degradation 7, 145–6, 150–1
Eisner, Elliot 121–2
Eliot, G. 4
empathy 123, 124, 146; *see also* teaching beyond empathy: the classroom as care community
empowerment 17, 52, 108; Naxalite movement 34–6, 38, 41; *see also* disempowerment
Engels, Friedrich 62
environmental degradation 7, 17, 145–6
Environmental Protection Agency 150
Enzenberger, Hans Magnus: *A History of Clouds* 143
ethics of representation and the figure of the woman: agency 46–54; agency 47; animality, subalternity and death 49–50; suicide 50–3
ethnic cleansing 120, 127
ethnic divisiveness 93
ethnic minorities 17, 29, 118, 124; *see also* minority discourse in postcolonial Indian English novel
ethnonationalist majoritarianism 17
exclusion 18, 134, 137; minority discourse in postcolonial Indian English novel 105, 106, 111, 113; racial 17; social 20, 22–3
existential conditions 4
exploitation 70–2, 76, 85, 86, 92–3, 97–8

failed states 17
family honour 23

Fanon, Frantz 40–1, 44, 68; *The Wretched of the Earth* 57
Faust, Drew Gilpin 132
Fein, Bruce 120
feminism 21, 23, 30; Naxalite Movement: female guerilla fighters 36–8, 43; postcolonial 37; teaching beyond empathy: the classroom as care community 133, 136, 139, 140
Fiji: precarity and resistance 6, 91–103; climate change 92, 93, 101; colonial capitalism 91, 94; colonial and post-colonial precarity 93, 94–6; cultural identity 92, 97, 100; cultural/socio-cultural precarity 91, 93, 94, 95, 99–100; displacement 97–8, 102; ecological precarity 91, 92, 93, 94, 95, 99–100; economic precarity 93, 95; environmental precarity 93, 100; ethnic divisiveness 93; exploitation 92, 97–8; fragmentation 102; geopolitics 91, 94, 99; globalization 92, 100; Indian indentured and forced labour 93, 94–5, 97, 98, 102; kinship and belonging 100–1; militarization 91, 94; nuclear testing 91, 93–4, 95, 98–99, 103; political precarity 9, 94, 95, 98; power 91–6, 98, 99, 102; protectionist policy 95; radiation effects 95; resilience 93; resistance 100–2; segregationist policies 92, 95; sustainability 92; vulnerability 92, 93, 96–7, 100, 102; *see also* Hau'ofa, Epeli; Mishra, Sudesh
Fiji Labour Party 102
film industries 4, 23, 24–5; *see also* Bollywood (Hindi cinema)
filmic texts and critique of gendered bodies 24–5
flooding 3, 5, 18
Foucault, Michel 20, 22
Freire, Paolo 132
Frusetta, James 127–8

Gairola, Rahul K. 5, 18–30
Gajjala, Radhhika 30
Gajjala, Radhika: *Online Philanthropy in the Global North and South* 23
Gandhi, Indira: assassination 105
gang rape 30, 113
Ganguly, Sumit 71
gender/gendered 4; bias and domestic servant invisibility and precarity 85; bodies 18; chauvinism 24; clothing 26–7; equality and Naxalite movement 34–5; expectations 25; nature of war 123; norms and their subversion 124; oppression 21; performance 27; positions of victimhood 36
genocide: educating against 122, 124–5; educating to prevent 122; Holocaust teaching 121–2; pedagogy 6, 122–6
geopolitical issues 91, 94, 99, 132, 135
German Climate Diplomacy Group 147
German Federal Foreign Office 147
Ghosh, Amitav 147; *The Great Derangement: Climate Change and the Unthinkable* 146; *The Great Development* 4; *Sea of Poppies* 7, 144, 153; *Shadow Lines* 51
Ghosh, Amodini: 'Foska Gero' ('Loose Ties') 46, 51
Ghosh, Binoy 57, 68; *Banglar Nabajagriti* (*The Bengal Renaissance*) 58; *Biography of the Nouveau Riche* 58, 59–60, 61, 64; *Kalpenchar Rachanasamgra* 58, 64; *Kolkata Shaharer Itibritta* (*The History of Calcutta*) 58; *Musings, or the Collected Writings of the Black Owl* 58, 64–5; *Nabababu Charita* 58; *Naksha* 5–6, 56–64, 67–8
Gilbert, Sophie 132
Gilmore, Kate 127
girmitiya contracts 145
globalization 92, 100
'good' violence versus 'bad' violence 36
Goodale, Mark 93
Gopal, Priyamvada 43–4
Gordon, Sir Arthur Hamilton 94
Gorman-DaRif, M. 5, 33–44
Gowalkar, M.S. 106
Guittari, Félix 20

Hai, Ambreen 6, 70–87
Hamid, Mohsin: *Exit West* 7, 130, 131–2, 134, 135–40; *The Reluctant Fundamentalist* 136
Handley, George: 'Climate Change, Cosmology and Poetry: The Case of Derek Walcott's *Omeros*' 101
Haraway, Donna 144
Hariharan, Githa 116; *Fugitive Histories* 106, 109–11; *In Times of Siege* 106, 109
Hau'ofa, Epeli 91, 92, 93, 94, 102; *Kisses in the Nederends* 99; 'The Ocean in Us' 99–100; 'Pasts to Remember' 101
Hegel, Georg 50
hijabs, wearing of 136–7
Hindi cinema (Bollywood) 5, 19, 23, 24
Hindu woman's body 21
Hinduism 106–7
Hindutva 107
Hobgood, Allison P. 140
Holocaust teaching 121–2
Hopkins, Katie 151
Hosain, Attia 86
human rights 46–7
Human Rights Council 127
Human Rights Watch 127
hurricanes 3, 18, 145–6, 149–50
Hutchings, Kimberly 35, 36, 38
hybridity 4, 5, 23

identity: cultural 92, 97, 100; domestic servant invisibility and precarity 75, 82; Fiji: precarity and resistance 91, 92, 93, 97, 100; honourable 40; literary lumpen 56, 57, 63; minority discourse in postcolonial Indian English novel 106; national 23, 93; politics of 22, 111; religious 106, 109, 110, 111, 113, 116; teaching

beyond empathy: the classroom as care community 136, 137
Indian indentured labour: in Fiji 93–5, 97–8, 102; in Mauritius 144, 145
indigeneity 62
individuality 75, 82
injustice 17; domestic servant invisibility and precarity 70, 72, 76, 77–8, 85, 87
international human rights organizations 121
International Tamil Centre 120
intolerance 113
invisibility *see* domestic servant invisibility and precarity
ISIS 7, 148
Islamist journalism 108
Iyer, Pico 3

Jackson, Reverend Jesse 149–50
Jain, Dhruv 34
Jayasuriya, Maryse 126
Jha, Raj Kamal: *Fireproof* 106, 111, 112–16
justice 115; subversion of 113, 116
justices, miscarriages of 116

Kant, Immanuel 50, 53–4, 65; 'Analytic of the Sublime' 48
Katrak, Ketu 22–3
Kennedy, Ellen 124–5; 'Redefining Genocide Education' 122
Keown, Michelle 91–2
Khobragade, Devyani 70–1, 85
Khurshid, Salman 71
kinship and belonging 100–1
Kona, Prakash: 'Notions of Gender in Hindi Cinema: The Passive Indian Woman in the Global Discourse of Consumption' 25
Kothari, Rajni 105
Kulbaga, Theresa A. 136

Lahiri, Tripti: *Maid in India* 72
lesbian relationships 26–7
'Let the Trump Team Eat in Peace' (*Washington Post*) 131
literary criticism 4, 6, 7
literary form, imbrication of 56
literary lumpen 5, 56–68; *Naksha* (Ghosh, Binoy) 58–64, 67–8; Other 57, 67, 68; representing the city and its underclass 56–8
literary writing 4, 92, 116
Lorey, Isabell 72, 131, 133; ciudad 8
lower-class idiom (*itar bhasha*) 59

McAdam, Jane: *Climate Change, Forced Migration and International Law* 149
The Mahabharata 30
'Maid's Dispute in India Erupts into Class War' (*New York Times*) 71
majoritarian populism 17
Majumder, Auritro 5–6, 56–68
Malamoud, Charles 53

Malreddy, P.K. 35
Mao Tse-tung: 'Problems of War and Strategy' 40
Maoist guerilla fighters 33, 34, 38
Maoist ideology 42
Maoist struggle 34, 36, 43, 44
Maoists 39, 41
Mara, Sir Kamisese 102
Markandaya, Kamala: *Nectar in a Sieve* 72
Martyris, Nina 44
Marx, Karl 20, 50, 56, 57, 62, 63
Marxism 59, 60–1, 66
masculinity 23
mass murders 3
material and structural violence 38
matters that embody 22–3
Mbembe, Achille 30, 41
Mehta, Deepa 25–29; *Earth* 18, 24, 28–29; *Elements Trilogy* 28; *Fire* 18, 24, 25–7, 29; *Water* 24
Meos of South-east Punjab 116
#MeToo hashtag activism 19
Michener, James: *Fiji: Return to Paradise* 95; 'Tales of the South Pacific' 102
migrants 3, 6, 7, 17, 20, 53, 72, 102, 136; climate change 149, 151, 153; Fiji: precarity and resistance 95, 98, 102
militarization 91, 94
mimicry 4
The Ministry of Utmost Happiness (Roy, Arundhati) 33, 34, 41–4
minority discourse in postcolonial Indian English novel 6, 105–17; Advani, Rukun: *Beethoven Among the Cows* 106, 112; communalism 106; Desai, Anita: *In Custody* 106, 107–9, 111, 116; dispossession 106; Hariharan, Githa: *Fugitive Histories* 106, 109–11; Hariharan, Githa: *In Times of Siege* 106, 109; Jha, Raj Kamal: *Fireproof* 106, 111, 112–16; resistance 106
Mishra, Pankaj 86
Mishra, Sudesh 91, 93, 94, 100, 101–2, 103; *Feejee* 91–2; 'In Memory of Jarek Woloszyn' 97; 'The Indo-Fijian' 96–7; 'Nightfall' 97–8
Mishra, Vijay 94
misidentified freedom fighter 21
misogyny 21, 136
modernism 59
modernity 62
Modi, Narendra 22
Mohan, Rohini: *The Seasons of Trouble: Life Amid the Ruins of Sri Lanka's Civil War* 6, 118, 122–6
Mohanram, Radhika 23
Morgan, Lewis, H. 62
Morris, Rosalind: *Can the Subaltern Speak? Reflections on the History of an Idea* 20
Motta, Sara C. 133–4
Mueenuddin, Daniyal 72, 87; *In Other Rooms* 74
Mukherjee, Neel: *Lives of Others, The* 44; *State of Freedom, A* 5, 38–41, 44, 85
Munda, Shanti 43
Munoz, Jose Esteban 30

Muslims 17, 22; in India 6, 107, 108–10, 115, 116
mythical body of a goddess 21

Nagappan, Ramu: *Speaking Havoc* 4
Nandan, Satendra 102
Narayan, R.K.: 'Annamalai' 78–85; 'Leela's Friend'
    76–8; 'A Snake in the Grass' 78–79; *Under the*
    Banyan Tree 73; 'A Willing Slave' 74–6, 78
nationalism 19, 59, 100, 106; chauvinistic 22;
    Hindu 63; postcolonial 56, 68; radical 145;
    ultra- 149
nationality 116
Nawa, Fariba: *Opium Nation: Child Brides, Drug*
    Lords, and One Woman's Journey Through
    Afghanistan 151–2
Naxalite Movement: female guerilla fighters 5,
    33–44; gender and Naxalite history 35–6;
    Gender and Radical Politics in India: Magic
    Moments of Naxalbari (1967–1975) (Sinha
    Roy, Mallarika) 33, 37–8; Naxalite icon 36;
    Other 46, 47, 48, 49, 52; patriarchy 36, 37,
    39, 41, 42; People's Liberation Guerilla Army
    (PLGA) 34, 36, 38–39, 41–2; representations of
    contemporary female guerilla fighter 38–43
neat philosophical universalism 46, 47
Nguyen, Viet Thanh 136
Nixon, Rob: *Slow Violence and the*
    Environmentalism of the Poor 146
nuclear testing 91, 93–4, 95, 98–99, 103

Obama, Barack 148
ontological conditions 4
opium cultivation in Afghanistan 151–3;
    forced eradication campaign 152; voluntary
    eradication 152
Opium War (China) 152
oppression 4, 7, 37, 112; economic and social 49;
    of female subaltern 5; gender 21, 38; habituated
    and systemic 74, 77; structural 134
Other 20, 133; domestic servant invisibility
    and precarity 72; literary lumpen 57, 67, 68;
    minority discourse in postcolonial Indian
    English novel 112; Naxalite Movement: female
    guerilla fighters 46, 47, 48, 49, 52; religious 6,
    105, 106, 107, 116; Sri Lankan civil war 124–6
outrage of modesty of foreigners in India 30

Paris Accord 3, 148
passivity on part of the state 114
patriarchy 7, 151–2; *Brooms of Doom: Notes on*
    Domestic Bodies Gendered to Death in Mughal-
    e-Azam, Fire *and* Earth 18, 19, 23, 24, 25, 26,
    27, 29, 30; domestic servant invisibility and
    precarity 75; ethics of representation and the
    figure of the woman: agency 51, 52; Naxalite
    Movement: female guerilla fighters 36, 37,
    39, 41, 42
People's Liberation Guerilla Army (PLGA) 34, 36,
    38–39, 41–2
Permanent Peoples Tribunal (PPT) 120, 127

philosophical universalism 5
philosophy and politics, short-circuit
    between 47–8
Pillai, Thakazhi Shivashankara: *Vellappokkathil*
    (In the Floods) 15
postcolonialism 4, 84, 145; *Brooms of Doom:*
    Notes on Domestic Bodies Gendered to Death in
    Mughal-e-Azam, Fire *and* Earth 18, 19, 21, 22,
    23, 27; ethics of representation and the figure
    of the woman: agency 48, 50, 53; Fiji: precarity
    and resistance 98, 100, 101; literary lumpen
    56–7, 59, 64–5, 66–7; Naxalite Movement:
    female guerilla fighter 36, 37
power 64, 153; *Brooms of Doom: Notes on*
    Domestic Bodies Gendered to Death in Mughal-
    e-Azam, Fire *and* Earth 20, 23; domestic
    servant invisibility and precarity 71, 75, 76, 79,
    84, 85; ethics of representation and the figure
    of the woman: agency 47, 52; Fiji: precarity
    and resistance 91–6, 98, 99, 102; Naxalite
    Movement: female guerilla fighters 38, 40,
    41; teaching beyond empathy: the classroom
    as care community 128, 131, 135, 138, 139;
    see also disempowerment; empowerment;
    powerlessness
powerlessness 71, 79, 107, 109, 112, 113
Precarias a la deriva (feminist activist
    group) 133–4
precarity 1, 3–7, 8; *Brooms of Doom: Notes on*
    Domestic Bodies Gendered to Death in Mughal-
    e-Azam, Fire *and* Earth 17, 19, 22, 29; climate
    change 147–8, 153; ethics of representation
    and the figure of the woman: agency 47–49,
    52–3; literary lumpen 62; minority discourse in
    postcolonial Indian English novel 105–6, 111,
    113, 115; Naxalite Movement: female guerilla
    fighters 38–39; teaching beyond empathy: the
    classroom as care community 131–2, 135–6,
    138, 140; *see also* Fiji: precarity and resistance;
    domestic servant invisibility and precarity; Sri
    Lankan civil war: teaching precarity, resistance
    and community

Qayum, Seemin: *Cultures of Servitude* 72–3
queer sexuality 5, 23, 24, 27, 66–7

Rabindranath: *Khata* ('The Exercise-Book') 50–1;
    Streer Patra ('A Wife's Letter') 50
race 4, 20
racial conflict 3, 95
racial difference 46, 47, 48
racial exclusion and evisceration 17
racial marginalisation 146
racial struggle 47
racialization 30, 151
racialized bodies 18, 23
racialized colonial practices 23, 95
racialized hegemony 22
racialized lumpen 57
Rajan, Rajeswari Sunder 51

Rammohan (social reformer) 60
rape 123; by police 37, 39, 41, 43; gang 30, 113
Ray, Raka: *Cultures of Servitude* 72–3
refugees/refugee crisis 3, 6, 17; climate change 144, 145, 149, 150, 151, 153; teaching beyond empathy: the classroom as care community 132, 134, 136, 138, 139, 140
resistance 3–5, 6, 7, 47, 140; *Brooms of Doom: Notes on Domestic Bodies Gendered to Death* in Mughal-e-Azam, Fire *and* Earth 19, 24; domestic servant invisibility and precarity 71–2, 74, 79, 82, 84; literary lumpen 60, 63; minority discourse in postcolonial Indian English novel 105–6, 111, 114–16; Naxalite Movement: female guerilla fighters 33, 44; *see also* Fiji: precarity and resistance; Sri Lankan civil war: teaching precarity, resistance and community
Richards, Sangeeta 70–1, 85
Rorotonga Treaty (South Pacific Nuclear Free Zone Treaty) 95
Roy, Arundhati: *The God of Small Things* 34, 44, 72; *Ministry of Utmost Happiness* 5, 38, 39, 43–4; *Walking with the Comrades* 43, 44
Roy, Srila 36, 38

Saldívar, Ramón 135
Sarkar, Sushobahan: *Notes on the Bengal Renaissance* 58
Sarvarkar, V.D. 106
Satchidandan, K.: 'After the Deluge' 5, 9–15; *Birds Come After Me* 7, 142–3; *Spaces* 6, 89–90
sati-suicide 46–7, 51–3
Scheidenhelm, Carol 131–2
secularism 50, 105–7, 110–11, 115–16
segregation/segregationist policies 19, 91, 92, 95
segregationist policies 92, 95
self-deprivation 52
Sen, Samar 58
sexual assault 3, 123; *see also* rape
sexual desires, prohibited 26–7
sexual deviants and queer sexuality 5, 23, 24, 27, 66–7
sexual harassment 86
sexual violence 22, 29, 30, 36, 42
sexualized poor 5–6
Shah, Alpa 34
Singh, Pratibha 36, 43
Singha, Kaliprasanna: *Hutom Penchar Naksha* (The Musings of the Barn Owl) 58, 59, 64
Sinha Roy, Mallarika: *Gender and Radical Politics in India: Magic Moments of Naxalbari (1967–1975)* 33, 37–8
skin of subalternity 20–2
sly civility 4
Sontag, Susan: *Regarding the Pain of Others* 4
South African apartheid 119
specific literary affects (*rasas*) 65
Spivak, Gayatri Chakravorty 4, 21, 22; 'Acting Bits/Identity Talk' 48; 'Can the Subaltern Speak?' 19, 20, 46–54, 137; *A Critique of Postcolonial Reason: Toward a History of the Vanishing Present* 47–8, 50; on 'Draupadi' 37; patriarchal assumptions 30; 'Righting Wrongs' 46–7, 50
Sri Lankan civil war: teaching precarity, resistance and community 6, 118–28; care communities 119–120, 123; educating against genocide 122, 124–5; educating to prevent genocide 122; ethical and moral convictions to identify manipulation 125; genocide pedagogy 6, 122–6; Holocaust teaching 121–2; individual and personal perspectives 122; manipulation and othering, presence of 125; Mohan, Rohini: *The Seasons of Trouble: Life Amid the Ruins of Sri Lanka's Civil War* 118, 122–6; null curriculum 121–2; personal courage of students to resist their own acts of classification, symbolization and dehumanization of others 126; teaching in the classroom 121–2
Sri-Skanda-Rajah, Usha S.: 'Sri Lanka's Genocide: Major Cover-Up Must Be Exposed' 120–1
Sridevi (feminist actor) 23
Stallybras, Peter 56–7, 66
subalternity 20, 46, 49–50, 53
subjectivity 53, 85; denial of 51, 52; discontinuity of 46, 47; gendered 63; precarious 56; rational 48
'sublime' (Kant) 65
subordination 72, 73, 78, 84
Subramani 92; 'Oceanic Imaginary' 93
subreption 53–4
suffering 3, 4, 21, 42, 49, 62, 67, 113, 124, 153
suicide 50–3
Sussman, Dana 85

Tantric rituals and magical practices 61–2
teaching beyond empathy: the classroom as care community 6–7, 130–40; affective and embodied praxis 133; agency and freedom 136, 137; civility 130, 131–5; class presentations 139; classroom *ciudadanía* 133, 134; collective action 134; Hamid, Mohsin: *Exit West* 130, 131–2, 134, 135–40; Hamid, Mohsin: *The Reluctant Fundamentalist* 136; identity 132, 136–7; metacognitive work 137; political engagement 131, 133; postcolonialism 136; power 128, 131, 135, 138, 139; refugees/refugee crisis 132, 134, 136, 138, 139, 140; relational and reciprocal collaboration 131, 134; 'Speculative Postcolonial Fictions: Alternative Realities Around the Globe' 135; student-centred approaches 133; symbolic action 135
Telengana People's Struggle (1946–51) 37
teleological judgment 48
terrorism 3, 145, 148, 152
Thoburn, Nicholas 57
torture 21, 37
Totten, Samuel 121–2, 127
transgressive femininity 25

Transnational Government of Tamil Eelam's (TGTE) Senate 120
Trivedi, Tana 6, 91–103
Trump, Donald/Trump administration 3, 20, 125, 131, 148
Truth and Reconciliation Commission (South Africa) 119

Umrigar, Thrity 72, 84, 87
United Nations Genocide Convention 121
United Nations Human Rights Commission 127
United Nations Report of the Secretary-General's Panel of Experts on Accountability in Sri Lanka 127
United States 3, 19, 23, 92, 95, 99, 103; climate change issues 143, 150, 153; Department of Defense 148–49; teaching beyond empathy: the classroom as care community 131, 132
Unrow Human Rights Litigation Clinic 121
Urdu journalism 107–8

visual arts 4
vulnerability 4, 6, 7, 17; climate change 149–50; domestic servant invisibility and precarity 76, 82; ethics of representation and the figure of the woman: agency 47–8, 53; Fiji: precarity and resistance 92–3, 96–7, 100, 102; minority discourse in postcolonial Indian English novel 109, 112; Naxalite Movement: female guerilla fighters 41; Sri Lankan civil war 119; teaching beyond empathy: the classroom as care community 119, 123

Walzer, Michael 151
war crimes and crimes against humanity 127
white supremacy 20
Williams, Raymond: *Marxism and Literature* 67
World Without Genocide 122

xenophobia 5, 17, 18, 22–3, 132, 134, 149